SUPERNATURAL ENGLAND

By The Same Author

The Dark World of Witches
The Realm of Ghosts
The Domain of Devils
Magic Medicine and Quackery
Superstition and the Superstitious
Witchcraft: The Story of Man's Quest for Supernatural Power
Deadly Magic

Paths to Inner Power Series:
　The Magic of Perfume
　Incantations and Words of Power
　The Ancient Art of Occult Healing

Supernatural England

ERIC MAPLE

ROBERT HALE · LONDON

© *Eric Maple 1977*
First published in Great Britain 1977
Reprinted with corrections 1988
ISBN 0 7091 6373 8

Robert Hale Limited,
Clerkenwell House,
Clerkenwell Green,
London EC1R 0HT

Printed in Great Britain by
St Edmundsbury Press Limited,
Bury St Edmunds, Suffolk
and bound by WBC

CONTENTS

1	The Romantic North	9
2	Mysteries of the Midlands (1)	31
3	Mysteries of the Midlands (2)	54
4	Eastern Journey	77
5	Horror in the Home Counties	113
6	The Sinister South	152
7	Ghouls of the Golden West	180
	Index	201

ILLUSTRATIONS

		facing page
1	Hilton Castle, Durham	48
2	Byland Abbey, Yorkshire	48
3	Peel Castle, Isle of Man, showing the cathedral	49
4	Newstead Abbey, Nottinghamshire	49
5	The Rollright Stones, Oxfordshire	64
6	Raynham Hall, Norfolk	65
7	Hill Hall, Essex	65
8	Reculver Church and Roman Fort, Kent	112
9	The Avebury Stone Circle, Wiltshire	112
10	Sandford Orcas Manor House, Dorset	113
11	Berry Pomeroy Castle, Devon	128
12	Chysauster prehistoric village, Cornwall	129

PICTURE CREDITS

Number 1, Bill Hardie; 2, John Edenbrow; 3, F. Leonard Jackson; 4, 8, 9 and 10, the British Tourist Authority; 5, Janet Bord; 6, National Monuments Record; 7, Richard Jemmett; 11, Roy J. Westlake; 12, Geoffrey N. Wright.

To DORA

I

The Romantic North

It was not until the close of the eighteenth century that Londoners first became fully aware of the English provinces. Until that time it had been customary to speak, rather, of town and country, the latter being regarded as a kind of backwater of uncouth behaviour, outmoded fashions and bizarre superstitions. With rapidly improving communications, however, there followed a dramatic transformation of the ideas which had hitherto dominated provincial life and the abandonment of beliefs which had remained relatively unchanged from medieval times. The process, alas, involved the loss of a unique peasant philosophy containing elements of paganism and strongly influenced by magical ideas.

The revolution was sudden, and dramatic. Among the educated classes ghosts and witches became outmoded, and at the same time the rural magician and healer began his departure from the life of the community, although he was not to make his final exit until the following century.

A new and far less comfortable world had been created and the old mystical realm of wish-fulfilment, dating back to pre-Reformation times began gradually to lose its influence until it all but vanished forever.

The legends which survived the holocaust were almost invariably dominated by the supernatural and consisted of tales handed down by generations of rural story-tellers who were the transmitters of tradition in the pre-literate era.

One of the more ancient legends has become famous as 'The Radiant Boy of Corby Castle' in Cumberland which was first committed to print in the last century by Mrs Crowe in her *Night Side of Nature*, a work which introduced generations of readers, for the first time, to the older mysteries of the British Isles.

In it we read of the beautiful golden-haired child, 'clad in white' who appeared to visitors at the Castle. Those who saw the spectre would be informed afterwards that they would either achieve great honours and power or would, alternatively, die tragically.

The source of the haunting remains a mystery: the identity of the 'Golden Boy' unknown.

However the ghost could well be accounted for by the ancient ritual of sacrificing beautiful children in the foundations of buildings for the propitiation of demons or as a form of blood rental to the spirits of the earth. A hint of this melancholy theme is to be found in Shakespeare's *King John*:

> 'There is no sure foundation set on blood,
> No certain life set by others' death.'

One finds, in the byways of archaeological research, a number of interesting references to this barbaric practice. While Darrington church near Pontefract was under repair about a century ago, a human skeleton was discovered embedded in the foundations of the tower where it had remained undetected for some six hundred years.

Many other legends are associated with earlier buildings than castles for in the north, as elsewhere, strange legends have been woven around relics of prehistoric ages. Little Salkeld, in Cumberland, has a circular temple known as Long Meg and her Daughters which has been described as second in size only to Stonehenge. The stones of the temple have long been associated locally with witchcraft and the black arts, for here the famous wizard Michael Scot interrupted a coven of witches who were celebrating their Sabbath and transformed them into pillars of stone. No one has ever been able to count the number of stones accurately but until this is done the witches must remain immobilized in their present state.

Westmorland has a reputation for the kind of melancholy curse which one would expect of the lonelier areas of Britain. To the south of Kendal is Levens Hall which is associated with the tradition that until such time as a white doe is born in the adjacent park no heir will succeed to his father's estate. The curse has proved singularly effective for a near relative is usually the one who has inherited the property. Lowther Hall, once the home of the half-mad Lord Lonsdale who demonstrated his immortality by sitting bolt upright in his coffin during his own funeral service is still haunted by his ghost and despite the strenuous efforts of exorcists to expel him from his old home, he is reported to be more active than at any time in the past.

Although Grayrigg Hall no longer exists its story is well worthy of re-telling. During the seventeenth century it was occupied by an inveterate foe of the Quakers named Duckett who rendered the lives of the normally tranquil Friends unendurable by harrying them from pillar to post. One of his victims named Howgill, driven to desperation placed a curse on the whole Duckett family which proved to be uncannily effective. Duckett soon lost all his money and his children were actually reduced to begging their bread in the streets.

Here too one finds embodied among the older traditions curious legends of giants like the monstrous Isir who lived by the River Eamont and ravaged the entire district to satisfy his craving for human flesh. The Devil, too, has left his mark on the folklore of Westmorland as visitors to Kirkby Lonsdale can discover for themselves by visiting the famous Devil's Bridge, spanning the River Lune where Satan's footprint is clearly imprinted on the masonry. The many boulders which lie scattered throughout this area were dropped by the demoniac bridge-builder at the same time.

As we shall discover later the devil is associated with the building of bridges in other counties in the British Isles and elsewhere. He built a bridge near Aberystwyth asking, in payment, a living soul but was fobbed off with a little dog. No doubt it was this ancient association with death and the devil which became responsible for the superstition that it is unlucky to pass under a bridge when transport is passing overhead.

Although witches, usually of the benign type, are known to have lived in Westmorland until comparatively modern times— where they healed sick human beings and provided a kind of occult veterinary service for cows, there is little to suggest that black magic was regarded as a problem even in the worst days of the witch mania. A solitary reference to the 'craft' appears in Ewen's standard work on the subject, *Witchcraft and Demon-*

ology. In 1669 Anne Tompson of Winton, a widow, was denounced as a witch by nineteen of her neighbours but apparently the judges were unimpressed by the evidence because they released their prisoner and sent her home.

Still in the north-west, we turn to Lancashire, that county of supposedly hard-headed and down-to-earth characters, whom on closer examination are found to be as romantically inclined and ghost-conscious as any other community in the British Isles. Lancastrians have a keen interest in their own folklore which they admittedly lace with their own specific type of humour, as when one solemnly assured the investigator that breweries now occupied the sites of every one of Manchester's traditional holy wells.

There is a tale, still told there, which relates to the unhappy conflict between the Catholic and Protestant factions in the years following the English Reformation. Sir John Southworth, the rabidly Catholic owner of Samlesbury Hall, on discovering that his daughter Dorothy had fallen in love with a young Protestant gentleman, put a ban on their romance and banned the suitor from the house. However, the couple continued to meet in secret and finally decided to elope. Their plans, alas, became known to the girl's two fanatical brothers who assassinated the young man at night and buried his body in the grounds, where a skeleton was discovered years afterwards by one of the garden walls. The girl was sent away to a convent on the Continent where she gradually went insane. Her ghost has been seen at Samlesbury standing near the road, while in the grounds of the hall itself two phantom lovers have been observed in the dusk walking side by side.

Lancashire, a Catholic stronghold, witnessed many cruel priest hunts in the sixteenth and seventeenth centuries, hence the large number of secret hiding places and priest holes which exist in its ancient houses. Persecution was by no means one-sided however as we shall discover from the curious story of Smithshills Hall near Bolton, which is haunted by the ghost of George Marsh, a priest burned by Bloody Queen Mary for heresy. In this house where he stood trial and where he received sentence, there is to be seen a bloody footprint on the spot where the martyr stamped on the floor. This is yet a further affirmation of the old-folk belief that the blood of those unjustly done to death can never be eradicated. George Marsh's ghost is still reported in the same house from time to time.

According to Jack Hallam, that redoubtable inspector of haunted inns, a spectral cross was once observed on the ceiling of the New Inn, Foulridge, not far from Colne. It is not altogether surprising to learn that the inn is haunted, in view of the fact that the garden wall of the original building was partly constructed from tombstones borrowed from a nearby Quaker burial ground.

It is one of the fundamental traditions of ghost lore that supernatural repercussions inevitably follow the desecration of graves for any purpose, let alone for inclusion in the fabric of a house.

Many rivers and lakes in Britain are haunted by elemental spirits which with the advent of Christianity were re-designated ghosts. A Lancashire example is the Ribble which is haunted at Bungerley stepping-stones not far from Clitheroe, by the spectral Peg O'Neill, who demands tribute in the shape of a human life, every seven years. Even today it is sometimes said, in this locality, that once Peg has received her dues no one else need fear drowning until the requisite period has passed. A further hint of old-time human sacrifice to water deities is suggested by legends associated with Jenny Greenteeth, the monster who haunts streams and silent pools throughout Lancashire. Many an anxious mother whose child has wandered over close to a pond's edge has been heard uttering the fearful warning, 'Come back or Jenny Greenteeth will get you.' Almost certainly Jenny Greenteeth originated as a horrific green-haired, green-toothed water sprite of Celtic mythology who had a passion for human flesh and lurked in the dark depths of still pools for anyone incautious enough to wander within reach of her claws. As a matter of interest it should be pointed out that in other places in northern England apart from Lancashire Jenny Greenteeth is a local name for duckweed.

Green hair seems to have been much favoured by aquatic spirits including the marine variety, hence the lines of the poet Browne referring to

> Ye mermaids fair
> That on the shores do plain
> Your sea-green hair.

It is in the northern areas that one discovers the most interesting example of the earlier pagan religious beliefs of the English people. The survival of many curious legends of this type in Lancashire indicates that Christianity could have retained no more than a superficial hold on the imagination of the inhabitants until a comparatively late period.

Belief in sorcery of the black and white variety has long been a prominent feature of the counties' occult history. Among the practices of the old-time enchanters we find poysoning of the ayre, blasting of corne, killing of cattell, and the raising of storms and tempests'.

Relatively late in history, and more particularly in the seventeenth century, Lancashire became the hunting-ground of Protestant heresy hunters, who seem to have included witches among their legitimate prey. To addicts of the supernatural Lancashire is, *par excellence*, the county of witchcraft, a somewhat dubious honour which it shares with Essex in south-eastern England. The old fear of witches can hardly be said to be extinct in the county today for one occasionally comes upon the surprising belief in rural areas that the hare has the power to change itself into a woman and vice versa. A statement to this effect was made in all seriousness to the author in the Pendle Hill area several years ago.

Lancashire witchcraft is closely connected in popular tradition with Pendle Hill which became notorious in the early years of the seventeenth century for black magic. Here in 1612 two covens of witches, with their high priestesses bearing the incredible names of Old Chattox and Old Demdike, were brought to book as the result of a general belief in the district that they had murdered some of their neighbours by magic. A number of ghoulish charms were said to have been utilized by the witches, one of whom, James Device gave evidence that three skulls had been removed for this purpose from the graveyard at Newchurch for use in certain ceremonies. Ten persons in all were found guilty and hanged at Lancaster Castle.

Eight Samlesbury witches who were tried at the same assizes for similar offences were found not guilty and acquitted.

Tourists who might be tempted to visit the witch country will note how ancient Newchurch in Pendle continues to survey the witch-haunted countryside from the huge eye which is carved in the church tower. According to a well-established belief, the mysterious eye protects the neighbourhood from the malicious glance of all witches.

The tradition still survives in nearby towns that one must take one's child to the summit of Pendle Hill before it reaches the age of five years in order to ensure its good health. Many of the older generation remember participating in this custom, which is called 'trampling on the witches'.

Lancashire is not only famous for its witches and imps but also for the demon dogs which have been reported for centuries loping along lanes leading to ancient churchyards.

These canine horrors are almost invariably jet black and headless and the sound of their howling is a portent of death.

Such dogs have a long and curious history in folklore. Among the Romans they were condemned as devils. In ancient India they were offered as sacrifices to the earth spirits.

The headless hound of Preston usually materializes before a local tragedy, while old Shriker, the devil dog of Burnley, performs a similar role by standing in the parish churchyard.

Lancashire can boast a number of intriguing occult manifestations of a less sinister character, however. For example the bride who cares to seat herself in the Bride's Chair, a rocky formation at Warton, can anticipate having a baby within the foreseeable future.

To conclude the Lancashire saga on a light-hearted note one turns to the occult traditions associated with the Winwick Pig which can be clearly seen carved on the tower of Winwick church. During the construction of this church a diabolical pig, emulated the devil, by stealing the building material and replacing it on another site where the church was ultimately erected. Its pathetic cries of 'We-ee-wick' are commemorated in the name of this parish. In some folk-traditions the pig is synonymous with Satan, although not one would hope the whimsical little Winwick pig.

As a county Cheshire shares a common heritage with neighbouring Lancashire, for each has a similar background. Alike they long resisted the invasions of the Welsh and Scots; however it is in their passion for the older legends that this affinity is most pronounced. The central shrine of Cheshire magic is undoubtedly Alderley Edge, that sheer cliff ascending from the Cheshire plain, for this was the ancient home of Merlin.

Merlin the British enchanter who lived in King Arthur's time, was in all probability a Celtic bard who was demoted in Christian tradition to the rank of a sorcerer and declared to be an offspring of Satan. However there appears to have been more than one Merlin, which may help to account for his presence in so many different places, including Alderley Edge.

It was here that Merlin touched what at first sight appeared to be solid rock but which immediately sprang open, revealing within it King Arthur and his knights awaiting the call to rise to the defence of England once again. A wishing-well here which is fed by a natural spring is believed to have supernatural qualities. It bears the curious inscription:

> Drink of this and take thy fill
> For the water falls by the wizard's well.

Wizardry of one kind or another remained a feature of Cheshire life until comparatively recent times although it was in the main, limited to the healing arts. During the nineteenth century a Cheshire healer would staunch haemorrhages by quoting from Holy Writ. At Congleton a thirteen-year-old girl was in constant demand to charm away the pain from burns and scalds. The most famous of all Cheshire's magical healers was Bridget Bostock who practised her craft at Church Coppenhall in the eighteenth century. Her pharmacopoeial powers were of countywide renown for she not only charmed away warts but remedied a wide variety of minor disorders by a judicious combination of prayer and spittle. Bridget, who was usually known as 'the Pythoness' (after the priestesses of the Temple of Apollo at Delphi), was particularly careful never to describe herself as a witch and she invariably refused to charge for her services, relying entirely upon voluntary offerings. This was well within the tradition of the white witch, for these women sincerely believed that their supernatural powers would decline were they to be exploited for money.

The cult of the bee, those tiny winged messengers of the gods, was observed in most parts of the county until fairly recently in a number of interesting rituals. It was essential to inform the bees of every change of domestic affairs including births, weddings and funerals and following a death in the family it was customary to lift the hive and turn it completely round. If this ceremony was omitted it was feared that a further death would take place shortly. At weddings the hive was bedecked with white ribbons and at funerals with black. It is not unknown even now for the bees to be informed when their owner changes his job.

The pleasing philosophy that the hive constituted part of the family is alas dying fast for there is little scope in a world dedicated to materialism for the survival of true feelings of kinship with the small creatures of the wild.

The darker superstitions had a long and active influence in this county; how else would it be possible to explain the presence on a wall at Bunbury of a group of stone images each representing, it is believed, a local official who was responsible for sentencing a poacher to transportation well over a century ago? On his release and return to the British Isles the poacher seems to have dedicated the remainder of his life to casting the most diabolical curses upon the effigies of his enemies from the safety of his front room. Whether or not they suffered any ill-effects from this dynamic form of revenge has never been recorded. All the same, it must have crossed their minds occasionally, particularly after some misfortune, that image magic, to give it its proper name, might sometimes work.

Among other historical curiosities available for study are the strange sandstone figures at Bidston Hill not far from Birkenhead, which include a cat-headed moon goddess and what is assumed to be the image of a sun goddess both dated by scholars to around A.D. 1000.

A number of shrines dedicated to ancient magic have survived the seas of change in out of the way areas of Cheshire. One is the 'holy' spring in Delamere Forest, where the waters are supposed to relieve blindness, deafness and arthritic disorders. Magically endowed springs played an important part in the pre-Christian religious life of Britain, and can be traced back to that ill-explored period of our history when every stretch of water was dedicated to a tutelary sprite who granted wishes in return for gifts from the worshippers, usually in the form of human sacrifices.

Combermere Abbey, close to the Shropshire border, is haunted by the spectre of a small girl whose presence was once regarded as an omen of forthcoming death in the Cottin family who occupied the building after the dispersal of the monks in the sixteenth century.

It is a lamentable fact that child hauntings are often indicative of child murder, or at worst child sacrifice, although it is not easy to associate this form of barbarism with a monastic house.

Cheshire seems to be blessed with more than the average number of hauntings, several being of comparatively recent origin. At Hoylake what is obviously the ghost of a golfer relives some traumatic experience on the famous golf course. One can assume from the fact that the ghost is garbed in knickerbockers that the match which resulted in this haunting must have been lost sometime prior to World War I.

Long-dead members of the Royal House of Stewart occasionally revisit their Cheshire subjects; Charles II presented himself at Marple Hall but Prince Charles, the Young Pretender, appeared in the flesh at the Old Parsonage, Handforth, in 1745 and scared a woman to death. The lady has now become the resident ghost.

There is a pleasing gregariousness about some of these spectres, as at Shocklach, where an annual conference of all the deceased members of the Brereton family takes place, their spectral coaches creating a great deal of congestion along the lane leading to the parish church.

The old superstition that an evil spirit could be conjured out of a diabolically possessed person and into the body of an animal or bird is the theme of the legend of Utkinton Hall, near Tarporley, for here the local flock of blackbirds is believed to be directly descended from a brood of devils who troubled the district during the Middle Ages.

Without doubt the most important of Cheshire exorcisms relates to 'the Boy of Northwich' who claimed to be possessed by devils for over a year, beginning with 1601. Seven clergymen, including a bishop, strove manfully to exorcize him, and in addition recommended private prayer and total abstinence from food 'for the comfort of the afflicted'. The boy behaved so wildly (for he really was insane) that one of his interrogators, overcome by terror, fell into the pigsty during his frenzied endeavours to escape.

The Isle of Man, set in the Irish Sea, preserves a number of

Norse and Celtic traditions, which give it an important role in the history of the occult. Sometime known as 'Britain's Magic Island', Man is in more than one of its aspects a fairy kingdom. Visitors crossing Ballona Bridge are expected to salute the fairies with the deference that is their due, and on more than one occasion an entire contingent of mainlanders has been heard murmuring politely 'Good morning, fairy' as they crossed.

The magicians of Man were supposed to have power to control the weather and to create impenetrable mists which obscured the route of the invader. The witches, too, were credited with similar supernatural powers over the forces of nature, for they could control the winds and still the storm-tossed waves. A curse from a Manx sea witch meant a rough voyage for the seaman: her blessing, a calm sea and a speedy and safe return to port.

Old writers occasionally disclosed how this was done. The Isle of Man witches tied up the wind in three knots of thread and as each was untied the wind blew stronger; untying the third knot brought a howling gale. Not surprisingly, a number of sea witches were burned at the stake in the seventeenth century. The older superstitious fears persisted until a very late period of Manx history and included general acceptance of the superstition that a witch had power to change herself into an animal, a belief which is not even now absolutely extinct.

The white witches of Man were famous healers. Old Tearle of Ballawhane, generally recognized as the most remarkable of the Manx 'witch doctors', was credited with a remarkable expertise in treating the sick with his charms and incantations. However, unless the patient fasted for a period stipulated by the magician and also maintained a strict silence on the nature of the treatment, he could never hope to be cured.

A wizard's supernatural powers were usually hereditary, being passed down the generations from father to daughter and mother to son, which was a relationship typical of witchcraft generally and has an interesting correspondence with another supernatural manifestation, for it is a common belief that there exists a powerful psychic link between mother and son and father and daughter, in that order. As most students of the occult are aware, a mother is frequently conscious of serious troubles affecting the son, although the two might be living far apart, and this includes premonitions of death. Daughters seem to be aware of a recently dead father's presence in the home for a considerable period after the funeral.

While still on the subject of the earthbound dead, we must turn to one of the most haunted sites in Man, Peel Castle, a main tourist attraction which has acquired a firm place in the ghost hunter's itinerary by virtue of the presence of a phantom dog, the Moddy Dhu, an animal with most unpleasant characteristics, which has been reported on several occasions in one of the castle passageways. To see this dog is to die, and over the centuries both a clergyman and a soldier have succumbed after seeing the spectre. The best authenticated incident occurred in the seventeenth century when a member of the guard on duty who was, admittedly, somewhat the worse for drink, decided that he would track the canine horror to its lair. He saw the animal, collapsed from shock and was dead in three days. According to an old tradition, the skeleton of a dog was discovered here when repairs were carried out in 1871.

Despite the affection felt for the fairy kingdom by most of the islanders, it is generally conceded that the bulk of the elfin population fled from the scene following the introduction of the railways in the last century. Nevertheless a number of quaint old legends of Bugganes and Glashans and similar elementals have managed to survive in popular tradition. Near Ballabag, close to a roadside, is the Fairy Stone, which magnetizes automobiles, drawing them despite all the efforts of their drivers, towards this particular spot on the road.

Castletown is one of the most important shrines of the English witch cult, for Dr Gerald Gardner, founder of modern witchcraft, lived there at the Witch's Mill until his death in 1964. It can be justly claimed that, but for Gardner's book *Witchcraft Today*, magic, white and black, might never have been revived in Britain, nor for that matter would there have been the current mania for exorcists and exorcism. The islanders still remember Gardner with mixed feelings, and sometimes with affection, for this strange Master of Witches was an extremely likeable man.

Castletown has a dismal record of witch persecutions, including burning prisoners alive. In the witchcraft museum is a memorial to Margaret Quane who was burned at the stake here with her child after attempting to cast a spell to improve the fertility of the crops. A local form of witch punishment was rolling the culprit downhill in a barrel studded with iron spikes. The witch of Peel was treated thus for having prophesied that the herring fleet would never return to shore.

At Crosby the visitor will hear the tale of a Buggane, a monster who wrecked the roof of St Trinian's Church in order to still the sound of the church bells, and at Peel he will see the ghost of a dapple grey mare, which is a rarity in ghost lore.

For the romantically inclined, a trip to Berry Dhones Pool, near Corrany Bridge, is imperative, for here unmarried girls can look into the waters on Hallowe'en to see the faces of the men they will marry.

Addicts of the unusual in Manx folklore should pay tribute to the most remarkable phantom in history, the Talking Mongoose of Doarlish Cashen, or Cashens Gap, a lonely spot overlooking the sea. The story begins in 1931, when the occupant of an old farm reported the presence of a small furry animal on the premises and furthermore one that tried to communicate with him in fluent English. Psychic researchers investigating the case managed to obtain a photograph of the creature which appeared to be the split image of a mongoose.

The mongoose made banner headlines in the newspapers during the mid-thirties and even attracted the attention of an American showman, who offered fifty thousand dollars for the right to exhibit it in the USA. The outcome of the story, however, was truly tragic. The house changed ownership and the new proprietor reported having shot a mysterious little animal in the grounds without preserving its body. From that time forth, however, the talking mongoose ceased its communications with the human race.

Even today, the wildness of England's north-east border affects the imagination in the most dramatic fashion. It is almost impossible to depict through the written word the barrenness of the northern moorlands in winter as the bracken and heather are raked by the icy winds. Environment and history alike have left their indelible marks upon the characters of north-eastern folk, for here were fought those bloody border battles, accompanied by massacres which

> Spairt neither man nor wife
> Young or old, or of manhood that bore life.
> Like wild wolves in furiosite
> Baith brunt and slewe with great crueltie.

In the North-east, folk traditions display a strong Scandinavian influence, which is understandable in view of the invasions from Europe into this part of England. The occult lore has a melancholy quality and even the elemental spirits seem to be foreign to the general run of English beliefs. A famous character in north country folklore was the Hedley Kow, a sprite who distracted the villagers of Hedley in Northumberland with insane pranks reminiscent of the poltergeist. After a mad bout in which kitchen utensils were upset and domestic life rendered impossible, the Kow obligingly transformed itself into a horse and galloped madly out of sight.

The hamlet of Black Heddon near Stamfordham suffered considerably from the pranks of another visitor from the past, a spirit known as Silky who leaped on to the backs of passing horsemen. Perhaps it was due to the strong ale of the north that these curious spirits had so long a run in popular tradition. The advent of the big breweries and the corresponding reduction in the consumption of real ale must have had a considerable effect upon their activities.

As one would probably anticipate from a community where the way of life had remained unchanged for centuries, a number of historical tragedies have been preserved in popular tradition in the form of ghost stories. Typical of these is the haunting of a farm near Haltwhistle by the ghost of a thief who was done to death at this place well over six hundred years ago.

In the grounds of Featherstone Castle, in the same district, the ghosts of a long dead wedding party who were murdered centuries ago have been seen. Sir Reginald Fitzurze, a phantom of baronial times, occasionally groans loudly here. He was starved to death in the castle many centuries ago.

Some truly frightening monsters have ravaged England in their time but none so disturbing perhaps, as the Laidley Worm, which had its lair near Bamburgh. This monster laid the entire region waste until it was finally overcome by the local knight errant, the Childe of Wynde, who banished it once and for all from the abodes of man. It is possible that the story represents some fragment of European mythology brought to the British Isles by the Scandinavian invaders, the Worm being another name for the dragon, the evil spirit of the skies who brings tragedy and death to human kind.

Phantasies of this kind were for centuries the stock in trade of the travelling tale teller, who in return for readily given hospitality entertained cottagers with gruesome legends from the past. These folk earned their keep and our gratitude and we are indebted to them for keeping alive many strange old tales which might otherwise have been forgotten. In one of these we are told of a host of phantom huntsmen who rode furiously through the night sky in the district around Hadrian's Wall. These spectral huntsmen crop up time and time again in the mythology of the European peasants and are believed to represent a folk memory of the Scandinavian Wode, the god of death and his fearsome companions who flew through the storm-racked heavens in search of human souls. One has only to cry out, 'Share your spoils' as the riders thunder overhead and a corpse is likely to descend, amid a shower of soot, into the hearth.

Curious reminders of the barbaric practices of our ancestors occasionally come to light in Northumberland to reveal a little of the darker labyrinths of the human mind. At Elsdon, the relics of horse sacrifice have been found: skulls exposed by the excavator or spade. Similar skulls discovered in other parts of England link us folk-wise with the Tartars of Central Asia who continued to sacrifice horses until about sixty years ago.

Wallington Hall, a late seventeenth-century mansion built on the site of an old castle, is haunted by an as yet unidentified monster which flaps its wings against the window panes and awakens sleepers with its heavy asthmatic breathing. Blenkinsop Castle at Haltwhistle is haunted by one of the most persistent spectres of the British Isles, a white lady whose presence is a portent of death. There is a psychic kinship between the white lady and the spectral man in grey who haunts Bellister Castle, one of the Border fortresses, for in folklore greyness is the symbol of grief.

Visitors to Holy Island should keep a sharp lookout for the ghost of St Cuthbert, the seventh-century Scottish monk who sits alone making beads, using a rock as an anvil. He also gathers small-holed stones from the beaches to convert into lucky charms known as St Cuthbert's Beads. There are many ghosts in Northumberland but relatively few of them bear a saintly character, most being earthbound spirits condemned to live on like the vampire until released from their miseries by the prayers of the compassionate.

County Durham can be summarized in one word—industrialism. It was here in the early nineteenth century that the cultural pattern of rural life was transformed with such speed that a style of existence which had survived unchanged for centuries disappeared virtually overnight. Much of the county's occult traditions were overwhelmed by the avalanche, but sufficient has survived to remind the modern generation of its important heritage of monsters and dragons.

The tale of the Lambton Worm contains a moral, for it combines a solemn warning against fishing on the Sabbath with vestiges of ancient dragon lore. We are told how Sir Lambton, a Crusader of somewhat plebeian tastes, invariably angled in the River Wear when he should have attended Sunday Service and that furthermore always blasphemed violently if the trout failed to rise to his bait. On one memorable Sunday there came a violent tug on his line, but instead of the huge trout he expected a tiny black worm had seized the hook. Disgustedly Sir Lambton tossed the worm into a nearby well and, abandoning the gentle art, set off for the Holy Land in quest of martial glory.

During Sir Lambton's absence the worm gradually increased in size until it had grown into a huge dragon which could only be prevented from consuming the entire local population by daily libations of milk provided by nine cows. Whenever the milk supply fell short of the agreed quota the dragon ravaged the district and finally the authorities decided that something had to be done. Valiant knights sallied forth armed with swords and cut the dragon in pieces but invariably the severed parts became reunited, and the battle had to be fought all over again.

At last Sir Lambton returned from the wars and promptly decided to tackle the monster once more. On the friendly advice of a priest he clad himself in a special coat of armour set with razor-sharp blades, but before setting forth he made a vow that if he were victorious he would sacrifice the first living creature he met on returning from the fray.

The great battle took place amid the rushing waters of the River Wear. The dragon coiled itself round the knight but was cut to pieces by the sharp blades; however the pieces were unable to reunite since they were swept down river in the current. The dragon, defeated at last, died in mid-stream.

It so happened that the first living creature Sir Lambton met after the contest was his own father whom naturally the knight obstinately refused to kill. As the result of this betrayal of a sacred oath a curse fell upon the Lambtons and from that day to this a phenomenal number of tragic deaths have befallen members of this ancient family.

Tales like this were told in all seriousness and believed with conviction by the Durham peasants of two centuries ago. For they still lived in a kind of rural innocence in which dream and reality seemed to be curiously combined. A similar fusion of old ideas provides the basis for the curious legend of the Cauld Lad of Hilton Castle, a ghost who haunted what was one of England's most magnificent homes. When the story was first set down by the historian Surtees the castle was a ruin 'hastening to decay'. One of the castle rooms was never used for the simple reason that it was haunted by the ghost of a shivering child, in fact a stable boy named Roger Skelton who had been murdered by Robert Hilton, his master, early in the seventeenth century, the body being flung into a well. The ghost when seen produced great terror for something of the intense coldness of the child penetrated the bones while an icy chill pervaded the room, and remained long after the ghost had departed: some people insisted that they continued to shiver for the remainder of their lives.

Even prior to the murder there had been curious stories of a brownie or elemental sprite haunting the castle. The atmosphere in the building strongly affected John Ingram who remarked in his famous collection of antique ghost stories: 'With such ghastly and such ghostly traditions connected with it, it is no wonder that Hilton Castle is a haunted place.'

Durham has a number of haunted pools, mainly in Teesdale, which are tenanted by some unrecognized species of ghost whose cries are heard although the spectres are never seen. Similar dismal screams have been reported from Neville Castle where a bloody battle was fought between the English and the Scots in the fourteenth century.

Still pursuing the familiar gruesome theme, we note that the last gibbet in England was set up in 1832 at Jarrow Slake, later Tyne Dock. The body exhibited was that of William Jobling, a pitman who murdered a local magistrate. The gibbet was taken down in 1853 and many years later came into the possession of the Newcastle Society of Antiquaries.

Long after the abandonment of the more barbarous punishments the corpses of malefactors were left to rot on lonely heathlands, often in sight of their own homes, their rattling bones in the winter winds serving as a constant reminder to passers-by that crime did not pay.

Until the abolition of public executions in the sixties of the nineteenth century the hangman's rope was a marketable commodity since it was supposed to have valuable therapeutic qualities. It was frequently used as a bandage for the relief of severe headaches. John Aubrey, the antiquary, recommended keeping a strand of hangman's rope inside the hat as an antidote to ague. A length of the rope with which a suicide had taken his life was a highly prized remedy for fits.

The best known ghost of Durham is the bloody faced spectral horseman who has been seen riding like the wind through West Auckland to vanish from view among the trees of Hamsterley Forest. Ghostly transport is also represented by the spectral coach pulled by headless horseman and guided by the inevitable headless coachman which haunts the area around Langley Hall to the north-west of the city of Durham.

Witchcraft does not seem to have troubled the Palatinate overmuch, although several cases were apparently of sufficient interest to find a place in the records. In 1651 two sorcerers were executed in the city of Durham for some unspecified form of witchcraft and at the beginning of the same century there are accounts of the prosecution of a white witch for attempting to heal the sick by inserting the beaks of white ducks into her patient's mouths. By and large the county seems to have escaped the full rigours of a regular witch hunt, doubtless because of supernatural influence of the famous Durham Ritual, which pitted the full powers of Heaven against the Satanic forces in the See.

Devils and demons of every kind seem to have by-passed the Palatinate almost completely during their journey southwards, although as we shall see they gathered a splendid harvest of lost souls in Yorkshire.

So generally accepted were the principles of magic in that county that during the nineteenth century burglars continued to use a ghoulish type of illumination known as a Hand of Glory or corpse candle when breaking into occupied premises. The candle which was manufactured from the fat of a body, taken from the gallows, was supposed to render the one who carried it completely invisible, and furthermore to send the occupants of the house into a hypnotic sleep in which they remained until after the intruder had departed. The candle quite literally lulled the householder's family and servants into 'the sleep of the dead'. A corpse candle which is exhibited in Whitby Museum, was previously employed as a charm to keep evil spirits from the home.

It was long the practice among witch fearing Whitby folk to protect their homes from the invasions of witches and devils with upright posts carved with mysterious symbols. Once these were set in place before the hearth no witch had the power to cross the threshold. Specimen witch posts are on display at Rydale Folk Museum at Hutton-le-Hole.

Terror of witchcraft extends far back into Yorkshire history. In the seventeenth century a woman named Isabella Billington was hanged and burned on a pyre at Pocklington for crucifying her own mother and sacrificing a cockerel and a calf to Satan. In John Mayhall's annals of Yorkshire there is a reference to the execution of Mary Pannell in 1603 for bewitching to death William Witham at Ledston. The place of her execution continued to bear the name Mary Pannell Hill for more than three centuries afterwards. Even fortune tellers might find themselves hailed before a court of law as suspected witches as in 1605 when Ralph Milner, a yeoman, was sentenced to confess his guilt before the congregation of Mewkarr church during Sunday service.

Wherever the fear of the witch has taken root one finds its effectiveness enhanced. Once Hester Spivey, a Huddersfield servant, became convinced that she had been cursed by Hester Frances, the Huddersfield witch, she lost the power of speech. The terror sometimes reached manic proportions as in 1654 when Elisabeth Roberts of Beverley transformed herself into a cat before the very eyes of John Greencliffe and struck him violently with her paw. Another 'witch', Katherine Earle, merely said to a young man she favoured, 'You are a pretty gentleman. Kiss me,' whereupon he collapsed and very soon died.

The best known of all Yorkshire witches was Mother Shipton,

the prophetess whose cave continues to be one of the tourist attractions of Knaresborough. This far-seeing lady whose vision of the future embraced many hundreds of years, lived in the early sixteenth century and was of so grotesque an appearance that from her earliest years she had been branded by those who knew her as 'the child of the devil'. Her visage in old age was even less endearing for she was described thus: 'Her head was long with fiery eyes, her nose of an incredible and unproportional length and encrusted with luminous pimples.' Mother Shipton has been credited with prophesying the downfall of Thomas Cromwell, the outbreak of the Fire of London and, among other catastrophes, the end of London which was due to take place on 17th March 1881. The ghost of the ancient crone must have chuckled into its beard when in that year vast numbers of English folk having disposed of all their possessions at rock-bottom prices waited in vain for the hour of Armageddon.

The time has gone forever when an English publican would fight shy of mentioning his resident ghost out of fear that it might adversely affect trade. In fact the opposite now prevails and the modern hotelier will often stress the presence of his spectre when advertising the attractions of his premises. Jack Hallam refers to an interesting case of this character in his *Haunted Inns of England*, relating to the Fleece Inn, at Elland Halton, immediately east of Leeds which was the scene of an atrocious murder in the distant past. Today not only are ineradicable bloodstains pointed out on the inn floor but one is told how that murder victim is occasionally seen driving his spectral coach past the premises and along an adjacent road.

Turning from blood to ghostly skulls we visit Burton Agnes Hall near Bridlington which has an honoured place in the annals of the occult. It was here in the seventeenth century that Anne Griffith was mortally injured by a gang of thieves and before dying extracted a promise from her family that her head should be removed from her body and kept within the house. Inevitably perhaps the wish was disregarded. The family must have considered it to be the ravings of delirium, but they were soon to be disillusioned in a most macabre fashion. The ghost put in an appearance and manifested its displeasure by slamming doors and uttering doleful groans, whereupon the family opened the grave and brought the skull inside where it remained until a thoughtless servant threw it into the garden. The uproar was resumed immediately and finally for the sake of peace the skull was taken inside again and bricked into a wall, where it remains today. The ghost of Anne Griffith still appears in Burton Agnes Hall from time to time but no one living there now has cause to be afraid.

Another ghastly skull once housed at 400-year-old Bowland Hall belonged to one of the victims of Henry VIII's fearful massacres in Yorkshire following the failure of the revolt known as the Pilgrimage of Grace. Its removal from the hall was followed by a series of deaths in the family accompanied by other disturbing manifestations which only ceased when the skull was returned to the building. The reason for keeping skulls indoors has never been adequately explained. There could possibly be some remote connection with primitive foundation sacrifice or, on the other hand, the practice might have had its roots in the Celtic custom of head-hunting. Folklore offers a large number of superstitions associated with skulls for they were once regarded as 'seats of the soul' and therefore founts of psychic power. In the seventeenth century a moss which grew on old skulls was used for the treatment of various nervous disorders.

Headlessness is one of the features of many hauntings, as we find in the story of the Headless Lady of Watton who was decapitated by a half-mad Roundhead during the Civil Wars because of her adherence to Roman Catholic principles. Bearing her murdered babe in her arms the mournful phantom continues to walk the ruins of Watton Abbey at night.

Elemental spirits seem to have had long life and great vitality in Yorkshire since they have been reported in Upper Wharfdale by men and women now living. Hart Hall in the moorlands of the north-east housed a Hob, a rustic sprite who occasionally lent a hand at bringing in the harvest. Other psychic manifestations, sometimes of a curiously modern character, have been reported from the county from time to time. For example in the year 1290 at the Feast of St Simon and St Jude a large silver disc-shaped object was observed drifting through the clouds by a monk of Byland Abbey. This phenomenon was regarded as a portent of evil at the time, but with hindsight we can clearly recognize it as one of our earliest flying saucers.

A road between York and Norton is haunted by a protective spirit who guides lost travellers to safety through the dense mists which are common in that part of Yorkshire. Many local people believe the spirit to be that of a girl who died of exposure in that place long ago, but it is far more likely that the story incorporates some ancient tradition of a guardian spirit who, over the centuries, has been transformed into a ghost. A less happy sprite from the wayfarer's point of view is a minor devil who is often held responsible for road accidents in the Whitby area.

Demon dogs crop up time and time again in our survey of occult England but special mention must be made of the Barguest, a canine horror which materializes in many Yorkshire churchyards immediately prior to an unexpected death in the parish: one of these is still supposed to haunt Egton, lying above the Esk valley. Yorkshire has also suffered from the intrusions of a far more sinister breed of phantom animals called Gabriel Hounds, frightening creatures with the bodies of dogs and the heads of human beings, which were described by old writers as 'Goblins of frightful appearance which sometimes took the shapes of huge dogs'. They favoured churchyards for their activities and were accompanied by a type of companion which few would care to meet.

> Grisly ghosts have leave to play
> And dead men's souls with courage brave
> Skip from out each several grave
> And walk round when the Barguest comes.

Even more horrific than the Gabriel Hounds is the three-headed dog (shades of Cerberus) who haunts Dobb Park Castle near Bradford, while at Flixton there is a rarity, a werewolf with blood-red eyes. On a lighter note we mention the Cottingley fairies, of which photographs still exist including one delightful portrait of a gnome in black tights.

In view of the foregoing examples of Yorkshire's more macabre traditions we need hardly be surprised at the survival of a very curious custom in the parish of Dewsbury, dating back to the thirteenth century. Here each Christmas Eve the bellringers toll the 'nine tailor' for every year of the Christian era. Unless this ceremony is religiously performed Satan can be expected to invade the parish during the following year.

2
Mysteries of the Midlands (1)

Ancient history remains a living force in Derbyshire which contains a large number of stone circles and other similar memorials to long vanished prehistoric races. Arbor Low, one thousand feet up on the moors, with its strange circle of recumbent stones, is perhaps the most impressive of these. At noon when a strange quiet descends upon the site there is sometimes an atmosphere which can only be described as magnetic. Seen at night, under the full moon, every huge stone seems like a battery of imprisoned psychic power.

A number of the more ancient stones of Derbyshire are credited with a kind of supernatural energy one well-known example being the Lumsdale Wishing Stone at Matlock.

The Holy Wells for which Derbyshire is renowned are associated with interesting religious ceremonies which are performed each Whitsuntide, when they are decked with religious symbols and flowers. The well at Tissington is said to date from the Black Death in the Middle Ages being dug as an act of thanksgiving for the salvation of the village from the plague.

The worship of sacred wells and streams had an honoured place in the cults of our remote ancestors, and like the stones of Derbyshire, the waters speak with the voices of another age. To our ancestors every cavern, river and stream represented a shrine of nature housing some subterranean spirit with strange supernatural powers. A cave beneath Topley Pike is supposed to shelter the elfin guardian of a nearby magic spring, where the waters have power to heal the sick. Over the centuries there has been a modification of the superstition and to be cured today one visits the spring only on Good Fridays. There are other shrines with the most unholy associations, for instance the deep Eldon Hole in the Peak Forest, where the sprite in possession is none other than Satan complete with horns, cloven hooves and forked tail. Although the belief in evil spirits must be as old as man, the Satan of theology is a comparative newcomer, arriving with the Christian missionaries to satisfy the permanent need for a scapegoat upon whom could be unloaded all the problems, perplexities and disasters of life, including the mystery of the crooked spire of the ancient church of All Saints, Chesterfield.

According to a well-known local tradition Satan happened to be clinging to the spire at the very moment when a virgin entered the church to be married. This rare phenomenon so astounded the Devil that he twisted his body round to obtain a better look, bending the spire in the process, with the result that it is now eight feet out of true.

The citizens of Chesterfield have supplied a supplement to the legend, for they say that if ever a virgin should pass the church the spire will automatically straighten itself.

Halter Devil Chapel near Mugginton provides a further reminder of Satan's less sinister activities in Derbyshire. Long ago a farmer named Brown, when somewhat the worse for drink, took a solemn oath that he would personally place a halter around the Devil's neck. He ventured forth amid a raging storm and, seeing a cow looming before him in the deluge, mistook the animal for Satan and attempted to cast his halter over its horns. The indignant cow thereupon knocked him to the ground. After this amazing adventure Farmer Brown took the pledge and built a chapel to commemorate the events of that remarkable night.

If the Devil was regarded as a somewhat jocular character, witches most certainly were not and any woman suspected of trafficking with Satan could expect a very dismal end. In 1650 Anne Wagg of Ilkeston cast the evil eye upon a young maid, and then repeated the operation on Farmer Elliot's calf which died within a matter of hours. Like so many other hapless agents of the Devil, Anne was handed over to the magistrates, who committed her for trial. Although the outcome does not seem to have been recorded in the county archives it can almost be taken for granted that Anne would have been hanged.

Horrors of every kind seem to have found Derbyshire a convenient headquarters for hauntings. An old skull, bearing the nickname 'Dickie', was once kept at a farm at Tunstead Milton and it was firmly believed in the neighbourhood that if it was ever removed from the building calamities of all kinds would befall. There is some doubt today as to whether the skull still exists, let alone retains its supernatural powers.

An omen which an early writer described as 'one of the most bizarre superstitions of any time or clime' is associated with Chartley Castle, the ancient home of the Ferrers family. Here was preserved a herd of remarkable cattle which were apparently extinct elsewhere in Britain. Their appearance was distinctive, 'their colour invariably white, muzzles black; the whole of the inside of the ear and about one third of the outside, from the tip downwards red: horns white with black tips, very fine and bent upwards'. There is an ancient tradition that the birth of a black or parti-coloured calf would be followed by the death within the year of a member of the Ferrers family. According to the *Staffordshire Chronicle in* 1835 this dismal omen invariably proved true. The famous Chartley herd no longer grazes amid the castle ruins nor are the Ferrers now associated in any way with their ancient home. In the year 1900, in the absence of a male heir, the estate passed out of the family forever.

Well over a century ago a correspondent writing in *Notes and Queries* described how Derbyshire folk became 'perfectly horrified when a child or other person unwittingly brought a peacock's feather into the house'. The supernatural penalty for doing so was, it appears, 'loss, and various disasters, including even illness and death'. This ominous superstition still retains its hold in the county. To the writer's personal knowledge a Derbyshire woman ascribed the near bankruptcy of her husband's business to the acceptance of an inlaid tray with a peacock motif. Only when the tray had been removed from the house did his financial affairs improve. This terror of peacocks' feathers, which is also shared by members of the theatrical profession, was originally based on the fear of the evil eye as represented by the 'eyes' in the peacock's tail. A peacock's cry incidentally is supposed to herald a shower of rain.

Industrial Derbyshire still retains its superstitions particularly among those working in the coalfields. It is a strict rule among miners that following an accident everyone has to cease work for the remainder of the shift, a custom which is carried out to break the run of bad luck and as an act of respect for the dead and injured. Miners throughout Britain share similar attitudes when it comes to coping with the hazards of the unknown in the bowels of the earth. It is sometimes said that pit accidents are more likely when beans are in flower.

The lead miners of Derbyshire have always refused to work on Good Fridays, a day which is also tabooed in other superstitions. It is unlucky to wash clothing on that day in case one should 'wash the head of the household away'.

Not every superstition held by Derbyshire folk is committed to death and disaster however for one can still visit the Mermaid's Pool at Kinder Scout at dawn and watch the fish-tailed maiden swimming gracefully in the dark waters below.

Nottinghamshire is a county with a remarkable history of hauntings, many of them having an extremely bizarre character. Newstead Abbey, for instance, can offer a variety of ghosts only comparable with Borley Rectory in Essex which was once declared to be 'the most haunted house in England'.

At some period following the Dissolution of the Monasteries by Henry VIII the Abbey of Newstead came into the possession of the Byron family and it was among its melancholy ruins that the poet Lord Byron wandered in soulful soliloquy accompanied in spirit at least, by another lost soul, a phantom friar, a lone survivor from the monastic era:

> A monk, arrayed
> In cowl and beads and dusky garb appeared
> Now in the moonlight, and now lapsed in shade
> With steps that trod as heavy yet unheard.

The Black Friar as he was known, was an ominous figure whose appearance invariably foreshadowed a crisis in the Byron family.

There were, however, other spectres who presented themselves to the Byrons: an ancestral spirit, the heavily bearded Sir John Byron, who occasionally emerged from his framed portrait and promenaded the state apartments in the afternoons, and was sometimes seen seated in his favourite chair perusing a heavy black-letter book.

'Devil' Byron, the poet's immediate predecessor, was actually haunted by the ghost of his own sister to whom, following a dispute, he had refused to say a single word right up to the moment of her death, despite her pathetic endlessly repeated pleas, 'Speak to me, my lord, do speak to me.' In the words of the poet Ebenezer Elliot her pathetic ghost continued to cry out above the elements,

> On winds, on clouds, they ride, they drive,
> Oh hark thou, heart of iron.
> The thunder whispers mournfully
> Speak to her, Lord Byron.

Newstead's other ghosts include a phantom woman in white and the poet's pet dog, Boatswain, who is understandably restless since he was sacrilegiously buried on the site of the monastery altar.

In conformity with the eternal law which decrees that desecrated shrines are doomed to suffer from continued hauntings, Rufford Abbey, a former Cistercian monastery near Ollerton, is haunted by a skull-headed monk. According to an old story told in the district, a man who came upon the monk unexpectedly collapsed and died from shock. The monk had the disconcerting habit of peering over the shoulders of members of the household while they admired their reflections in the dressing-table mirror. The Savilles, who once owned the property, must have suffered the tortures of the damned from these intrusions, and the City of Nottingham, the present owners are unlikely to require the services of a night watchman for this particular building.

Nottingham Castle, has long been the focal point of curious hauntings which continue even now to mystify the investigator. The ghost of Regent Mortimer, who was imprisoned in one of the dungeons prior to his execution at Tyburn in 1330, has been heard, although not seen here. Over the centuries curious footsteps have resounded from within the solid rock upon which the castle stands, and it has been suggested that this is the tread of the long-dead prisoner in the cell. The anguished cries of a woman, believed to be Isabella, Mortimer's tragic mistress, have also disturbed listeners from time to time. Isabella actually witnessed her lover being dragged from her chamber to his death by armed guards.

Robin Hood and his band are inseparable from Sherwood

Forest but whether the outlaw was a real historical personage or a figure from folk mythology remains a matter of debate among historians and folklorists alike. The late Margaret Murray, that learned authority on historical witchcraft, believed that there existed a positive link between the warlike Robin Hood and the elfin character Robin Goodfellow, one of the personifications of the elemental spirit we know as Puck. Should this be so, we have an interesting example of the evolution of a nature spirit into a human being in traditional lore.

Robin Hood and Maid Marian survived until fairly late in history as stock characters in the old May Day games which in all probability originated as fertility rites. The link with arboreal sprites seems to be even more firmly indicated when one visits the one thousand-year-old Major Oak in Birkland Wood near Edwinstowe in which Robin and his entire band were supposed to have concealed themselves from the forces of the Sheriff of Nottingham.

Nottinghamshire seems to have been somewhat inadequately researched ghost-wise, for the ever-popular ghost gazetteers contain relatively few references to the restless dead of the county. Andrew Green's interesting book *Our Haunted Kingdom* mentions two modern hauntings; in one a council worker, having apparently forgotten to clock off, continues to promenade the corridors of the Automobile Association headquarters in Nottingham City, and in another a phantom soldier occupies a council house.

Nottingham became the scene during the late sixteenth century of a series of spectacular exorcisms carried out by one John Darrell of Mansfield, who acquired the type of notoriety which has ensured him a place in the calendar of infamy with Matthew Hopkins, the Essex witch finder.

Darrell began his career by expelling devils from children and became a nationally known figure when he attempted to drive the Devil out of Nottingham boy named William Somers who, later, under interrogation disclosed that the exorcism was fraudulent. Darrell was investigated by Dr Harsnett, later Archbishop of York, an outcome of the enquiry being the virtual outlawry of exorcism from the year 1604 onwards. In fact, little was heard of this curious ritual until the revival of witch belief in England some three hundred and fifty years later, in 1951.

One of the curious features of English occult lore is the wide variations in the type of psychic phenomena from county to county. As one moves southwards there is a distinct change in the supernatural climate. The restless dead remain, as one would expect, the most frequent source of psychic disturbance, but other horrific entities tend to monopolize the stage and in the case of Shropshire it is usually Satan and his imps.

The deeply rooted terror of Devildom always most strong in Protestant dominated areas was the main cause of this situation, as was the determination of the old-style clergy to assign almost every supernatural phenomena to evil spirits. In the curious legend of the outlaw of Kynaston's Cave near Great Ness, for example, this theme is given special emphasis. This particular area was the headquarters during the fifteenth century of a Robin Hood-like character known as Wild Humphrey Kynaston, an athletic fellow whose exploits included leaping on horseback a distance of nine miles to escape his pursuers. Local mythmakers insisted that he had actually jumped the River Severn and doubters were directed to the very spot where the miracle took place, which is still known as Kynaston's Leap. Alas it was not sufficient for this remarkably agile Shropshire lad to retain his place in local lore as a miracle man, for the legend had to be remoulded by the church into an argument in support of the Christian position—in short Humphrey had acquired his supernatural powers in return for selling his soul to Satan.

Any abnormally shaped outcrop of rock might equally be associated with the Devil, a well-known example being the Devil's Rocking Chair on Stiperstone Ridge. The manic obsession with the powers of evil created a curious situation in which people occasionally lost the capacity to differentiate between ordinary water spirits and demons, as when a mermaid emerging from a pool at Child's Ercall was mistaken by onlookers for an evil spirit. When one of the observers gave vent to his amazement with an obscene oath, the mermaid in disgust plunged to the bottom of the pool and was never seen again.

It is not now generally known that one of the original reasons for the ringing of church bells was to drive thunder and lightning out of the parish, together with the devils who caused storms. A reference to this curious tradition occurs in an ancient poem 'The Popish Kingdom':

If that the thunder chance to roar and stormy tempest shake
A wonder it is for to see the wretches how they quake
How that no faith at all they have nor trust in anything
The clerk doth all the bells forthwith at once in the steeple ring.

Shropshire's church bells were particularly notable for their 'conversational powers', as we can judge from the following jingle:

Roast beef and mutton say the bells of Church Stretton,
Hop skip and run say the bells of Clun,
You're too fond of beer say the bells of Ellesmere
Why don't you ring louder say the bells of Hope Bowdler
Because we are beaten says the big bell of Eaton ...

Although witches were easily expelled by the ringing of church bells, Shropshire seems to have been encumbered with more than its fair share of the sinister sisterhood which incorporated that well-known character Mother Garve of 'Castle Foregate' Shrewsbury who cured sick sows by transferring their diseases into the body of her unfortunate cat.

Shropshire ghosts run true to form, the principle underlying the majority of hauntings being that the souls of those who suffer a violent death (whether self-inflicted or otherwise) or are denied Christian burial must remain earthbound until they are released from bondage by the prayers or exorcisms of some holy man. Suicides were interred at crossroads with stakes through their hearts to offset the danger of the shades returning to torment the living.

However, there exists a tranquil type of spectre who is rarely mentioned in ghost stories: for example the phantom pianist who gave midnight recitals at Whitchurch Civic Centre a few years ago. The council officials who investigated the case hazarded a guess that the ghost might be that of a Whitchurch musician who had disappeared mysteriously some years previously.

Far closer to the rigid standards demanded by contemporary ghost-hunters is the haunting, which dates from the Middle Ages, at Ludlow Castle. The local story tells how a love-sick maid unwittingly betrayed the castle to its enemies by secretly admitting her lover, one of the force besieging the castle. Accompanying him was a horde of enemy soldiers who overcame the garrison and put it to the sword. Overwhelmed by remorse the girl flung herself from the battlements, meeting a bloody death on the rocks below. Now, in accordance with well-known tradition relating to suicides, her anguished spirit wanders through the castle ruins at night earthbound to an eternity of regrets.

John Timbs, in his classic *Abbeys, Castles and Ancient Halls of England and Wales* refers to a curious psychic manifestation reported from the long vanished priory of Austin Friars at Ludlow. According to Timbs' informant 'at night, the old Priory seemed to be occupied by its former inhabitants', and on fine nights 'the Prior and his brethren, all habited in white, might be seen walking along Friars Lane'. The monkish spectres seem to have been banished over a century ago by a Mr Pritchett when he demolished what remained of the ruins and converted the site into a meadow.

Yet another of Ludlow's historic ghosts is the tall grey-haired woman of unknown identity who haunts the churchyard and whose cries are heard occasionally after dark.

We must include in our study of Shropshire byways a visit to the church of Astey Abbots to see the maiden's garland of Hannah Phillips who died in 1707. Chaplets or garlands of flowers were borne at the funerals of virgin girls until the end of the eighteenth century and represented a survival of a pre-Reformation rite originally instituted to signify the triumph of spirituality over carnal lust.

It is remarkable that maidens' garlands should have survived in any of our churches but this can perhaps be explained by the old superstition that it is unlucky to disturb or remove them. The ultimate origins of the rite may be found in the belief held by our pagan ancestors that any virgin who died young became the bride of Death, god of the underworld. Garlanded as for her wedding the virgin consummated her nuptials in that ghoulish bridal chamber beyond the grave. The garland superstition forms a part of a whole group of traditional ideas relating to churches and churchyards, which have survived as a somewhat depressing folklore of death.

As most sextons will be aware, any human bones disinterred during grave-digging must be re-interred at once or their owners will follow you to your home and give you nightmares. It is considered most unlucky to disturb a grave in any way, while even treading on one brings misfortunes. Far more dangerous from the supernatural point of view is leaving a newly dug grave open over a Sunday as this ensures that there will be another funeral in the parish within a short space of time. Once dug, the earth around the grave must settle evenly. If it begins to subside a death can soon be expected in the same family.

To end the Shropshire saga on an appropriately melancholy note the visitor should visit the ruins of Lilleshall Abbey which are said to resound at night to the most horrifying screams and groans, accompanied by the chanting of long dead monks. An archaeological excavation carried out on the site some years ago was headlined by the Press as 'a ghost hunt with Government sanction'—'Watch out for the murdered monk'. Even today it is firmly believed locally that this grim-visaged spectre from the Middle Ages wanders amid the crumbling masonry and occasionally enters a nearby cottage where it peers earnestly at the occupant as he lies trembling in his bed.

Those familiar with traditional Staffordshire must have felt somewhat overwhelmed on reading a recent newspaper report that a Newcastle-under-Lyme citizen had choked himself to death 'with a garlic clove he left in his mouth overnight to ward off Dracula-like monsters'. As it happened the sufferer was a Polish emigrant, but it should not be imagined that Staffordshire is without its proper quota of supernatural horrors.

As recently as the last century witchcraft was practised quite openly in the county, albeit with a commercial tinge. In 1823 Sarah Roxborough, a seeress, was charged with fraudulently claiming she had power to 'rule the planets, restore stolen goods and get in bad debts'.

Today, with the revival of witchcraft, magic and sorcery as a way of life among many otherwise impeccable English citizens, it might be salutary to refer to a case which, although occurring as long ago as 1620, brought supernatural Staffordshire into the lurid light of notoriety.

William Perry, a schoolboy then living in Bilston, began to vomit pins, which at that time was regarded as symptomatic of bewitchment. His parents, both Roman Catholics, sought the aid of several priests who announced they had expelled three demons from the boy's body. The need for a scapegoat was satisfied by the arrest of an old woman for sending demons to attack the boy and she would probably have been executed had it not been discovered that the entire affair was a put-up job organized by the priests in order that their church might have the honour of exorcizing him. The case of the Bilston boy became a *cause célèbre* in the annals of English witchcraft.

Even the most prosaic Staffordshire citizens seem to have had a predisposition for occult beliefs. A classic historical case was 'Iron Mad' Wilkinson, the eighteenth-century Bilston iron founder and a pioneer of the Industrial Revolution, who was responsible for building the world's first iron bridge, and launching the world's first iron ship and who advocated iron-paved roads. Wilkinson was incapable of writing a letter without incorporating the 'magical' word iron, and he even constructed the iron coffin in which he was duly buried. His workmen were so overwhelmed by Wilkinson's enthusiasm for his subject that they waited, in vain, by his grave on the first anniversary of his death in the hope that his ghost would appear no doubt to utter a brief homily on the supernatural properties of iron.

It was said that an exorcism was actually performed in a Bilston coal mine in the late eighteenth century to expel an evil spirit which had been responsible for a number of accidents.

The miners marched in procession led by a man carrying a Bible in his right hand and a key in his left, and chanting the Lord's Prayer backwards, after which the evil spirit made a rapid exit from the pit.

Much of the Black Country's legendary lore perished with the industrialization which engulfed the area during the eighteenth century; however a number of medical superstitions have survived.

A child's stomach-ache can be eased by rubbing in the light of the waning moon and chanting at the same time,

> What I see may it decrease
> What I feel may it decrease
> In the name of the Father, Son and Holy Ghost.
> Amen.

Another survival from ancient times is the famous Abbots

Bromley Horn Dance which takes place every September, being an almost unique example of an ancient fertility rite. The performers, who are known as Deer Men, carry reindeer heads complete with horns and engage in mock combat with one another. Some of the old magic retains its potency it appears for local farmers regard a visit from the Deer Men as a harbinger of good luck.

An interesting custom with obvious links with primitive religious beliefs takes place at Endon each spring when the well is 'dressed' (or garlanded) and at the same time a sack of straw heaved over a raised bar. This ceremony, which is known as 'tossing the sheaf', is in fact a nineteenth-century revival of a much older rite dedicated to ensuring crop fertility.

Turning from ancient rituals to ghost stories, one discovers instances representing several historical periods. The White Hart Inn at Caldmore Green, Walsall, is haunted by a servant girl who committed suicide in Victorian times. Peter Underwood declares in his *Gazetteer of British Ghosts* that her ghost was once observed near a former licensee's bed.

Staffordshire's most interesting haunting however is much older and is associated with Tamworth's Norman castle, now a museum, which occupies the site of a monastic house erected by a daughter of Alfred the Great. The builder of the present castle, Robert de Marmion, a follower of William the Conqueror, ruthlessly expelled the local nuns to nearby Oldbury but shortly afterwards the ghost of St Editha, the founder of their order, appeared at his bedside threatening him with a dreadful death unless he returned them their rightful home. To emphasize the point she struck him with her crozier causing blood to flow. Robert de Marmion was so shattered by the experience that he immediately made full restitution of the stolen property.

Despite the many centuries which have elapsed since this remarkable occurrence, Editha's ghost continues to haunt Tamworth Castle and, strange to say, it is not the only spectre in occupation, for a mysterious White Lady has also been seen on one of the terraces. She is said to be the ghost of a girl who witnessed her lover being killed in mortal combat beneath the castle walls. In recent years Editha has become known as the Black Lady to distinguish her from the White Lady who also wanders at night through the same ancient building.

The relative absence of ghosts in Staffordshire, compared with other counties could well be accounted for by the deliberate policy adopted by the clergy during the seventeenth century to allay superstitious fears. As long ago as 1637, largely as the result of an enquiry instituted by the Bishop of Bath and Wells, it was decided to place a kind of interdict upon the activities of 'certain apparitors who go about the country frightening the people'.

Lincolnshire is a county of rural contrasts: it contains a good third of England's fen lands and its highlands or wolds which rise above the plain are reminiscent of cliffs emerging from the sea. It is also a county of the most interesting psychic manifestations, many of which are associated with prehistoric burial mounds, among them those mysterious hillocks known as the Giants Hills near Skendleby.

The innumerable boulders, or to give them their popular name, puddingstones, which are found in the Lincolnshire countryside are associated with curious legends. In the old churchyard of Anwick, to the north-east of Sleaford, may be seen the famous Drake Stones which are reputed to conceal a hoard of buried treasure which is under the protection of the Devil. According to an oft-repeated local legend a farmer searching for his missing horse discovered a huge stone resembling a drake, hence the name given to the stones. The site is also supposed to be haunted.

Not far from Caister is another stone which is not associated with the Devil, as is more usual, but with Jesus Christ. The Saviour during one of His journeys is supposed to have found Himself in Lincolnshire where He begged a small quantity of corn from a farmer who was sowing seed from a bag. The man callously replied, 'I have no corn, this is a stone,' to which Jesus replied, 'Then stone it shall be,' and the bag was immediately petrified into a lump of rock. Efforts have been made over the centuries to remove the stone from its present position but each attempt has been followed by crop failure on the farm accompanied by the mysterious deaths of cattle, and for this reason it is now left severely alone.

Lincolnshire was once famous for the audacity of its demons which, if legend be true, often entered parish churches with little or no hindrance. One of Satan's favourite spots was the parish church at Holbeach where his activities are still remembered.

The story belongs to that period of Lincolnshire's history when the fens were largely undrained and the villagers had little to occupy their long, dark winter evenings apart from gambling, using the 'Devil's Picture Books' as playing cards were then known. One night three cronies, being somewhat the worse for drink, found their minds constantly turning to the fourth member of their party who had recently died. After a drunken discussion it was agreed they should pay respects to their departed friend at his tomb in Holbeach churchyard, and while there someone suggested that the corpse should be disinterred and taken into the church for a game of cards, the dead man acting as dummy. The body was disinterred and the game began. It went merrily enough until about midnight when to the players' horror the corpse suddenly disappeared and was replaced by a grinning Satan. They rubbed their eyes in amazement, but when they opened them again Satan had vanished and the corpse had resumed its place. They continued the macabre game but this time it was interrupted by the arrival of three fearsome fiends who leapt out of a vault and dragged the sacrilegious card players off to Hell.

This does not seem to have been the end of the story, however, for there were subsequent reports of four dismal spectres seen standing in the porch, providing a gruesome warning to anyone who felt tempted to indulge in a game of cards in church.

Like the devils, witches and warlocks found Lincolnshire a congenial area for their operations until very recent times. Some of their descendants dispensed herbal remedies and chanted medieval-style incantations accompanied by prayers within the memories of people now living. However, much of this art would today be described as suggestion or faith healing. The awe which magic arouses in the minds of some people seems to have its own therapeutic quality for it certainly works miracles.

The Wise Man of Louth, one of the more famous of the Lincolnshire healers of the last century, ascribed most of the illnesses he came upon to black witchcraft, and his remedies consisted largely of boiling the urine, finger and toe-nail clippings and hair of his patients in a pot on the hearth fire at midnight.

During the Middle Ages monks were known to dabble in the black arts in the hope of discovering a short cut to preferment in the Church, but one of these, Thomas Wright, the monk of

Soulby, came to grief when his books of magic were discovered in his cell. His punishment was almost certainly very light, however, for the worst penalty a priest might expect to undergo in pre-Reformation times would have been a severe penance.

Strange sounding incantations and words of power, usually in metrical verse were employed by rural healers to banish the quartern ague which was a common ailment in the Fen districts. One of these 'quacks' forced her patients to drink a hell-brew of gin, treacle and snuff, whilst she chanted the following spell up the chimney:

> Tremble and go
> Tremble and quake
> Tremble and die
> Never return.

There is a curious mound between Boston and Horncastle which was long reputed to be an assembly point for night hags. It was, however, in all likelihood a tumulus which folk tradition had invested with an aura of magic over the centuries.

Fear of witchcraft was responsible for many injustices in old-time Lincolnshire where hostility towards scapegoats was easily aroused among devil-fearing communities. Poor Fan of the Fens, the witch of Louth was chased out of the village where she lived by an army of hysterical cudgel-waving farmers, while Meg of Cranwell, another suspect, was actually murdered by a labourer with an old sword. Nor has one famous case of historical witchcraft been forgotten by Lincolnshire folk. This was the trial and execution of Margaret and Phillippa Flower for bewitching to death the young son of the Earl of Rutland. They suffered on the gallows at Lincoln in 1619.

Lincolnshire can boast a surprising number of occult characters, but doubtless the best known of all is the Lincoln Imp which is carved on one of the pillars of the Angel Choir of Lincoln Cathedral. Like others of his kind the Imp created an incredible amount of disorder in the cathedral by his misdemeanours and was finally exorcized by an angel by the simple act of turning him to stone.

For every half-remembered folktale still treasured by Lincolnshire folk, there are a dozen ghost stories which are not only retailed with zest but discussed with the utmost conviction.

The most famous haunted house in Lincolnshire is undoubtedly the old parsonage at Epworth, once the home of the Wesley family of whom the preacher John was a younger member. For two months, from December 1715 to the following January the household was subjected to constant invasions by a poltergeist, to use a familiar term for a noisy elemental spirit. Members of the family caught fleeting glimpses of a white figure, and in addition a most alarming manifestation described as a 'headless badger' which 'gobbled like a turkey-cock'. A spectre of this type would, at an earlier period of Lincolnshire history have been automatically classed as either a demon or a witch's imp for the latter were notorious for assuming grotesque animal shapes. Just sixty years earlier in the same county a wizard had actually claimed to have under his command an imp in the guise of a hare.

Thorpe Hall near Louth is haunted by the mysterious Green Lady whose appearances are regularly reported in the local Press. This particular haunting has acquired nation-wide renown as one of our most melancholy love stories, in which a heartbroken girl commits suicide for love and is condemned henceforth to haunt the scene of the tragedy for ever. She was a Spanish lady named Leonora Oviedo who fell hopelessly in love with the sixteenth-century Sir John Bolles of Thorpe Hall during his military campaign in Spain. The two parted and she took her life in far-off Cadiz. Her spirit followed her lover to England however and as long as the Bolles family were in possession of the Hall the ghost of a raven-haired woman in a green dress wandered through the gardens. More recently she has returned, still searching for her lost lover. The story first acquired its niche in folklore's hall of fame as the result of its inclusion in Bishop Percy's classic work *Reliques of Ancient English Poetry*.

An apparently unpublished ghost story was collected by the present writer whilst researching in the Brigg district of Lincolnshire. There is a well-known account here of a poor woman of Brigg in her eighties who set off one foggy Christmas Eve to beg money to buy a Christmas dinner. She became completely lost and wandered in misery until she collapsed from exhaustion and was later found dead from cold and hunger. Her cries have been heard at night immediately before Christmas pleading in despair, 'Which way do I go? Which way do I go?' Those who stumble upon the ghost in the mist say that 'her face is a dreadful picture of anguish—her eyes staring in horror'.

Whilst on the more macabre aspects of Lincolnshire's occult traditions we must refer to the legendary curse of Crowland Abbey. One Christmas in the ninth century the discipline of the monks got completely out of control and they began to indulge in debauchery, blasphemy and devil worship, deriding the shocked protests of their Abbot and rebuffing all his efforts to restrain them. They were, in fact, celebrating the semi-pagan Festival of Fools which was based on the Roman Saturnalia. The priests, still in their vestments, began dancing back to back around the altar, one of the recognized methods of conjuring up the Devil. The Abbot fled to his cell in horror and only just in time for the Prince of Evil suddenly materialized in the midst of the revellers and in a thunderous voice demanded of God divine authority to lay his curse on Crowland Abbey and its obscene priests. Satan then announced to the monks that within a twelvemonth not one stone of the Abbey would rest upon another and that all present would have been consigned to the horrors of the bottomless pit. Before disappearing in the usual cloud of brimstone and flames the Devil declared that at some time in the future a new abbey would rise upon the foundations of the old but that none present would live to see it. In the year 870 the curse was fulfilled to the letter when hordes of ferocious Vikings invaded Lincolnshire, murdering the monks and reducing Crowland Abbey to a scorched ruin. Years later a new and more beautiful building was erected in its place, but true to the prophecy none of the monks who had indulged not wisely but too well at the Christmas festivities ever lived to witness the momentous event.

In this interesting instance of what cynics might call retro-history we recognize a well-known device of the Church to lay the ultimate responsibility for human calamities upon the sinfulness of man.

Many of Lincolnshire's older traditions and beliefs almost certainly emanated from the European mainland for they display bizarre aspects which are rarely found elsewhere in Britain. Near Owston Ferry the River Trent is haunted by a seal-headed woman, while Knaith plays host to a ghost with the face of a dog. Westwoodside goes to the other extreme for there the local ghost is a woman minus her head.

Thomas Fuller, the seventeenth-century English divine once observed, unkindly, that of all English counties 'Gloucestershire was the one most pestered with monks'. It was this particular characteristic which gave rise to the old saying 'As sure as God's in Gloucestershire'. From the vast array of pagan beliefs which seem to have survived into modern times it becomes obvious that the Christian brotherhoods must have had all their work cut out to uphold Christ's banner against the tide of infidelity in the county. Gloucestershire is even today a veritable museum of unusual and extremely interesting customs inherited from the remote past, some of them of a bizarre character.

For example, every Whit Monday Birdlip witnesses the rolling of a gigantic cheese down Cooper's Hill pursued by hordes of yelling children eager for the lump of cheese awarded to the one who succeeds in capturing it. Some folklorists consider the custom to be a modern version of a very ancient pagan ritual connected with sun worship. The huge cheese, which represents the sun replaces the flaming wheel which was at one time sent rolling down Cooper's Hill.

Another ceremony of which only a single example has survived is Painswick's ancient 'clipping' ritual in which members of the parish walk around the church deosil—that is from left to right or 'the way of the sun'. Actually the term 'clipping' is quite unrelated to the trimming of the yew trees which takes place in the churchyard on the Feast of the Nativity known locally as Clipping Sunday. Various theories have been advanced to account for this event but it seems to be generally agreed that it is a survival of the Roman Festival of the Lupercalia which was dedicated to Pan.

Gloucester has a number of similar links with Britain's ancient past in the ancient barrows and 'pagan stones' which can be seen in many parts of the county and which are usually associated with curious legends. Torbarrow Hill near Cirencester is associated with a strange story involving two local men who entered the hillside through an aperture and discovered within it a warrior in armour accompanied by two corpses. Many English hillsides and tumuli are believed to be the abodes of horrific spectres and demons but there are cases in which ancient sites are credited with powers of a beneficent character, a well-known example being the Bambury Stones on Bredon Hill.

Hilton Castle, Durham

Byland Abbey, Yorkshire

Peel Castle, Isle of Man, showing the cathedral

Newstead Abbey, Nottinghamshire

Two of these, the King's stone and the Queen's stone, are supposed to have supernatural healing powers, the sufferer having to squeeze his body through the aperture separating the two in order to be cured of his ailments. The Bambury Stones, in common with others of a similar type owe their preservation not merely to their therapeutic attributes but to the fear of our ancestors that some kind of misfortune or curse might descend upon anyone who attempted to remove them.

The 'Grey Geese' of Addlestrop consist of a large number of stones which, according to ancient legend, were originally geese transformed into their present shape by a witch after a goosewoman had refused her alms. It is almost certain that large stones and curious natural rock formations played an important part in early religious life and the mystery surrounding them has given rise to the modern superstition that they are batteries of psychic power which were charged with energy at some unknown period in the past. Another intriguing theory, first advanced more than half a century ago and now acquiring a new lease of popularity, relates to pudding stones. It is often suggested that the presence of these stones on hilltops, in alignment across miles of open country, indicates the routes of ancient trackways.

Alfred Watkins, author of *The Old Straight Track* in which these theories were first put forward, mentions one such stone, the Long Stone near Staunton, as forming part of such a trackway. He also refers to the curious tradition that if the stone is pricked with a pin at midnight it immediately sheds blood. This could possibly indicate that the stone once played a part in some bloody ritual or even human sacrifice. In another legend the stone was seen moving over the fields at midnight. The famous Buck Stone (also at Staunton) which is set at an elevation of 900 feet is believed by those living near it to have been used as a sacrificial stone and as the site of a beacon.

Folklorists tell us that hill sites which originated as centres for pagan religious ceremonies were later utilized for the popular May Day games. At Mayhill, on the Gloucestershire/Herefordshire border, for example, a May Day contest waged between the young people of adjacent parishes for the possession of the hilltop, continued until well into the nineteenth century. This particular ceremony is believed to have originated as a ritual contest in which the spirits of summer and winter, personified as youths and girls, vied with one another to determine whether life was to triumph over death in nature.

The occasional monster crops up in the supernatural history of Gloucestershire as elsewhere in the English countryside. At Deerhurst the entire population are said to have been tyrannized by a huge dragon until a man of the people named Smith severed its head from its body with his axe, for which he was rewarded with a piece of land which was held by his descendants until the sixteenth or seventeenth centuries. A pleasing bit of folklore this and one which defies easy elucidation. However if Gloucestershire fails to offer very much in the realms of monster lore it compensates for the omission with curious stories relating to wayside and other graves.

At the crossroads between Poulton and Ready Token may be seen the grave of a supposed witch which is known far and wide as Betty's Grave. There is another version of the story in which it is described as the grave of Elizabeth Barstowe who either committed suicide or was hanged for theft, her body being buried at the crossroads to prevent it returning from the dead to haunt its old home.

Eighteenth-century Gloucestershire folk seem to have displayed a morbid interest in the bodies of the illustrious dead, for the tombs of the old nobility were frequently desecrated by ghoulish-minded antiquaries and their contents examined and noted. In 1782 during one of these necromantic orgies, the mortal remains of Catherine Parr, the last of Henry VIII's wives, was ripped from its lead coffin in the chapel of Sudeley Castle. The body was described by its discoverers as: 'white and moist, and wrapped in 7 sere cloths of linen, entire and uncorrupted although it had been there upwards of 280 years'.

The most eloquent shrine to deceased royalty, however, must be Berkeley Castle, the scene of the dreadful murder of King Edward II in 1327. It was here that the king was tortured to death with a red-hot spit, his shrieks of agony being heard in the town of Berkeley despite the immense thickness of the castle walls. The body was laid to rest in Gloucester Cathedral after the heart had been extracted for preservation in a silver casket. For centuries afterwards the night of death was remembered with horror by the local peasantry, and the castle still echoes with the cries of agony which are sometimes heard at night by people in the locality.

It is with relief that one turns from the morbid traditions associated with Gloucestershire's stately dead to the lighter lore of its belfrys, although here as elsewhere church bells were rung to banish the forces of evil from the abodes of man—as we read in the poet Herrick's well-known lines:

> From noise of scare fires rest ye free
> From murders Benedictie
> From all mischances that may fright
> Your pleasing slumbers in the night
> Mercie secure ye all and keep
> The goblin from ye while ye sleep
> Past one o'clock and almost two
> My masters all, good day to you.

According to a curious tradition preserved at Cherington, if one of the bells were stolen from one belfry and placed in another, undetected, the thief would escape punishment. This illusion was rudely shattered however when the treble was stolen in 1810 and set up in the Avening Tower. Ernest Morris mentions the dire consequences for the thief in his 'Legends of the Bells':

> Those Cherington bells, those Cherington bells
> What a sad tale their jingling tells.
> Alas, their now imperfect chime
> Proclaims our folly and our crime.
> ... O that we were out of the cells.
> We'd ne'er again take Cherington bells.

One of the less advertised pursuits of old-time Gloucestershire adventurers was digging up tumuli for buried treasure, and by doing so braving the anger of the spirits under whose protection it had been placed. In order to outwit the treasure dragon or spirit it was necessary to employ a highly skilled sorcerer, but even so if there occurred a single error in the ceremony the treasure hunter could expect to be blasted to perdition by the outraged guardian.

Sorcery was obviously very prevalent in Gloucestershire for as long ago as 1551, Bishop Hooper (later to be burned at Gloucester) lambasted otherwise orthodox churchgoers for putting their faith in 'prophesies, palmistry, forbidden arts and damnable crafts'.

In the seventeenth century a young witch of Tewkesbury was accused by a pig-farmer of transforming herself into a polecat, which says a good deal about contemporary standards of hygiene; but long after witchcraft had ceased to agitate the people, there remained a marked aversion among wayfarers to passing through Fairford where some of the inhabitants were suspected of casting spells upon all strangers including pedlars. Mercifully there appears to have been at least one day in each week when the threat could be disregarded since, according to the well-known Gloucestershire axiom, 'Monday's curse is no curse'.

The good folk of Gloucestershire were great believers in the principle of direct action when confronted with the possibility that operators of the black arts were at work in the community. Even to fall under suspicion of uttering an incantation often meant a visit to the courts where the accused would be fortunate to escape a conviction for witchcraft, since it was taken for granted that one could kill an enemy by an oral spell. However, the majority of the cases concern the middle years of the seventeenth century, and long before its conclusion most executions, as elsewhere, had been brought to an end.

Gloucestershire ghosts had a deeply-rooted affection for their old homes, and at Prestbury for instance there are reports of multiple hauntings. The ghostly Black Abbot is often seen in the grounds of the ancient Priory and in the parish church, while a highly cultured female phantom occasionally plays the spinet in a local garden. Occasionally hoof beats are heard as a frantic cavalier thunders through the town to deliver a somewhat overdue report on the outcome of the Battle of Worcester, while a sinister shadowy figure waits at Cleves Corner with the avowed purpose of strangling strangers. Whatever might be said of the amenities of ancient Prestbury it is generally agreed that its night life is rarely dull.

Yet another ghost with an affection for its ancient habitation is the Winchcombe monk who wanders in the vicinity of the abbey ruins, and whose arrival usually augurs some kind of tragedy in the locality. One must not depart from the Gloucester scene, however, without honourable mention of the ghost of Gloucester jail. This prison is haunted, it is reliably stated, by the ghost of a girl who was immured centuries ago in one of the cells of the abbey which stood on the adjacent site. The ghost is said to have pointed an accusing finger at one of the more sceptically-minded inmates of the jail, since which time no one has had the temerity to express doubts as to its authenticity.

3
Mysteries of the Midlands (2)

The traveller who passes through rural Herefordshire, a county seemingly untroubled by tumult and basking in tranquillity finds it difficult to imagine it as the scene of bloody warfare in bygone days.

Yet that great earthworks, Offa's Dyke, provides visible evidence of a time when it was necessary to erect a county-wide bulwark against the intrusions of the savage tribes of the west. The entire border echoes to old legends of those troubled times. Even its later ghost lore repeats the melancholy theme of violence as in the tale of two young lovers crushed by the millstones of war and finding solace only in death.

The tragedy occurred at Goodrich Castle on the River Wye which was besieged by the Ironsides under Colonel Birch during the Civil Wars. Alice, the Colonel's daughter, fell deeply in love with a young Roundhead named Clifford and the two, fled to the imagined security of the castle, which soon came under devastating mortar fire. The couple then attempted to cross the Wye on horseback, the girl riding pillion. Alas the raging current swept them both to their deaths, but this was not the end of the story. Even now, it is said, the two ghosts are occasionally seen on horseback struggling against the raging waters.

The problem of the troublesome ghost was adroitly solved by the Herefordshire clergy by the simple expedient of commanding the spirit to enter a bottle in which they confined it for 999 years. At Aconbury a spirit of greater ingenuity than usual succeeded in escaping from its bottle and revenged itself upon its persecutors by haunting the district for many years afterwards.

The Wye, like many other British rivers, is associated with a ghost which at an earlier period of our history would have been classed among the water spirits. Today, the sight of a spectral woman rowing down river is regarded by local fishermen as an omen of death. The ghost is said to utter the most heart-rending cries.

Bransil Castle was once said to contain a secret hoard of treasure under the guardianship of a demon crow. Only when the bones of Lord Beauchamp, a former owner, had been displayed to the bird would it surrender the gold. During the nineteenth century Lord Beauchamp's skeleton was said to be in the possession of a local man but he seems to have made no attempt to claim the hoard.

A good many years ago Avenbury church was haunted by a phantom organist who continued to play long after the building had been locked up for the night. The musician seems to have wearied of his exercises for although still remembered by older churchgoers his music is no longer heard.

A number of curious traditions belonging to the pre-Reformation age of poetry, magic and legend are still remembered in this border country. One is the story of the Mermaid of Marden who seized a church bell which had fallen to the bottom of the river and refused to surrender it. Even today it is sometimes stated that the bell has been heard ringing on the Sabbath when the other bells of the district are summoning worshippers to church.

Among the older Herefordshire traditions recorded by John Aubrey, the antiquary, is the pleasing 'pagan' rite in which young men and girls of the villages danced in the churchyards on holy days and holidays, this being one of the customs later outlawed by the joyless Puritans. The festivities took place on the north side of the churchyard, which was rarely used for burials since it was believed by many to be associated in some mysterious fashion with hellfire and damnation.

The witches on both sides of the border had an uncanny reputation for transforming themselves into bats and, thus disguised, to flit through open windows to cast spells upon the household. In Hereford itself there were innumerable witches of the 'white' or helpful variety like 'Dr' Coates the magical healer who operated during the nineteenth century and who was adept at tracing the whereabouts of lost or stolen objects by reading the stars and similar forms of divination. Characters like this were without any doubt, the last of a dying race of medieval magicians.

The prefix 'Dr' would have been self-awarded in the vast majority of such cases but it was not uncommon for a seventh son of a seventh son to be given the title as one of his Christian names for no better reason than that persons so born were supposed to have inherent healing powers.

It would perhaps be unwise to treat Herefordshire witchcraft too lightly or to regard it as extinct, in view of a macabre incident of black magic reported by the newspapers a few years ago. Apparently an irate ratepayer deposited the waxen image of his councillor, pierced with pins, on the doorsteps of the municipal offices.

However it was the Devil, rather than the witch who seems to have created the greatest consternation in this particular county. In fact instances of persecutions of witches were much rarer here than elsewhere in England.

Matthew Paris, the thirteenth-century English chronicler mentions a case which caused great alarm in his day, when a Herefordshire woman gave birth to a devil: in fact a baby born with a full set of teeth. The child attained the height of a seventeen-year-old youth in six months. Not surprisingly the mother's health collapsed and she died soon afterwards.

A more typical devil tradition is associated with Brampton Bryan Castle, the scene of a famous siege during the Civil War. Sir Robert Harley, whose home it was, had changed sides and although originally on friendly terms with Oliver Cromwell maintained from that time forth an intense hostility to the Dictator which lasted until Cromwell's death on 3rd September 1658. On that day a terrifying storm struck all England and as it raged through Brampton Bryan uprooted many huge trees. According to Sir Robert, Satan was actually observed dragging a struggling Cromwell through the castle park *en route* to Hell. On each anniversary of his death Cromwell's ghost is supposed to return to haunt the castle grounds.

This is a further reminder of the well-known story that Cromwell sold his soul to the Devil before Dunbar in return for political and military power, and that he received the support of Satan until the day he died.

One of the best known Herefordshire devil tales relates to the building of Kentchurch Grosmont bridge by the Herefordshire wonder-worker Jack of Kent. Keeping to precedent in such matters, Jack offered Satan, in return for his assistance, the first individual who crossed the bridge following its completion. Jack, of course, had no intention of honouring the bargain and lured a dog onto the bridge instead, much to the Devil's chagrin.

Bridge-building devils seem to have been more dim-witted than most. The annals of folklore are filled with stories in which they were easily deceived in this particular fashion.

Not far from Kington, at Stamore Rocks, there is a piece of waste land called The Devil's Garden which tradition insists is destined to remain barren until the end of time. Similar plots, often known as 'Devil's Acres' have been reported from many other parts of England; they are usually covered by weeds and more particularly thistles, which are plants supposedly dedicated to the Devil. Incidentally a thistle-covered patch of ground near the village of Canewden in Essex on the other side of the country was a shrine dedicated to both devils and witches.

A variant of the popular children's graveyard game in which one dances around the oldest tomb to conjure up the Devil, is suggested by the well-known legend of Weobley churchyard, where the same result is achieved by circumnavigating the preaching cross. For maximum effectiveness one has to recite the Lord's Prayer backwards.

Demoniac human beings seem to have created a reign of terror at many places in the British Isles and but for the once commonly employed rites of exorcism would doubtless be troubling the localities in which they lived to this day.

Such an exorcism provides the theme of a curious legend still told at Kington on the River Avon. After the death of the local tyrant, Thomas Vaughan, better known as Black Vaughan who was killed at the Battle of Banbury in 1469, his spirit refused to leave Kington Church and had to be coaxed into a box by a group of clergymen which was then cast into a pool where it apparently rests to this day. However, the spirit must have escaped for the haunting has resumed recently. Hergest Court, the fifteenth-century home of the Vaughans, later converted into a farmhouse, was long haunted by a demon dog which materialized prior to the death of any member of the family.

Demon dogs, in their role of harbingers of doom, are no rarity in Britain, well-known examples being Black Shuck the one-eyed hound of East Anglia, and the packs of canine horrors haunting Dartmoor and Bodmin Moor. The traditions of the demon dogs which haunt the Welsh border however are reminiscent of the legendary hounds of Annwyn which ushered the spirit of death into the realms of man, and also of the Greek Hecate who stood at the crossroads to give warning of death and whose presence was announced by howling dogs.

Herefordshire's famous Three Choirs Festival which was first introduced as long ago as 1715 has a rightful place in the nation's folk calendar and has even attracted a visitor from the other world. This was a phantom monk who invariably arrived at midnight during the first week of September, becoming a firm favourite with the other tourists until alas driven off by an amateur exorcist reciting the Lord's Prayer.

Among the legends of Leicestershire there is the story of a curious and macabre miracle based on the ancient folklore of blood.

It was long believed that if innocent blood were shed a curse would fall upon those responsible. Not only were the bloodstains irremovable but they also 'cried out for vengeance'.

At Wistow in Leicestershire, in the days of the Saxons, the Lord Britfardus callously murdered Wistan, the heir to the Kingdom of Mercia and buried his body secretly. Some time afterwards there came the first manifestation of divine anger, when tufts of hair began to sprout like grass from the grave of the murdered man. On seeing the 'miracle' the murderer's conscience was tormented by an overwhelming sense of guilt. He lost all self-control, raved like a madman and died utterly insane. The murdered man's bones were reverently transferred to Repton and placed in a shrine in which they remained until the Reformation when they were ejected as superstitious relics.

For years afterwards visitors to Wistow in June, the anniversary month of the murder, claimed to see human hair springing from the earth where the dead body had lain.

Hinckley, a town better known for its association with the hosiery industry than with the older superstitions, has a grisly churchyard memorial, the gravestone of Richard Smith which is supposed to sweat blood every 12th April, the anniversary of the day of his murder in 1727 during a quarrel with a recruiting sergeant. Among other graveyard superstitions which continue to linger on here and there in the county is the belief that removing a corpse from a grave for any reason whatsoever, including transferring it to a family vault in another churchyard, ensures a further death in the same family.

It is remarkable that so few Leicestershire hauntings have found their way into the standard works on ghost-lore. I find only three mentioned in the Pan *Guide to Haunted Britain*, two in Peter Underwood's *Gazetteer of British Ghosts* and one in Andrew Green's *Our Haunted Kingdom*. The most interesting story relates to Bosworth Hall near Market Harborough which is haunted by the ghost of a woman who refused to permit a priest to hear the dying confession of one of her servants and is now earthbound. A bloodstain, said by some to have been caused by the spilling of sacramental wine, and seemingly ineradicable, can be seen in the house.

Donington Hall, described as 'a very ancient foundation of Leicestershire', and the erstwhile seat of the Marquess of Hastings, was haunted by a phantom coach which was heard, but never seen, in the drive immediately prior to the death of the heir. According to Henry Blyth's *The Pocket Venus*: 'When the master of the house, sitting at the head of his table, twice heard the sound of a carriage outside when none was there then his death was certain before the year was out'.

The ghost of a skull-headed monk accompanied by a phantom dog has been reported from Beacon Hill not far from Woodhouse Eaves, said to be the second highest hill in the county. The scene of the haunting is the site of an Iron Age encampment and one is tempted to hazard that the legend must have very ancient roots. Yet another ghost is the headless warrior who haunts the lanes of Market Bosworth, and who is believed to be one of those who died at the Battle of Bosworth Field in 1485.

Inevitably, perhaps, a phantom Dick Turpin rides his ghostly Black Bess down the Leicestershire highways. The highwayman complete with tricorne hat and heavy cloak has for years been an established feature of local folklore.

Leicestershire is far more notorious for its witches than its ghosts as historians of the black arts are well aware. Over 350 years ago in 1619 Margaret and Phillippa Flower, both servants at Belvoir Castle, ancestral home of the Earls of Rutland, were executed (at Lincoln) for the crime of bewitching to death the

Earl's eldest son, the young Lord Roos, after Margaret had been dismissed from her post for some misdemeanour. The technique employed for this foul deed will be familiar to those conversant with the principles of black magic. Margaret first obtained a glove belonging to the young man and rubbed it on the back of Rutterkin her cat. The glove was then boiled, pricked with pins and buried in a dungheap. According to the theory of witchcraft the heir would then gradually waste away, which he did. Three other Leicestershire women, Anne Baker of Bottesford, Joan Willemot of Goodby and Ellen Greene of Stathorne, were also involved in the case. The principal accused, Margaret and Phillipa Flower, fully avowed their guilt and were hanged, to the relief of all respectable members of the community.

Twenty-three years earlier Thomas Darling, a fourteen-year-old Burton boy, reported that he had been cursed by an old woman named Alice Gooderridge and as a result had suffered from recurrent attacks of fits. He also insisted that a green cat accompanied by green angels had invaded his bedchamber. John Darrell, the exorcist who took over the case, created a sensation when he produced the voices of devils from the boy's mouth. An independent investigation into the case revealed that the boy had fabricated the entire story, but the revelation came too late to save the 'witch' who had in the meantime died in jail.

Leicestershire preserved an unenviable reputation as a witch-hunting county long after fear of the black arts had ceased to trouble the adjacent counties. As late as 1679 Mistress Margaret Herbert, a young widow, was accused of sending devils into a neighbouring home where loud knockings were heard by the terrified householders, and sheets plucked from the beds by unseen hands. According to a contemporary account Mistress Herbert was sentenced to be burned at the stake, which is highly unlikely, since the legal penalty for witchcraft was hanging. Many years later one of the so-called victims of the spell declared on his deathbed that he had fabricated the evidence against her from spite.

The last case of this type in England and Wales was recorded in Leicestershire in 1717 when an old woman and her son and daughter were denounced as witches by twenty-five of their neighbours. The jury to its everlasting credit refused to send the case for trial.

While the matter was under investigation an interesting anti-witch remedy came to light. Apparently all one had to do to obtain relief from a spell was to suspend a small bag containing rosemary and marigold petals close to one's chest, and mingle a little human blood with one's ale.

Many curious rituals dating from early history continue to linger on in Leicestershire and the neighbouring county of Rutland. One custom which some people believe to have originated as ancient fertility magic takes place annually on Easter Monday at Hallaton, when hare pies (they are usually beef-steak) are scrambled for on a mound called Hare Pie Bank.

According to one school of thought the scramble is the last surviving link with a local springtime rite in which a sacred animal was sacrificed to the spirits of fertility.

Rutland, like Leicestershire, has an ancient custom of which it is justly proud. At Oakham the monarch and peers of the realm must present the lord of the manor with a horseshoe when passing through the county. Horseshoes (representing tribute covering many centuries) are on view at Oakham Castle, among them specimens 'as vast as a horse collar'. In contravention of the usual custom the shoes are suspended with the points downwards which, as most people will agree, is unlucky. When hung with the horns upwards the horseshoe is a talisman against the malice of witches, a superstition derived from the luck-bringing qualities of the crescent moon. The only variation of the popular practice is connected with blacksmiths, who have the traditional right to suspend horseshoes points downwards without any detrimental effect upon their fortunes.

Rutland seems to have preserved a number of curious beliefs which are not now found elsewhere. Among the hunting fraternity one finds stories of foxes which when pursued by the hounds transform themselves into ancient crones, a tradition harking back to shape-shifting powers once credited to witches. It is interesting that this rare superstition should have survived into modern times. During the Middle Ages the fox was often believed to be a demon which could take the shape of a woman, the better to deceive human kind.

To provide a safeguard against the powers of darkness it was customary in Rutland as recently as the last century to nail a cross of rowan wood or mountain ash 'up and down the cowhouse' for protection against witches.

Rutland, like neighbouring Leicestershire, has recorded comparatively few ghosts. One is a spectral witch who haunts the parish church at Stoke Dry where long ago she was deliberately starved to death, while at Stretton in the south of the county a phantom white lady has been seen; and nearby a grisly suicide swings eerily at night from the branches of an old oak tree.

Northamptonshire, once generally known as the county of 'spires and squires', lies now well within the London commuter orbit yet fortunately remains a terrain of pleasant towns and quiet villages. It is in fact an ocean of tranquillity where the population is, largely free of the tensions suffered by those living nearer to London. Despite the county's long-established connection with the footwear industry, there remains a great deal of non-industrial folklore to be collected by the connoisseur of old-time trifles.

One finds examples of curious traditions associated with particular villages, a well-known one being represented by the saying 'Faxton was cursed by murderers'. The Faxton story takes us back to the beginning of the seventeenth century when Judge Nichols, Lord of the Manor of Faxton, was about to pass sentence of death on a prisoner. To prevent this, four women relatives of the accused cast a spell not only on Judge Nichols but on the village itself. This curse was not only held responsible for the judge's sudden and mysterious death but for the subsequent decline in the prosperity of the village. Faxton church contains an effigy of the judge supported by four figures representing the cardinal virtues: Justice, Prudence, Temperance and Fortitude which, local people once believed, to be the images of the four cursing women. The scales of Justice which dropped long since from the judge's monument were thought by villagers to represent the Divine scales on which the souls of the murderers were weighed on the Day of Judgment.

Northamptonshire featured prominently in the English Civil War and not surprisingly its ghost lore incorporates a number of morbid tales relating to the time when the county families were cruelly divided in politics and religion.

Woodcroft Castle at Elton near Peterborough was the scene

of a curious tragedy involving Michael Hudson, known as the 'plain-dealing chaplain', who was entrusted by King Charles with many important secrets. After being taken prisoner by the Parliament, Hudson with other Royalists fled to the safety of Woodcroft where they were besieged by a powerful army. The chaplain and the more courageous Royalists defended themselves valiantly for a time but were finally compelled to surrender under promise of quarter. However, once the Parliamentarians had been admitted to the castle they treacherously resumed the assault upon the now helpless defenders. Hudson was thrust over the battlements, to which he clung desperately as his hands were hacked again and again by enemy swords. He fell into the moat and endeavoured to swim to the bank but sank after being felled with the blow of the butt end of a musket. Long after the Civil War had receded from the memories of most Englishmen, those living near the castle claim to have heard the chaplain's screams of 'Mercy! Mercy!' Even now, it is said, the clash of swords is sometimes heard at night on the anniversary of the crime.

One of the most famous Civil War hauntings occurred at Daventry where the army of Charles I was encamped shortly before Naseby. The King was awakened from sleep in the Old Wheatsheaf Inn by a spectre which materialized in his room and solemnly warned him to withdraw from the battle or suffer defeat. The ghost, it appears, was Thomas Wentworth, Earl of Strafford whom Charles had surrendered to the Parliament for attainder and execution in 1641. The King was sufficiently troubled by the haunting to consult Prince Rupert, his brilliant cavalry leader, but was advised to ignore the warning and enter the battle. Charles' subsequent defeat at Naseby is a matter of history. Although the haunting was apparently limited to this one occasion, the story is still current in the Daventry area.

For the benefit of those with morbid inclinations the remains of those who died in the battle were first buried in a field and later transferred to the crypt of Rothwell Church where some 30,000 human bones may be seen laid down in regular order, layers of bones alternating with layers of skulls. It is thought that some of the dead of Bosworth Field might also have been deposited in this mausoleum of horror.

Northamptonshire has several contemporary ghost stories of interest to those in pursuit of the occult. At Absworth, near

Silverstone, the cowled figure of a monk has been seen recently, and another was photographed in Woodford parish church as recently as 1966. Woodford was the scene of a curious haunting at the time of the Civil Wars. Among the surviving Assize records for the Midland circuit in the Public Records Office occurs the case of Anne Goodfellow, the witch of Woodford who confessed that a white tom cat which haunted her home had declared itself to be 'her aunt's spirit'. The cat initiated Anne into the black arts after drinking some of her blood. The fate of the much haunted witch of Woodford and her cat is unknown; but her confidant, Cherrie of Thrapson 'a very ancient man' was left to die in Northampton jail.

Two Guilsborough women, Agnes Browne and her daughter Jane were hanged in 1616 for bewitching several young persons to death. The accused who were described during the trial as being 'as far from grace as Heaven is from Hell' had discarded their more familiar broomsticks to ride about the district on a sow's back.

Northamptonshire gipsies, like their fellows elsewhere, often came under suspicion of pratising the black arts, and as a result were regarded with some enmity. At Broughton there is a noisy annual parade of villagers known as the Tin Can Band which is believed to have been introduced in the first place as a device to keep gipsy witches out of the neighbourhood. The ceremony is held on the first Sunday after 12th November at midnight. Taking into account the changes in the calendar introduced in 1752 which resulted in a variation of eleven days, it seems certain that the ceremony was originally held on 31st October, or Hallowe'en, the traditional night for driving away witches, devils and ghosts.

Loud Noises were always anathema to evil spirits; in modern Germany whips are cracked and pots sent smashing to the ground on the eve of weddings to protect the bride and groom from bewitchment. In Romany witchcraft, one finds that the Dukkerers, as the fortune-tellers are called, will often hint to a client that he or she is bewitched and then offer to remove the spell in return for crossing their palms with silver.

Perhaps only in our own day has it been fully realized how closely paganism lies beneath the surface of our minds. This helps to explain the modern preoccupation with magic and the

Rollright Stones, Oxfordshire

Raynham Hall, Norfolk

Hill Hall, Theydon Mount, Essex

fascination felt for civilizations that have 'vanished in the midst of time'. The historic fact that the early Christians built their churches on pagan sites often enhances the mystery attached to these holy places. All Saints Parish Church, Lilbourne, stands close to an earthworks which suggests that those who built it saw the value of 'cashing in' on the sanctity of a pagan shrine. The curious mazes of which so few remain today are believed to have played an important role in the mystical life of the Bronze Age. They were sufficiently popular to be adopted by Christian builders, for the maze motif appears in the marbled floors of churches from the twelfth century onwards, often fashioned in the form of a cross combined with the figures of angels and bishops. Until about sixty years ago one of the most interesting mazes was still in existence at Boughton Green. Known as The Shepherd's Race and some thirty-seven feet in diameter, it was perambulated annually at the time of the village fair. Now nearly all the old mazes have vanished, and we are left to mourn with Titania in *A Midsummer Night's Dream*:

> The nine men's morris is fill'd up with mud;
> And the quaint mazes in the wanton green,
> For lack of tread, are undistinguishable ...

During the Middle Ages the bones and tusks of fossil animals were often assumed to be the remains of an extinct race of giants and were exhibited in churches together with such awe-inspiring 'supernatural' souvenirs as meteoric stones.

Stanion Church in Northamptonshire possesses a curious relic which is associated with one of the best known English legends, the six-foot long bone, the rib it is said of a gigantic Dun Cow. According to an old legend the Dun Cow promised to supply milk to all who were kind enough to feed it. However, the arrangement was complicated by the arrival of a witch who instructed the animal to fill a sieve with milk. The cow attempted to carry out the impossible task and died from exhaustion.

Most authorities are agreed that the presence of huge bones in churches is not fully explained. However it should be borne in mind that the cow was a sacred animal among all Indo-European peoples which include the Aryan race to which the English belong. It was once believed that you could ensure a place in

Heaven by giving a cow to a pauper, and in the folklore of northern England the Milky Way, is known as Cow Lane, and is supposed to be the route taken by the soul on its journey to the other world.

It would be fair to say that of all the Midland counties Warwickshire has been the one most influenced by witchcraft and the black arts. The traveller in this fascinating countryside can taste a wide variety of pleasures, including delightful woodland scenery and the cult of the Bard while those who venture off the beaten track will be intrigued by the tenacity of superstition among the country folk. If a recent report in surviving folk beliefs in the county can be regarded as significant, there can have been little real change in the pattern of some of their ideas since the last century.

In 1975 the newspapers published the result of a survey carried out among Warwickshire country folk which produced the following 'old wives' tales':

To ensure that a baby grows up strong and healthy it must be rolled in the first snow of the winter following its birth. Another curious survival relates to boy and girl twins. It is imperative to baptize the boy prior to the girl for if the process is reversed the girl will eventually grow a beard.

More than a century earlier in the days of Queen Victoria the *Gentleman's Magazine* of 1859 published a list of Warwickshire beliefs then current which included the following gems of county lore:

> The only certain remedy for the bite of an adder is to kill the offending reptile and apply some of its fat to the wound. If a pig is killed in the wane of the moon, the bacon will be sure to shrink in the boiling; if, on the other hand, the pig is killed when the moon is at the full the bacon will swell.

There is an almost medieval quality about the surviving remnants of Warwickshire witchcraft, for while there is little trace of the modern doctrine of the witch coven with naked maidens dancing to the gods of fertility upon lonely hilltops, there is instead devildom, bloody murder and occult mysteries which seem destined never to be solved.

On St Valentine's Day 1945 a seventy-four-year-old farm labourer named Charles Walton of Lower Quinton set off to work as usual in the fields on the slopes of Meon Hill, and on the same evening his corpse was discovered saturated with gore. A gash in the shape of a cross had been hacked in his chest and his throat had been impaled with his own pitchfork to the blood-stained soil. Despite exhaustive police enquiries neither murderer nor motive was ever brought to light and the Coroner's jury were forced to bring in a verdict of 'murder by a person or persons unknown'.

Scotland Yard's famous detective, Fabian of the Yard, who investigated the case in depth, found himself working on completely unfamiliar lines for there was now the suggestion that Walton had been murdered by some neighbour who suspected him of witchcraft on no stronger grounds, it appears, than that he kept toads as pets.

There was, however, a curious parallel between the Walton case and a similar murder in the same district some seventy years earlier in 1875 when Anne Turner, a suspected witch who also kept toads, was murdered by a man who believed she had bewitched him. Her throat was slashed with a billhook and her body, like Walton's, was pinned to the earth with a pitchfork.

Long Compton village, the scene of the murder of Anne Turner, is destined to remain dominated by supernatural forces for a long time to come if the well-known legend holds true. 'There are enough witches in Long Compton to push a wagon-load of hay up Long Compton Hill', goes the saying. The local contingent of 'pale Hecate's team' are supposed to hold their nocturnal revels just over the county border at the famous prehistoric site, the Rollright Stones. The presence of these mysterious characters in Long Compton plus a phantom coach which is regularly pulled by six headless horses up Harrow Hill in the same parish, suggests the existence of a somewhat neurotic night life in this haven of rural tranquillity.

This is only one of the fascinating phantom coach stories which are told in Warwickshire, for the county is second to none in its deference to the old doctrine that the souls of the restless dead will sometimes linger on in the physical world for centuries on end.

Ilmington, near Shipston on Stour, famous as the home of

Bennett the Cotswold Fiddler who died about a quarter of a century ago, is now more renowned as the scene of a haunting which has become national property following its inclusion in the majority of ghost gazetteers. From as long ago as the eighteenth century a phantom coach pulled by spectral horses has been reported moving in complete silence through this part of Warwickshire. Observers declare that the coach leaves the road and takes to a rough trackway where it presently dissolves into the mist. However, more recently, the 'night coach' as it has been called has been seen in daylight following the same route. Local residents fail to show any real interest in this phenomenon being far more impressed by the ghost of a former churchwarden who wanders among the pews.

A wide variety of spectral transport is known in Warwickshire: there is a phantom lorry on the road between Coventry and Rugby which vanishes into thin air after crashing into the vehicle ahead of it and a spectral pedestrian has been observed crossing the stretch of road between Atherstone and Shipston on Stour and marching fearlessly through a brick wall. This ghost is linked in local tradition with the death of a farmer whose horse carried him at too great a speed into the overhanging branch of a tree near this particular spot.

Perhaps there ought to be a haunting there but there is none at Blacklow, re-named Gaversake, the site of the execution of Piers Gaveston, King Edward II's evil genius whose influence over the monarch was ascribed to sorcery. Gaveston, popularly known as the Witch's Son, died dreadfully, continuing to scream for mercy until the headsman's axe silenced him forever. For some seemingly inexplicable reason Gaveston's ghost has recently returned to haunt the scene of his capture at Scarborough Castle, Yorks.

There is an old tradition at Long Lawford that the ghost of a one-armed man was trapped in a bottle by a dozen local clergymen many years ago. The spectre had haunted the now vanished Lawford Hall from Elizabethan times onwards and had become so troublesome that the church was called in to eject it. Astounding as this might seem, exorcizing a spirit into a bottle was once a recognized procedure. The ritual is an interesting one and worthy of describing in detail. The exorcist had to stand at the centre of a circle inscribed in chalk on the floor, with a Bible in his hand and a bottle of water at his feet. He muttered either a prayer or a magical incantation commencing in a low tone but gradually increasing in volume until his voice arose to a terrifying scream. This part of the ceremony was known as 'witching the ghost small enough to enter the bottle'. A candle was next lit and inserted into the neck of the bottle. The exorcist cried out at the top of his voice 'I conjure you into this bottle to remain there until the candle burns in water'. Afterwards the bottle was cast into the nearest stream, which completed the exorcism.

A bottle-conscious ghost haunts the Blue Lias public house at Stockton near Rugby. The inn was originally a farm and here a labourer was discovered in bed with his master's wife and murdered on the spot. According to recent reports a spectre with red hair has been seen flitting through the public bar leaving chilly emanations in its wake.

The majority of English battlefields have their ghost stories and Edgehill is no exception. This battle, fought not far from Kineton in Warwickshire on 23rd October 1642 between the Royalists led by King Charles I and the Parliamentary army under the Earl of Essex, was the first of the Civil War and incredibly bloody. Of all conflicts civil war is the most shattering both psychologically and psychically, and the blood guilt will often find its outlet in legends of macabre hauntings which are told centuries after the principal characters in the struggle have been forgotten.

The Edgehill ghosts were reported about two months after the battle by shepherds who declared they had seen two phantom armies re-enacting the horrors of war. They had clearly heard the clamour of arms, the beating of drums and the cannon's roar and had observed the rival war-standards borne by spectral warriors floating above the sea of blood. When the report reached King Charles I he dispatched a number of officers to the scene with instructions to verify the story, and these affirmed that they were genuine, for they also had witnessed the ghostly battle. This news, alas, was regarded by the Royalists as ominous of even worse horrors to come.

It is said that Edgehill field remains a haunted place to this day. The hoofbeats of invisible cavalrymen thunder at night down the nearby roads and across the hillside accompanied by the screams of the wounded and dying which rise shrilly above the clash of steel.

Inevitably a number of macabre legends have survived among those living in the Edgehill district, one of the most interesting being the tale of the soldier and the devil. A villainous corporal of Dragoons named Jeremiah Stone having looted the dead and dying on the battlefield, filled his pockets with a large amount of stolen money. Although wounded he had sufficient strength to find his way to the Anchor Inn in Warwick where he confided his ill-gotten gains to the landlord, promising to return when he had recovered. After his wounds had healed the corporal arrived at the Anchor Inn to collect the loot, and as one would expect, the landlord declared he had never seen him before and ejected him from the premises. The soldier next tried to break into the inn to recover the money but was arrested and thrown into prison. So far the story seems perfectly credible, but at this point fantasy takes over and it develops on lines familiar to students of seventeenth-century superstitious ideas. While the soldier lay miserably in jail contemplating his forthcoming end on the gallows no less a personage than Satan entered his cell and, recognizing a soul mate, offered to represent him at the trial. The deal was agreed and on the appointed day the Devil arrived in court and put it to the judge that in fairness to his client the inn ought to be searched for the money. On hearing this the landlord leapt to his feet and declared, hand on heart, 'May the devil take me if I lie.' Opportunities like this are no everyday occurrence and the astounded Devil grabbed the terrified innkeeper in his talons and, leaping into the air, flew with him over the rooftops of Warwick, leaving in his wake what was described in a contemporary account as a 'terrible stink'.

Devildom can claim a veritable stronghold in Warwickshire legendary lore.

Between Alcester and Stratford there is a conical hill known as Alcocks Arbour where, according to local tradition, a robber named Alcock once had his lair. For centuries following his death the robber's hoard of gold was believed to lie under the protection of a diabolical cockerel. An Oxford scholar, no doubt trusting that his educational qualifications secured him from all supernatural hazards, sought and discovered the treasure chest but inadvertently awakened the cockerel and was torn to pieces. Had the scholar possessed a better knowledge of folklore his life might have been spared. According to local belief, he had only to present the cockerel with one of Alcock's bones and he would have been given the treasure without any further enquiry.

Another name given to the same hill is the 'Devil's Bag of Nuts'. According to an old legend Satan had been gathering nuts on Devil Nutting Day (otherwise Holy Rood Day) when the Virgin Mary ordered him to drop his sack immediately. He complied but the harvest of nuts falling in a heap to the ground formed this conical hill.

At the root of this odd little story can be detected an intriguing tradition with a pre-Reformation flavour. Holy Rood Day (14th September), was an ancient church festival coinciding with the popular rural custom of gathering nuts. The gatherers were usually young couples who found it an opportune occasion to tarry awhile in the woods.

> The Devil as the common people say
> Doth go a-nutting on Holy-rood day
> And sure such lechery in some doth lurk
> Going a-nutting do the Devil's work.

Nuts have been traditionally regarded as symbols of fertility and in Roman Britain they were presented to newly-weds to ensure a plentiful harvest of babies. There were villages in the British Isles where the bride was actually given hazel nuts as she left the church, hence the country saying, 'A good nutting year brings plentiful boy babies'.

The legend of the Dun Cow of Warwick is almost the same as that of the Dun Cow of Northamptonshire. The legend was recorded in a curious black letter book entitled *The Noble and Renowned History of Guy Earl of Warwick* in the library of Warwick Castle. The story tells how an enormous 'dun-coloured cow at least four yards in height and six in length and a head proportionable' devastated Warwickshire villages until it was combated by the folk hero Guy of Warwick who had the pleasure of seeing the monster expiring before his eyes amid vast torrents of blood.

On learning of this remarkable victory the King of England conferred a knighthood upon the champion and gave orders that one of the Dun Cow's huge ribs was to be displayed in Warwick Castle. Dr Caius, the sixteenth-century Cambridge scholar, claimed to have seen the creature's enormous head in the castle together with a vertebra of great size, its circumference being not less than three Roman feet, 7 inches and a half'. Another rib, was on view at Guys Cliffe, the chapel of Guy of Warwick 'the smallest part is nine inches, the length 6 feet and a half'.

No doubt history will go on recording fantastic battles between supernaturally endowed mortals and monsters from the primeval slime, even if they have now been projected into the realms of Science-Fiction.

In Christian symbolism the dragon represents evil incarnate which is destined to be overcome by the spirit of good. Some early chroniclers believe Guy of Warwick to have been a real person who lived during the reign of King Athelstan in the ninth century and that the Dun Cow legend symbolizes the battle royal fought by him against the Danish champion, the African warrior Colbran in which the latter was defeated.

Geographically Worcestershire may be compared to a huge saucer, for it consists of a central plain almost entirely rimmed by hills. The county offers many vistas of breathtaking beauty, delightful river scenery, the Vale of Evesham, forest land and the fascinating Malvern Hills.

Historically speaking the county remains linked in most people's minds with two important battles relating to two civil wars. The first, Evesham in 1265, saw the defeat of de Montfort's forces, and the second, Worcester, which was fought four hundred years later, resulted in the overthrow of Charles II by the Parliamentary army. Neither of these bloody conflicts is likely to be forgotten in a county where old memories live long.

The trauma of civil war must be held accountable for the apparition which presented itself to a sentry at Worcester Cathedral in the 1640s. The mysterious manifestation for which no adequate explanation has been submitted from that day to this, was a phantom bear, or at least this was the excuse offered by the soldier for his absence from his post.

Far less emotionally disturbing, however, is the well known occult presence frequently reported from Dudley Castle now reduced to little more than a magnificent ruin as the result of a disastrous fire in the eighteenth century. The castle ghosts indicate their presence by emanating an icy wind which sends shivers down passing spines. This is followed by the arrival of two figures in 'historical costume' walking arm in arm near the gate house.

That famous beauty spot, the Cotswolds village of Broadway, acquired a merited place in the calendar of the macabre as the result of the gibbeting here in 1661 of three innocent persons at the crossroads, a spot clearly marked by the Cross in Hand signpost. Self-ringing church bells or better, perhaps, bells rung by long-dead hands, are a fairly commonplace feature of English village folklore, and Broadway is no exception in offering a similar legend to posterity. According to a well-established tradition the bells of the Broadway church were heard ringing during the Second World War at a time when all bellringing was banned in Britain. The local view is that the sound emanated from the heart of a beech wood where the parish bells, which were removed from the belfry after the Reformation, are thought to lie concealed.

Taking into account the well-known fact that a church is almost invariably the oldest building in any locality it is hardly surprising that it should often be linked with very ancient legends. There is a curious story on record relating to the rebuilding of Inkberrow church which took place, presumably during the Middle Ages. As fast as the stones were down by the workmen the local demons, who rejoiced in the name of Arcubs, took them away. Finally, discovering that all their efforts were completely futile the Arcubs gave vent to their anger by scattering the haycocks around the farmers' fields and making the night hideous with their doleful laments.

It was through legends of this type that our ancestors commemorated the bitter struggle between the rival religions of paganism and Christianity at the dawn of English history. Treading firmly in the footsteps of St Paul, the early Christians maintained the principle that all the gods of the pagans—as well as most of those who worshipped them—were devils who had to be destroyed. One can sympathize with the frantic and futile pagan priesthood struggling vainly against the tide of the Christian advance, only to be condemned as imps of Satan once they had been overthrown.

Although Worcestershire's devils seem to have enjoyed a long and active life, their intrusions into the county's affairs were largely confined to the medieval period. Ancient chroniclers tell of a particularly harrowing invasion in 1355 when 'many men were driven mad by the sight of demons'. Innumerable countryfolk were suddenly struck down by an unknown malady 'as it were from the assaults of evil spirits'. Those afflicted lost their reason and ran like madmen about the villages, sometimes taking refuge in fields and woods, but many were brought into the churches to be exorcized by the clergy.

There survives in Worcestershire not only an extensive devil lore but also some curious beliefs concerned with other unearthly visitants of devilish origin. According to an old Bromsgrove tradition, six phantom birds of fate fly occasionally over the town in search of a seventh. Should they find it, continues the cheerless legend, the world will come to a sudden and dramatic end. Some hold the view that Satan rides a devilish pack of hounds through the same district and that their fiendish howls are heard at night in the vicinity of Lickey Hills.

The Devil adopted all manner of disguises in the past the better to deceive the peasants of Little Comberton. On one occasion, dressed as a labourer, he obtained employment on a farm where he unwittingly betrayed his supernatural identity by working at phenomenal speed. Suspecting that this was no human workman the farmer decided to be rid of him by setting him a number of seemingly impossible tasks. The labourer was first instructed to fill a water barrel from a sieve, and next to mow a field covered with iron spikes. He succeeded in both tasks and was then ordered to straighten a curl in a lock of a woman's hair. He failed this task dismally and retreated from the farm in disgust, never being seen in that part of the county again.

With such a vast number of Worcestershire devils at work it is hardly surprising that the county should have had an unenviable reputation for witchcraft. As recently as the nineteenth century there was an infamous white witch at Kidderminster who owned a devil masquerading as a huge black cat. The woman is supposed to have disappeared mysteriously up her cottage chimney followed by the cat which left a powerful aroma of brimstone in its wake.

The villagers of Tardebigge (on the Birmingham and Worcester Canal) are almost certainly unaware of the importance of their area in the annals of witchcraft. Tardebigge was the home in the seventeenth century of the infamous Dr John Lambe who began his career as a wise man or white wizard and graduated from rural witchery to metropolitan sorcery, becoming personal magician to the Duke of Buckingham. On 16th December 1607, Lambe was charged at Tardebigge with practising 'certain evil diabolical and execrable arts' on Thomas, Lord Windsor which had caused his lordship to waste away. Lambe was found guilty and would have been hanged but for an outbreak of jail fever which killed off most of the court officials and the jury. He was transferred to the Kings Bench Prison, where he resided in luxury, being consulted by the nobility and gentry of London. Had he kept his head he might have remained in security and comfort for the remainder of his life, but his passion for the drama led to his undoing; he was detected by a London mob making his way to a theatre and torn to pieces.

A witchcraft mystery which has hitherto defied elucidation is brought to mind by the singular haunting near Harvington Hall not far from Bromsgrove. It is the ghost of the witch Mistress Mary Hicks who was executed early in the eighteenth century for causing her neighbours to vomit pins and for capsizing a ship by her magical arts. A contemporary pamphlet published in 1716 has led to a great deal of confusion by suggesting that the events took place in Huntingdonshire. However, the presence of her ghost in Worcestershire indicates fairly clearly that the Harvington Hall area was the real scene of her operations.

No doubt Worcestershire is endowed with the usual quota of ghost stories but relatively few of these appear to have gone on record. Jack Hallam mentions in his interesting book *The Haunted Inns of England* a Kidderminster pub where an adulterous wife who was murdered long ago by her jealous husband continues to search frantically at night for her dead lover, and at Upton Snodsbury a phantom baby protests with frantic screams at its murder at the hands of its father who had been driven mad by its crying.

Few lovers of the Malverns are unlikely to be deterred from their visits by the melancholy story of the curse of Raggedstone Hill. During the Middle Ages a monk died there from exhaustion while undergoing a penance which involved crawling to the summit on his hands and knees. With his last breath the monk took a long hard look at the rocky hill top and declared: 'May all those upon whom the shadow of this stone shall fall die an untimely death.'

A number of phantom carriages and coaches crop up in the annals of occult Worcestershire. One of the former hurtles across the lawns of the court house at Shelsea Wash and sinks gracefully into the moat, and another has been seen on the road between Lenchwick and Norton. Worcester has also an eccentric ghost consisting of a pair of phantom hunting boots which have been seen marching over a field at Besford. They are said to have belonged to a kennelman who had the misfortune to be eaten by his hounds.

4
Eastern Journey

Cambridgeshire is far more renowned for its university than its ghosts although the latter, one is happy to say, are at last receiving the recognition that is their due. The countryside, despite its many uninteresting aspects, provides a favourable environment for extremely macabre manifestations, in particular the fenland areas which have become happy haunting grounds for visitors from beyond the grave.

Here are to be found many survivals based on the folk traditions of our ancestors: for the entire area is dominated by ghosts, ghouls, giants and witches, not to forget their gibbering imps. When the mist lies low over the fenlands Cambridgeshire is indeed a haunted place.

Commencing our journey into the unknown with the city of Cambridge itself, one visits Corpus Christi College to hear the sad tale of a suicide of long ago, the unhappy Dr Butts who hanged himself on Easter Sunday 1632. His disturbed state of mind, which resulted in this tragedy, was brought about by an epidemic which carried off many acquaintances and students alike. Occasionally the spirit of Dr Butts, which was at one time easily identifiable from its shoulder-length hair, is observed staring mournfully from a window. An attempt to exorcize it many years ago seems to have failed for, as Christina Hole says in her *Haunted England*, 'the ghost still haunts his old quarters'.

A nineteenth-century ghost has been reported in connection with Trinity College, in this case the spirit of a child whose cries were actually heard by one of the students when Christopher Wordsworth, brother of the poet, was master there. Dr Wordsworth had recommended certain lodgings to the youth, who later returned to him complaining that a spectral child with hands turned outwards had appeared in his room time and time again and depressed him with its groans. William Wordsworth who also knew the story says that the rooms had a long-standing reputation for being haunted.

Seats of learning have attracted unearthly visitants from earliest times since scholars, in seeking to unlock the mysteries of nature, often unwittingly open the doors to all kinds of demoniac forces. Learning, like intelligence, has always been suspect, hence the curious story of the seventeenth-century Cambridge undergraduate who sold himself to the Devil in return for his degree. (A pamphlet published in 1646 refers to a visit to one of the colleges by Satan in the guise of a Master of Arts.) The student it is said passed his examination with honours but was later seen soaring over Cambridge in the arms of the Devil, *en route* to Hell.

It was no doubt because of the strong Puritan influence in the university that Cambridge scholars always displayed a keen preoccupation with the supernatural, the Devil and Hell. The original chapel of Emmanuel College, the cultural centre of Puritanism, was deliberately built in a north and south orientation instead of the customary east and west as a visible protest against the traditional practice of erecting churches in alignment with the sun which seemed to imply a tacit allegiance to sun worship. Cambridgeshire, as one would perhaps expect, was an area where the persecution of witches reached epidemic proportions. Typical of the seventeenth-century witch hunts was the curious case of a woman of Cambridge who was wooed by a devil disguised as a 'young man' who vanished into thin air leaving a puppy in his place. Accepting an invitation to meet her lover at a party the girl discovered that all the guests were witches, including an ancient warlock who had flown to the assembly on the back of a pig.

There are occasional references in old records to witches who hurtled through the skies at night on hurdles, sometimes whisking innocent bystanders into the air as they flew. In 1612 two Quakers were said to have transformed a Long Stanton woman into a mare and have sailed on her back through the heavens to a coven meeting at Dinton near Cambridge. Fortunately the Quakers were acquitted of the charges of witchcraft which had been brought against them, otherwise it is just possible that their organization might have gone down in history as the Society of Fiends.

This story appears in greater detail in the seventeenth-century pamphlet *Strange and Terrible News from Cambridge being a true relation of the Quakers bewitching Mary Phillips*, a case which created something of a sensation at the time particularly when a number of Cambridge theologians declared the acquittal to have been a traversty of justice. Among those who opposed the verdict was John Bunyan, author of *The Pilgrim's Progress*.

As recently as the first quarter of the present century, Horseheath could boast a witch in Mother Red Cap who is still remembered in the district. After her death in 1926, which was widely reported in the Press, it was disclosed that she had owned five witch's imps, all of them in the traditional shapes decreed by the folklore of witchcraft—namely a cat, a toad, a ferret, a mouse and a rat.

Since it is also traditional that a witch is unable to die until she has passed her imps to her successor it must be assumed that someone in the locality has inherited Mother Red Cap's powers together with her curious menagerie. Only in the realms of the Devil presumably could a demon cat lie peaceably with a devil mouse.

Cambridgeshire witches, when brought to book, were usually offered a last minute opportunity to vindicate themselves by reciting the Lord's Prayer word perfectly while they stood with the rope around their necks at the foot of the gallows on Castle Hill. The Lord's Prayer was also employed in Cambridgeshire as an antidote to black magic spells until comparatively recent times. In remote areas of the fenlands a 'bewitched' person would boil a bottle containing his own urine and blood, his nail parings and snippets of his hair at midnight whilst reciting the Prayer backwards. The purpose of this counter-spell was to so torment the witch through the power of white magic that she consented to release him from her spell.

All kinds of devilish creatures, many of them fairly obviously fiends from Hell, have been reported from the quieter areas of the county from time to time.

At West Wratting, for example, there is an imp called Shrug Monkey a pop-eyed shaggy-coated monster of unknown species with (curiously) the head of an ape. In the Willingham area more demoniac mice are supposed to lurk. Their original owner, Jabez Few, who is firmly believed to have sold his soul to the Devil, seems to have left his fiendish pets to fend for themselves. One of them, obviously starving, was last seen chasing a terrified cat down the Cambridgeshire lanes.

Until about a hundred years ago the villagers of Leverington held an annual supper to commemorate that dreadful occasion in the eighteenth century when an evil spirit whirled a woman into the air as a punishment for baking cakes on Easter Sunday. A special cake, known as a whirling cake was long one of the culinary delights of this feast.

Cambridgeshire folk, in common with those of other counties, had a tendency to attribute their ancient earthworks and prehistoric sites to Satan, hence the prevalence of place names bearing the prefix 'Devil', most of which are reputed to be haunted by very ancient ghosts. The Cambridgeshire Devil's Dyke has a spectre of fairly recent vintage, however, the ghost of a murderer who was gibbeted at Reach Fen some two centuries ago.

Felon's bones can never rest, nor for that matter can that canine horror, the phantom Black Shuck who haunts Devil's Dyke. This demon dog, which is reputed to be the size of a pony, surveys his prey from a single red eye. Those who have the misfortune to see him (which is usually at dusk) can anticipate dying within the year.

Giants are a rarity in the folklore of the eastern counties, their natural habitat being the mountainous areas of the north and west. Cambridgeshire, however, once possessed a well-known character belonging to this species named Tom Hickathrift, a seven-foot monster man who is buried in the churchyard at Tilney. Possessed of incredible strength Tom could lift the trunks of immense trees with ease and was even known to carry a wagon-load of straw on his back without pausing for breath. Although Tom was born in the eleventh century, stupendous deeds reminiscent of the giants of Celtic mythology were attributed to him, including a duel with a rival treasure-guarding giant whom he battered to death with the axle of a cart, using its wheel as a shield, finally making off with his enemy's gold.

To those unversed in esoteric matters, the name Gog Magog probably conjures up visions of that well-known Cambridgeshire golf course '18 holes, 6,286 yards set in ideal surroundings of heath and parkland'. To others it will possibly suggest the mythical giants Gog-Magog who were overthrown in battle by the legendary Brut, first king of the Britons and brought to London to serve their master in his ancient palace where Guildhall now stands. To the religiously-minded Gog and Magog are recognizable as the Biblical names of the enemies of God, but to lovers of folklore Gog-Magog was a giant who was miraculously transformed into that mighty heap of earth which we know as Gog Magog Hill.

In the 1950s excavations carried out on the site which lies southeast of Cambridge, revealed hill figures cut into the chalk which were believed at the time to symbolize the cosmic conflict between light and darkness fought by the Sun God against those who sought his destruction. Although the hill has subsequently lost much of its significance as a place of pilgrimage, it retains a place in ghost lore, for it is said to be haunted by a spectral horseman.

Cambridgeshire's monastic houses are almost invariably haunted by one or more of their former cloistered inmates who have never forgiven the iconoclasts for robbing them of their sanctuaries. Spinney Abbey, once a thirteenth-century monastery, is haunted by phantom monks who seem to be completely unconcerned with the fact that their ancient home is now a farmhouse.

The ancient vicarage at Elm near Wisbech is still occupied by a long-forgotten ecclesiastic who mournfully tolls a bell prior to any forthcoming death in the parish.

Cambridge, as one would expect of a shrine of learning and the arts, boasts the presence of two phantom poets. One is Rupert Brooke who haunts the old vicarage at Grantchester, while a spectral Lord Byron occasionally swims in a local pond. Why this restless soul should have preferred the idylls of Cambridgeshire to the Gothic splendours of Newstead Abbey is somewhat mystifying. It is difficult to reconcile Grantchester's tranquil moods with the author of *The Giaour*:

> But first on earth as vampire sent
> Thy corpse shall from its tomb be rent:
> Then ghastly haunt thy native place,
> And suck the blood of all thy race.
> Then from thy daughter, sister, wife,
> At midnight drain the stream of life ...

The most famous ghost in this much haunted county is Queen Mary Tudor, who is said to have slept awhile at Sawston Hall, and to have resided there in spirit ever since. Here at night there are sounds of a latch being lifted by invisible hands, while the musically attuned have detected a spinet played by an unseen presence. Bloody Mary must have regarded the original house which stood on this site with great affection for it was here that she was protected by faithful friends from those who would have imprisoned her.

As an appropriate conclusion to our morbid tour through the Cambridgeshire countryside we turn to the Caxton Gibbet Public House on the Old North Road. The inn was once owned by a landlord who in true Sweeney Todd tradition murdered his customers for their money. The gibbet which stands nearby marks the site where footpads, highwaymen and sheep stealers were suspended in chains in the eighteenth century.

Essex is sufficiently close to London to provide a very accessible area for touring and, disregarding that part of the county now absorbed into Greater London, one finds large areas of unexpected interest, not the least being Epping Forest now under the custodianship of the City. Few who choose to visit this six thousand acres of splendid woodland are aware of its interesting history. As the surviving remnant of the Royal Hunting Forest of Waltham it is a focal point for curious traditions and customs as well as for melancholy ghost stories, some of them centuries old.

Not far from Epping, which was known to the gipsies as the 'Town of the Big Tree', there is an Iron Age earthworks where, according to local belief, Boadicea, the Iceni queen, fought her last battle against the Romans and where she and her two daughters are supposed to have taken poison rather than fall alive into the hands of their enemies. Even today there are rumours that three phantom women have been seen in the dusk walking side by side close to the public road.

In view of the fact that much of the forest was originally owned by the monks of Waltham Abbey it is not unduly surprising that a cowled spectre is occasionally seen in the area called Monk Wood. Every now and again there are reports that the phantom monk crosses the forest roads where he has recently become an accepted traffic hazard.

The Abbey itself, which now lies beyond the forest area, is supposed to be haunted by the ghost of a young girl who committed suicide in the River Lea in order to escape the attentions of a lustful cleric. Visitors to the Abbey have sensed a sinister atmosphere at this place: a common experience being a shiver running down the spine. Lights have also been seen within the Abbey church at night accompanied by the faint sound of chanting from a long-dead choir emanating from the ruins at the rear of the building.

A local ghost story, thought to be at least three hundred years old, is associated with one of the forest ponds and its haunted willow tree. It was here many centuries ago that a young couple met secretly, concealing their relationship from the girl's father who insisted that they must part. Their secret was betrayed and the father in an insane rage killed his daughter to prevent her from keeping her tryst. The girl, however, appeared at the usual meeting place, standing beneath the willow tree, but as her lover embraced her she melted away in his arms. This area of forest was long shunned by courting couples as a place of unmitigated doom.

There are many other haunted sites in this mysterious forest, one being Queen Elizabeth I's ancient hunting lodge, now a museum, which has a spectre so horrific that it once scared a tramp to death. A wild huntsman accompanied by spectral hounds rides at night through the gates of Copt Hall, to the north of the forest, in search of human prey.

During the eighteenth century Epping Forest became the happy hunting ground of many highwaymen, including Jack Rann, better known as 'Sixteen String Jack', who has a public house named after him. However, it was the villainous Dick Turpin who provided the area with its most famous ghost story. Turpin and his gang set up their headquarters in the forest in the 1730s and engaged in an orgy of deer stealing, highway robbery and housebreaking. In 1736 they invaded the isolated farmhouse home of Widow Shelley at Loughton and compelled her to disclose the whereabouts of her money by holding her over an open fire. The old woman finally revealed the hiding place and the thieves decamped with about four hundred pounds, an immense sum of money in those days.

As a penance for his abominable crime Turpin's ghost must

ride down Traps Hill, Loughton, past the old widow's home three times every year with his victim's ghost clinging to his back. To meet these spectres at night is regarded as an omen of disaster in the district. Details of the robbery are recorded in that curious compendium of eighteenth-century infamy—*The Newgate Calendar*.

It is rare to discover dragon legends within commuting distance of London, but Essex rejoices in several for Essex has always been a county of surprises.

At Henham, to the north of the county, lying close to the Hertfordshire border, a nine-foot-long mini-dragon 'with eyes as big as a sheep's' was once seen in a field near the village. Apparently the monster was perfectly harmless and shortly afterwards disappeared from the scene, but up to a generation or so ago the dramatic incident was commemorated by the sale of miniature dragons at the annual fair. A life-sized model of the dragon, with a boy inside it, was one of the features of Henham's May-Day pageant.

The only reliable Essex antidote to death from a dragon's fangs was apparently a curious beverage called Snakebite which was sold at the village inn. The well-known public house, 'The Essex Dragon', in Covent Garden, London, commemorated this remarkable affair.

According to a manuscript in the Library of the Dean and Chapter of Canterbury two mighty dragons were once seen advancing upon each other from opposite sides of the Essex/Suffolk border, one being reddish brown and the other jet black. After hours of futile flutterings and screaming each retreated to its own side of the border, to the intense relief of the peasantry.

Not long afterwards an immense dragon with hypnotic eyes threatened the ancient town of Saffron Walden, but after killing sundry defenders was itself overcome by a man in a suit of armour constructed from mirror glass. On seeing its reflection in the mirror the creature collapsed and died from shock.

A third dragon which lurked among the tombs in East Horndon churchyard, rejoicing in the name of the Great Worm, was finally cut to pieces by the local knight-errant Sir James Tyrell. Yet another dragon was once seen flying over the ancient village of St Osyth. It had 'short wings and very large teeth' and belched spumes of fire, setting light to some of the houses.

The devil was very fully employed in Essex if the tales still circulating about him are to be believed. In 1402 he arrived at Danbury church, which stands on the tallest hill in the county, dressed 'in the likeness of a grey friar'. Entering the building he 'put the people in great fear, and in the same hour with a tempest of whirlwind and thunder the top of the steeple was broken down and half the chancel scattered abroad'. The cowled devil leaped like a madman from side to side on the altar and departed from the church leaving 'an intolerable stench' in his wake.

Another intriguing devil legend is associated with the little village of Tolleshunt Knights near the North Sea coast where a man once decided to build a house on a spot previously dedicated to Satan. Somewhat put out by this intrusion the devil arrived on the scene after dark and enquired politely 'Who is there?' The night watchman on duty answered equally civilly 'God and myself and my two spayed bitches.' The devil returned on the following night and received the same answer. On the third night he turned up yet again and repeated the question. However this time the watchman, being somewhat the worse for drink, replied clumsily 'Myself and my two spayed bitches and God'. Alas, by placing God last the watchman had fallen from grace and could no longer protect himself from Satan. The devil rejoicing tore the man's heart from his body and seizing the great beam from the building flung it a distance of several miles, crying out as he did so, 'Where this beam shall fall, there shall they build Barn Hall.' Strange to say there is a house not far from here called Barn Hall which contains what is said to be the original beam cast by the devil, which is now reputed to cure the ailments of those who touch it. The night watchman's heart is said to be bricked into one of the corners of Tolleshunt Knights church.

Witchcraft is still a matter for concern in parts of rural Essex despite the fact that much of the county lies within working distance of the City. It can even be said without risk of denial that some women in the county regard the subject with a degree of fear. To trace the anxiety to its roots, however, it is necessary to step back several centuries in time to the days of Elizabeth I when the county first acquired notoriety as a centre of the black arts. The earliest statute against witches, which was introduced in 1563, was followed by a spate of executions which ravaged Essex from end to end. Many suspects confessed to selling their souls to the devil and inflicting injuries and death upon their neighbours and their cattle. The panic subsided a little at the turn of the century but was revived dramatically during the Civil Wars when the little town of Manningtree on the Essex/ Suffolk border became the scene of a persecution which is a classic in the history of witch-mania.

It was here in 1645 that Matthew Hopkins, a Manningtree lawyer, began witch hunting on a freelance basis, charging a fee for every witch he succeeded in sending to the gallows. As the result of one such operation no less than nineteen women were executed in the market place at Chelmsford on a single day.

One village which suffered acutely from the ravages of the self-styled Witch Finder General was St Osyth near Clacton which had lost many of its women to the witch hunters during the previous century. Here, some three hundred years later in the 1920s a grisly souvenir of those terrible times was discovered buried in a garden, the skeleton of a woman whose bones had been firmly riveted together by, it is presumed, her executioners to prevent it from leaving the grave to attack those responsible for her death.

St Osyth has another haunting presence in the ghost of the martyr of that name. She stands in front of the parish church on the anniversary of her execution carrying her severed head.

Great Leighs near Chelmsford became the scene of a macabre discovery during the Second World War when the skeleton of a witch was found beneath a boulder during the construction of an airfield on the outskirts of the village. This was followed by a curious sequence of events which convinced the villagers that the witch's curse was still potent. Haystacks collapsed, hens ceased laying, and the clock in the church tower refused to give the correct time. A nearby pub, 'Ye Olde St Annes Castle' was reputed to have been haunted from that time forth. Another skeleton was discovered, impaled, at the crossroads at Little Waltham, several miles away.

Prior to World War I the village of Canewdon in the southeast of the county acquired considerable notoriety as a centre of witchcraft, nor can one say with certainty that its weird sisterhood is yet extinct. Known in local folklore as 'The Witch

Country', Canewdon has a permanent establishment of six witches under the leadership of a male master of witches. It is said locally that 'every time a stone falls from the church tower one witch dies and another takes her place'.

The villagers possess a photograph of George Pickingale, the last master of witches, taken just before his death at the age of 105 in 1909. A tall gaunt man with staring eyes, he is a reminder to iconoclasts of the present day that the power of the evil eye can still arouse intense fear among Essex folk.

There are many ancient legends in circulation in the area relating to the witches' imps, which were usually white mice. It was traditional that a Canewdon witch was unable to die until she had passed on her mice and with them her power to her successor. To become a witch in the first place a Canewdon woman had to dance twelve times round the church at midnight, when the Devil would appear.

In the folklore of witchcraft occurs various techniques for acquiring the power to bewitch. In one secret ritual it was necessary to obtain a piece of consecrated bread and on the following night carry it round the church widdershins, that is anti-clockwise. On the third time round a huge venomous toad would appear with its mouth wide open to receive the bread. Once fed the toad breathed on its benefactor who then became 'a strong witch for ever more'.

A well-known preventative against witchcraft was holy water and consequently church fonts were kept securely locked to prevent sacrilegious thefts of this kind. Those who care to follow up this aspect of the supernatural should examine the font at Bobbingworth church near Ongar which was originally padlocked 'as a precaution against the theft of holy water by witches'.

The last ten years or so have witnessed a sinister revival of witchcraft in many parts of rural Essex where the hearts of animals have been found on tombstones pierced with pins or thorns and often accompanied by such disturbing features as the desecration of church interiors and the damaging of bibles.

In the Canewdon 'witch country' a grave was dug on the golf course at night with the obvious intention of frightening the players, and a ventriloquist's dummy was discovered pierced with a knife after a midnight black mass in the local museum.

In view of the present situation it is hardly surprising that

England's last witch doctor, Cunning Murrell, ran a flourishing business removing spells in the area up to the middle of the nineteenth century. There appears to be some need for services of a similar character today.

Visitors to Essex churches will no doubt have noticed that many of the north doors have been bricked up in the distant past. The alterations appear to have been carried out in the post-Reformation period, when the unorthodox use of church buildings came under official censure. Historically the north door had an important function in exorcisms as may be seen from the following passage from the pamphlet available to visitors to St Mary's Church, Great Baddow, near Chelmsford: 'The north door is blocked up due to the suppression of superstition. It was believed that when a witch or bedevilled person was exorcised in the church, the escaping devil used the north door.'

Essex has very few castles and only one of these, Hadleigh, has a firmly established tradition of hauntings. Built by Hubert de Burgh as an Essex stronghold, it is now little more than a melancholy shell with its towers precariously shored up against subsidence. The ruins are reputed to be haunted by the devil—described locally as the Black Man—who is accompanied on his rounds by a spectre known as the White Lady. The latter has the unpleasant habit of compelling strangers to dance with her if she finds them trespassing upon her terrain at night.

Pleshey Castle, of which nothing remains apart from the bridge, the mound and the moat, is believed to be the site of a buried treasure which is apparently unprotected by either devils or ghosts and which has so far eluded archaeologists working there.

One is aware that many nationally known ghost stories have arisen from very real events in history, a well-known example being the ubiquitous phantom of that unhappy Queen Anne Boleyn. It is therefore likely that other ghosts whose origins are no longer remembered relate to some significant local event of the past, usually of a tragic character, which an investigation in depth might bring to the light of day. A deserving field for research would surely be the well authenticated hauntings at the World's End Fen near East Tilbury. Apparently the ghosts of three monks have been seen crossing the busy road to dissolve into the mists of the adjacent fields. We have a possible clue in the fact that in the year A.D. 630 St Cedd founded a monastery somewhere near the World's End Fen.

St Mary the Virgin at Little Baddow is not normally included among our haunted churches, but there have been occasions when visitors have felt a cold chill, suggesting an uncanny presence in the building. The experience was described thus, by a visitor: 'I was overcome with a morbid depression. The air grew colder. I shivered and my spine began to crawl.' Now for a possible historical basis for the story. In Clifford Bax's book *Highways and Byways in Essex* we read how in 1615 Lady Alice Mildmay, wife of a local dignitary who lived at Graces in this parish, drowned herself because of her husband's unkindness, and that her ghost haunts a pathway in the parish called Grace's Walk. Does Alice also haunt St Mary's? There is a strong likelihood that she does for her effigy can be seen in the church.

Moving westwards we reach Hill Hall, an Elizabethan mansion in the village of Theydon Mount which is associated with a pathetic legend concerning a foolish girl and her seven lovers. The girl, who lived in Elizabethan times and whose identity is unknown, was courted by seven brothers whom she kept at bay by playing one against the other. Finally they fought a bloody duel, all seven of them, while she stood by delighting in the spectacle, having promised to marry the one who survived. Unfortunately all seven died from sword wounds either immediately or soon afterwards, leaving the minx suddenly aware of the enormity of her crime. Even now her ghost is occasionally seen creeping through the ruins of the house which was once her home. Grey-haired, white-faced and grief-stricken she searches in vain for the seven lovers whom she sent to their deaths.

The surviving monastic remains in Essex are haunted as one would expect by one or more of the original inmates as, for example, the phantom monk who walks the cloisters of Prittlewell Priory near Southend, now a museum. This ghost has also been seen near the fishponds and his arrival is usually signalled by a terrific outcry from the waterfowl. A possible clue to the monk's identity is suggested by the discovery several years ago of a skeleton in the Priory graveyard. The skull, which was detached from the body, was found facing downwards in the direction of Hell. It was not unusual during the Middle Ages for a priest who had dabbled in the black arts to be decapitated and buried in this peculiar way.

A common factor in Essex coastal hauntings has been the necessity felt by local smugglers to scare away troublesome interlopers. The phantoms they created on the marshlands were of a singularly horrific kind whose shrieks at night were almost capable of raising the dead. The River Stour, near Manningtree, scene of the witch hunts of Matthew Hopkins in the seventeenth century, is still haunted by a witch whose cries of agony were reported again and again by listeners from the opposite shore on nights when 'a run of tubs' was under way.

The most notorious Essex smuggling area, however, was the ancient village of Virley of which only a fragment of the church now survives. This district was the headquarters of an extremely bloodthirsty gang of smugglers and wreckers who terrorized everyone who blocked their path. A group of excisemen whose throats they cut lie buried beneath the remains of their boat, among the weeds of the lonely churchyard.

The ancient village of Coggleshall south-east of Colchester can boast the presence of a phantom monk who makes the round of Coggleshall Abbey carrying a lighted taper at night. The ghost, white-faced and wrinkled like old parchment, glides silently through the lanes towards the nearby River Blackwater. Near here wanders Coggleshall's other ghost, Robin the Woodcutter, who is famous locally for having saved a beautiful carved effigy, *The Angel of the Christmas Mysteries* from the Protestant iconoclasts who despoiled the Abbey in the sixteenth century.

Mersea Island, on the Essex marshland fringe, once possessed a Roman garrison and, as one would expect, a phantom legionary is occasionally seen at dusk marching across the Strood, as the causeway linking the island with the mainland is known. According to one authority this is the oldest ghost story in England, although, possibly, the ghosts of Boadicea and her daughters in Epping Forest have a better claim to this honour.

Basildon New Town would seem at first sight to provide an unlikely setting for a ghost of pre-Reformation vintage, yet it continues to be haunted by a former Rector, robed in red, who is known widely as the Red Monk. The ghost which has been reported making its way to the parish church of Holy Cross, is believed in the district to be 'a lost soul waiting release' but to date no aspiring exorcists have come forward to lay him. The same monk is occasionally seen crossing the busy highway *en route* to Laindon's hilltop church several miles away.

Further south the network of creeks which intersects this part of the coast provided ideal terrain both for the Thames and Crouch smugglers and their ghosts. The phantoms of Hadleigh Castle, once a favourite landing place for smuggled liquor, have already been mentioned but another horror, Old Moss's ghost bus, was if anything even more famous. The 'bus' which patrolled the lonely River Crouch area creating terror whenever it was seen was pulled silently by headless horses—in reality white horses hooded in black, and shod with shoes of sponge, the coach wheels being rendered almost soundless by swathings of old blankets.

Among similar occult manifestations utilized by smugglers were the goblins which were occasionally heard barking at night from a clump of trees and the headless woman wearing an old-fashioned poke bonnet who floated along the sea walls at dusk. The identity of this fearsome lady has never been properly established, although it was the consensus of local opinion that she was one of the emanations of the late-lamented Anne Boleyn, a lady who incidentally haunts Rochford Hall in the town of Rochford, and who has also been seen on the local golf course during the Christmas season.

No legendary giant has favoured Essex with his presence but the county seems to have attracted a number of dwarfs. At Gypsy Mead Fyfield lived Lavina, a female elf whose singing was occasionally heard in the meadows at dawn. Another elfin character nicknamed Rollicking Bill excited a good deal of local interest whenever he 'skipped over the rills and the dene' of Maldon Marsh at twilight. Yet a third character belonging to this now extinct species of fairy folk is the hideous dwarf of intimidating appearance who hovers around the graveyard at Springfield near Chelmsford, near the old house called Springfield Place.

Occult lore invariably flourishes on ancient battlefields and this is particularly true of Ashingdon, in south-east Essex, which stands on a hillside, once the scene of the bloody battle of Assandune in A.D. 1016. It is said locally that no grass will ever grow on this hill which was once stained red with the blood of Edmund Ironsides' army when it suffered defeat at the hands of Canute the Dane. Another curious tradition is associated with the parish church which was erected on the hilltop after the battle. Prior to the Reformation this church housed a wonder-working image of the Virgin Mary which had power to remedy female infertility and even now after the passage of centuries it is considered by local couples to be a lucky church in which to marry.

Many Essex churches were built, as elsewhere, on the sites of temples dedicated to the worship of heathen gods which usually took place under the open sky. The remote church at Beauchamp Roding bears witness to this pagan influence by the presence of a flat stone in the churchyard. According to the local legend, attempts were made in the past to remove the stone from the site by the church builders, but it was invariably returned to the spot where it stands today.

Similar relics of the older religions of the British Isles often go by the name of Devil's Stones. Among other Essex survivals are the stones at the villages of Alphamstone, and Ingatestone.

Tantalizing stories relating to the discovery of an ancient idol crop up from time to time in this haunted countryside. In the year 1847, according to Phillip Benton, the Essex historian, the remains of a huge statue described by its discoverers as 'a heathen deity' were dug up in a field in the parish of Canewdon in south Essex, and with it were found a number of 'bones which crumbled upon exposure to the air'. Alas, antiquarian interest must have been at a low ebb in that part of the county for 'this interesting relic of heathen worship was broken up to repair the road'. It is curious that 'the stone idol' (to give it the name by which it is still remembered) was not preserved from destruction through superstitious awe as in many other parts of the country. However Essex has long been Puritan territory with an in-built aversion to relics associated with paganism and Popery alike.

Every writer on the supernatural has sooner or later to face up to the perplexities of Borley Rectory in north Essex, universally known as 'the most haunted house in England'.

The village of Borley has been haunted for centuries by a phantom nun and a phantom coach but it was not until the ancient rectory was replaced by a hideous Victorian building in the nineteenth century that the rector's troubles commenced. The phantom coach was now seen trundling through the rectory library while the nun made her protest by peering mournfully through its windows as the incumbent tried to work. The problem was temporarily solved by bricking up the windows, and had not that celebrated ghost hunter Harry Price arrived on the scene in 1929 it is likely that the hauntings would never have become more than a local affair. From that time onwards, however, until 1939, when the rectory was destroyed by fire, Borley commanded nationwide attention. It was infested by hordes of spectators as well as by legions of spectres including a ghostly nun who haunted the gardens and scrawled the name Marianne on the walls. Most local people were even then convinced that a journalistic hoax was being perpetrated and those who still remember the incidents hold similar views today. However, a good ghost story can never be kept down. The spectres have long since adjourned to the parish church, while the phantom nun and the coach must have returned to their original beat—for they have been observed at night passing along the road by the graveyard wall.

Haunted Huntingdonshire if one might coin a title for this county's supernatural history, can offer the visitor a royal ghost, several haunted inns, a bevy of furtive demons, a giant or two, and a miscellany of the more familiar occult horrors. No doubt further investigation would bring to light a veritable host of hauntings for, like all fenland counties, Huntingdon provided an extremely favourable field of operation for the unquiet dead.

We begin our tour with Kimbolton, near Huntingdon, an attractive village possessing a number of interesting old houses and a parish church containing the memorials of the Montague family. Kimbolton's greatest pride, however, is its imposing castle, which was described by the nineteenth-century writer Hepworth Dixon as 'the centre of all the history and legends of the shire of Huntingdon'. He continued, 'The memories which hang about it are in the last degree romantic and imposing. There Queen Katherine of Aragon died'.

John Timbs in his *Abbeys, Castles and Ancient Halls of England and Wales* refers to her ghost which walked the rooms and corridors 'in the dull gloaming or at silent midnight, robed in a white dress and wearing her crown'.

There are, or were at one time, other ghosts in Kimbolton Castle, one of whom was the forbidding spectre of Sir John Popham, the ferocious Lord Chief Justice of Elizabeth I's reign, who after death (as in life) would lie in wait for poachers among the elms in the park or sit astride one of the walls ready to leap upon the back of any intruder. A third haunting arose from the dreadful murder of a child (the name and circumstances are unknown) who was flung long ago from one of the castle windows to meet a dreadful death on the flagstones below.

There cannot be the slightest doubt that the haunting of the Ferry Boat Inn at Holywell is among the best known of all English ghost stories, for over the years the phantom has been featured in magazine articles and television and the site has become a place of pilgrimage for ghost hunters from every part of Britain.

The story has very ancient roots and must therefore be considered one of our oldest, for it begins with an eleventh-century love affair involving a decidedly uncouth character named Tom Zoul, a man 'who preferred his game of ninepins to the company of girls'. His sweetheart, a young girl named Juliet, driven mad by neglect and unrequited love and finding it impossible to bear the strain of his indifference, hanged herself from a tree by the River Ouse one 17th March between the years A.D. 1050 and A.D. 1100.

Under the law then prevailing it was not possible for a suicide to be buried in consecrated ground and Juliet was therefore laid to rest where she had died, on the banks of the River Ouse, the spot being marked with a slab of stone. Long afterwards an inn was built on the site—the Ferry Boat Inn—which stands there today, Juliet's 'gravestone' becoming part of the inn floor as every visitor to the place can see. But this is not all: for many years it has been customary for visitors and local people to undertake a pilgrimage to the inn on the night of 17th March and wait for the midnight hour when Juliet's ghost is due to emerge from beneath the flagstone. Women tend to avoid the inn on this particular night despite the fact that there is no firm evidence that the ghost has ever kept the appointment.

A number of minor ghosts commemorate some otherwise forgotten events in Huntingdonshire's unrecorded past. One of these is the spirit of a murdered drummer boy who arose from the dead to revenge himself upon his murderer, a sailor named Matcham. Although the murder was actually perpetrated in Huntingdonshire, the spirit followed the sailor to Wiltshire where it shattered his composure by materializing before his eyes. Matcham was so emotionally disturbed by the apparition that he found himself unable to rest. He confessed his guilt to the authorities, was put on trial and condemned to death, being gibbeted by old Matcham Bridge, the very place where he had committed the murder.

Huntingdonshire phantoms seem to have conformed to the traditional pattern as laid down by some archetypal arbiter of the basic law of hauntings. Nearly always it is the restless spirit of the suicide or the murdered who assails the living in a persistent and often horrifying quest for post-mortem justice.

Serious students of the occult will be aware of changes in the types of hauntings over the ages. After the Reformation we rarely hear of ghosts returning to reproach the living for neglecting the Masses necessary for their soul's repose. Also less frequently reported were certain other sprites of the peasant world of yesterday, victims of times 'sea change', spectres mentioned by the poet Gay:

> Some say they hear the jangling of chains
> And some have heard the Psalteries strains.
> At midnight some the headless horseman meet
> And some espy a corpse in a white sheet
> And other things, fey, elfin and elf
> And shapes that fear creates into itself.

Yet assuredly the famous poltergeist of Barnack has every right to be classed as a genuine old-time spirit. Popularly known as Button Cap he haunted the old rectory when Henry Kingsley held the incumbency over a century ago. Button Cap was a good-natured, harmless little fellow who made queer noises, scratched the woodwork and occasionally stroked the heads of children. This particular sprite was accorded honourable mention in the elemental spirits' *Debrett*—Carrington and Fodor's *The Story of the Poltergeist* which referred to its playful habit of rolling barrels backwards and forwards in the rectory cellar. Charles Kingsley, who was present during one of these frolics, confessed himself not over-impressed by these inanities. Further details of the haunting will be found in Charles Kingsley's *Life*.

One of the most remarkable ghost stories ever told is connected with the Nuns Bridge which spans Alconbury Brook not far from Hinchingbrook House. On this spot at dusk, or shortly afterwards, a phantom nun has occasionally been observed by motorists standing at the roadside. Several minor accidents have been laid at her door as the result of drivers swerving to avoid her. Unlike the majority of highway spectres this is no phantom hitch-hiker, to refer to a type of ghost which has become extremely commonplace in the automobile age. On the contrary, the nun's objective, if she can be said to have one, seems to be directed to creating the maximum amount of havoc among night-drivers or alternatively scaring them to death.

This curious haunting has caught the imaginations of local residents and has also succeeded in arousing superstitious awe among some of the U.S. personnel at Alconbury Air Base. A number of service men and women attributed the ghost's presence to the discovery well over a century ago of skeletons beneath the floorboards of Hinchingbrook House, which occupies the site of a Benedictine monastery.

There are many haunted sites in Huntingdon where the ghost stories, as one might expect, have a somewhat monotonous similarity. Some of the county's inns can boast tragic ghosts, and in others historical characters seem to have enjoyed permanent hospitality, as for example the 'Golden Lion' at St Ives, which once housed Oliver Cromwell, and now occasionally resounds to his footsteps.

A letter in the *Yorkshire Evening Press* dated Monday, 20th October 1975, complaining of the neglected state of Dick Turpin's grave in St George's Chapel, York, is a timely reminder that both the notorious highwayman and his ghost are rated among the more precious assets of the English countryside. There are few areas of eastern England where Dick's spectre has not been reported, Huntingdonshire being no exception for the ghost regularly does the rounds of the Bell Inn, Stilton, on Wednesdays at midnight precisely.

Huntingdonshire in common with other Puritan dominated counties hunted witches until comparatively modern times, often with great ferocity. George Lyman Kitteridge, the great authority on English and American witchcraft, observed in his book *Witchcraft in Old and New England* how as late as 1808 'Anne Izzard of Great Paxton in the county of Huntingdon was scratched and wounded and threatened with ducking as a witch'. As visitors to the area of her operations will be aware, her ghost still flies above the local meadows astride the familiar broomstick.

The 'scratching and wounding' of a witch to which Kitteridge referred was not merely an expression of local ghoulishness but the normal technique employed for neutralizing an evil spell. The witch was held tightly by one of her neighbours while her victim scratched her forehead with a pin or with the fingernails until the blood ran freely. Once the blood had been released the spell was broken and the power of the witch temporarily neutralized.

The Devil cast his sinister shadow over Huntingdonshire at a very early period. In 1525 for example a peasant working on the lands of the Abbot of Saltrey declared that he had seen a black demon killing the parish priest.

The fiendish seventeenth-century East Anglian witch hunter Matthew Hopkins, self-styled Witch Finder General, extended his crusade to Huntingdon in 1646 and it was from a clergyman of this county that he received his first serious rebuff. John Gaule, vicar of Great Staughton, had the honour of branding Hopkins a hypocrite and rabble rouser in his pamphlet *Select Cases of Conscience Touching Witches and Witchcraft*, in which he wrote: 'Every old woman with a wrinkled face, a furrowed brow, a hairy lip, a gibber tooth, a squint eye, a squeaking voice, or a scolding tongue having ... a dog or cat at her side' was in danger of denunciation as a witch.

The most infamous and horrifying witchcraft story, however, belongs to the pre-Hopkins era and involved the persecution of three innocents who came under suspicion of having cast a spell upon members of an old established county family, the Throgmortons of Warboys.

The anti-witch legislation of 1563 had produced intense anxiety and fear throughout the eastern counties, reinforcing the conviction that the Man in Black, as the Devil was popularly known, was working actively against all God-fearing persons. This elusive gentleman was far too adroit to be arrested by the witch hunters, but his agents, the witches made an easy target.

In 1589 the children of the Throgmorton family were 'attacked by devils' and afterwards declared that old Agnes Samuel had bewitched them. Hysterical disorders are a common feature of adolescents but, alas, during the panic of the witch hunts they were often regarded as symptoms of diabolic possession.

Lady Cromwell, a member of the famous county family of that name, recommended burning a snippet of Mrs Samuel's hair to neutralize the spell, but the latter, justifiably aggrieved, protested angrily to her, 'Why do you use me thus? I never did you any harm as yet.' These words were thought to represent a curse and when Lady Cromwell was taken ill and died after many months of misery it was automatically assumed that she had been bewitched. The entire Samuel family now fell under suspicion and were accused of bewitching their neighbours and their cattle. During the course of her interrogations Mrs Samuel was chained to a bed-post and her forehead torn until the blood flowed. All were found guilty and hanged to the great satisfaction of the onlookers and the intense relief of their immediate neighbours.

The entire property of the Samuels was automatically forfeited to the Lord of the Manor, Sir Henry Cromwell, husband of the 'bewitched' Lady Cromwell, who used it to endow an annual sermon on the menace of witchcraft which was preached in Huntingdon until 1812.

East Anglian folklore is full of surprises for the area is a vast reservoir of the most macabre folk traditions, many of them traceable to the Danish and Norse invasions of the Dark Ages. Much of this lore is concerned with a race of demons possessing the macabre qualities we usually associate with the devils of south-eastern Europe.

Norfolk, from the psychological aspect is a jungle of occult horrors for not only is it the habitat of the Demon Dog, but ogres and ghosts of all types have managed at one time or other to settle down comfortably in this otherwise delightful county.

The most famous Norfolk haunting is connected with Raynham Hall, ancestral home of the Marquess of Townshend. It was here in the thirties or forties of the last century that the ghost of a stately woman in a brown dress and wearing a coif was seen on a staircase. Her features were perfectly normal with one important exception; in place of eyes were dark hollows reminiscent of the eyeless sockets of a skull. Earlier writers were agreed that although she was seen on several occasions, the identity of the Brown Lady remained an unsolved riddle. It has now been ascertained, however, that this is the ghost of Lady Dorothy

Walpole, sister of the statesman, who first haunted nearby Houghton Hall (described by Timbs as a 'melancholy fine place') and later transferred to Raynham. Among those who claimed to have seen the ghost was Captain Maryatt, the famous writer of adventure stories, who bravely discharged a pistol when it materialized in his bedroom. The most memorable haunting, however, occurred in 1936 when the ghost was actually photographed while descending the stairs. Since that time there have been many stories circulating in the district which suggest that the ghost has transferred its attentions from Raynham Hall to the adjacent roads where it has been observed standing in the shadows as if begging a lift from passing cars.

Norfolk always had close links with the Boleyn family and it is therefore understandable that unhappy Anne Boleyn should have acquired a firm niche in the county's ghost lore. Her body is said to have been interred beneath a marble slab in the ancient parish church at Salle near Aylsham and her ghost is supposed to haunt her old home, Blickling Hall, on 19th May, the anniversary of her execution. Anne has been seen in a phantom coach arriving at the door of the ancient mansion garbed in white. She enters the building headless and wanders in melancholy fashion from room to room.

Anne's father, Sir Thomas Boleyn, is condemned by the fates to perform an annual penance which involves travelling in a coach pulled by headless horses over no less than forty bridges in the neighbourhood of Blickling, followed by a pack of howling devils. It is fairly obvious that the circumstances of the Boleyn tragedy must have been grafted upon legends of a much older haunting. The manifestations were said to have first occurred following the execution of Anne's brother, Lord Rochford, who was beheaded before her.

> That very time, at dead of night,
> Four headless horses took their flight,
> Dragging behind them as they ran
> The spectre of a headless man.

It goes almost without saying that Norfolk possesses the normal complement of phantom coaches, pulled by headless horses, but it will be agreed that the coach loaded with headless bridesmaids which pelts along the Old Norwich Road is somewhat unique in the annals of ghost lore. The hauntings began long long ago after a wedding party had been upset into a wayside pond where they all drowned miserably. There is a generally held superstition in the locality that those who see this coach will soon die.

The Potter Heigham area on the River Thurne is reputed to be haunted by a number of strange spectres, some of them associated with real events as, for example, the Phantom Skater of Hickling Broad. The story had its origin in a tragedy belonging to the early years of the nineteenth century at the time of the Napoleonic Wars, when a poor drummer boy fell in love with the daughter of a rich man. Knowing theirs to be a hopeless romance, the two married secretly and arranged to meet in a small hut on the banks of Hickling Broad. In winter when the surface of the Broad was frozen hard the drummer would skate over the ice beating a rhythmic tattoo on his kettle-drum to announce to his sweetheart that he was on his way. Then, one snowy night the waiting girl heard the distant sound of drumbeats becoming louder and louder as her lover drew nearer—and then suddenly cease. The ice had given way and the drummer had plunged to his death in the frozen waters of the Broad.

In summertime when the Broad is alive with holidaymakers the old story is forgotten but in misty Februarys it is re-told in the local inns, for there are those who claim to have heard the drum of the phantom lover at night as he skates over the ice to meet his long-dead bride.

The Potter Heigham hauntings include the ghost of a woman in white who rows across Hickling Broad and another of a shrieking girl who travels with the Devil in a phantom coach. In this case the coach driver happens not to be headless but is equipped with a gleaming white skull.

In the Aylmerton district a number of mysterious circular hollows known locally as the Shrieking Pits are visited by a ghostly white lady whose identity remains unknown, and who is sometimes seen at night peering into the pits and crying as if her heart would break. Her dismal moans and frantic groans have been reported for centuries in this part of Norfolk. Part elemental spirit, part ghost, the white lady has more in common with an Irish banshee than with any recognizable English phantom.

A banshee has been defined as 'an Irish supernatural being of the wraith type' which manifests its presence by emitting dreadful shrieks, which are regarded as a death omen by those who have the misfortune to hear them. The banshee is usually 'attired in loose white drapery' and with the coming of dusk 'she pours forth her mournful wail'.

Norfolk ghosts are an admittedly noisy species; even the phantom monks announce their presence with distressing cries. William Dutt mentions in his *Highways and Byways of East Anglia*, written almost three quarters of a century ago, the screeching ghost of St Benet's Abbey which made the nights hideous with its howls. Then there was the shrieking spectre of Queen Isabella, consort of Edward II, who filled Castle Rising with lamentations of remorse for the death of her husband whom she killed in intention if not in deed.

Castle Rising seems to have become a focal point for other macabre happenings in recent years. About ten years ago a group of witches nailed sinister-looking puppets to its doors.

Among Norfolk's other noisier spectres are the Babes in the Wood who haunt Wayland Wood near Watton among the trees where long ago the two were said to have perished. In the words of the old ballad:

> Thus wandered these poor innocents
> Til death did end their grief
> In one another's arms they died
> As wanting due relief.
> No burial this pretty pair
> Of any man receives
> Til Robin Red-Breast piously
> Did cover them with leaves.

The cries or wails which are occasionally reported from Wayland Wood could well be the lamentations of the local 'laughing gulls' which fly above the adjacent fields.

It is not until one has wandered alone at dusk by Norfolk's lonely North Sea shore that one begins to sense its strange melancholy. At such times it is easy to give credence to the local belief that the souls of long-drowned sailors float along the sands, or that their voices sad and plaintive are mingled with the shrieks of the winds, the moaning of the tide forming a kind of death dirge which chills the heart. Norfolk has many drowned villages and beneath the waves the church bells of the long-vanished village of Shepden sometimes ring loud and clear as if the bellringers were yet alive.

This coast was once the haunt of some of the wildest smugglers in Britain, who operated ruthlessly upon the principle 'dead men tell no tales'. There is even a phantom coastguard patrolling the shore at Bacton, while the ghost of the murdered smuggler of Happesburg has become a part of local history.

Over the past two centuries the legless figure of a man has been seen here at dusk from time to time carrying a bundle. While not actually headless, his head hangs downwards from the neck presumably from a strip of skin. Presently the ghost sinks into the sands at a place called Well Corner which is the site of an ancient well. Some of the older folk here recall that when the well was excavated many years ago, out of it came a headless corpse and a bundle—the latter containing a pair of human legs. And the ghost of the smuggler is still around, they say.

Old Shuck, Norfolk's famous demon dog, which is about the size of a small pony and which surveys mankind from a single, bloodshot eye, is likewise reported from time to time. It is said in Norfolk that although Shuck's howls make the blood run cold, his footfalls are soundless. As always, his presence is an omen of death.

Shuck often put in an appearance at East Dereham and Sheringham. At Overstrand, Shuck's Lane has been named after him. One nineteenth-century writer described Shuck as 'a black shaggy dog who visits churches at midnight', and continued: 'One witness nearly fainted on seeing it. On bringing his neighbours to see the place he found a black spot as if gunpowder had been exploded there. Does one detect here the German Dog Fiend?' Shuck's unwelcome presence has been reported recently near Barton Broad at about dusk, although the clifftops between Sheringham and Cromer remain his favourite haunt.

A decidedly eccentric type of demon has occasionally been reported from Norfolk's more populated coastal regions. Known as Old Scarf and invariably invisible, it has the unnerving habit of prodding his victims playfully in the ribs. According to a well established rumour Old Scarf once crept into a Great Yarmouth holiday caravan and ruthlessly expelled the occupants.

A grim and humourless demon haunts Grimes Graves, the Neolithic flint mines at Weeting, where there is a local legend that the mines were only abandoned 'after Old Grimes had been seen in the workings'. Grim was in fact the name of a Scandinavian giant who guarded treasure hoards and occasionally ravaged human kind with fire and sword. He is the giant in Bunyan's *Pilgrim's Progress* and his name translated means the Evil One. Visitors to the British Museum will see on exhibition a Neolithic altar which was discovered in the mines.

The Devil, although never idle, seems to have had all his work cut out to maintain the rounds of his Norfolk diocese during the so-called Ages of Faith. Tunstall in East Norfolk (long since united with Halvergate), will never forget his last visit for he absconded with all the church bells, and was last seen plunging with them into a marsh which became known as Bell Hole ever afterwards. The numerous bubbles which rise to the surface of the marsh indicate that the bells must still be 'sinking, ever sinking down to the Bottomless Pit'.

Satan's heydey was of course the seventeenth century when his time was fully employed, if we choose to believe the evidence, in buying the souls of the foolish women whom he had tempted from the paths of righteousness. There was a very curious case of this type at King's Lynn in 1616 when Mrs Mary Smith, a cheesemonger, was hauled before a court to stand trial for selling her soul to the Devil in return for the elimination of her competitors in King's Lynn Market. She agreed that Satan had approached her robed in black and 'in a low, murmuring and hissing voice' had offered to look after her business affairs and more particularly help her injure her neighbours—all this in exchange for her immortal soul. Once endowed with diabolical powers Mrs Smith set about the community like a miniature Attila. A man who struck her child found his fingers dropping off one by one. When the witch expressed the hope that a pox would alight upon one of her neighbours, the affliction followed as a matter of course.

Her most devastating curses were reserved for her business competitors whom she attempted to undermine by bewitching their customers, one of whom complained that he became 'so grievously afflicted' that he was compelled to take to his bed which he discovered to his horror was occupied by hordes of crabs and toads. There must have been extensive rejoicing in King's Lynn Market when they hanged Mrs Smith the following year.

Norfolk has a number of curious legends which were in all probability introduced from the European mainland with the invasions of the Sea Kings of long ago. Possibly it is no more than a folk memory preserved in the form of a ghost story but there have been frequent accounts of a phantom Viking ship, blazing at night in the river near Walsingham, with a dead warrior chieftain aboard. This echo of the traditional Viking funeral rite could well have reverberated down the ages as an historical narrative, and then have become absorbed into the general body of the county's lore of ghosts.

There is also a phantom Roman centurion who escorts a column of spectral prisoners who are condemned to die in the arena to make a Roman holiday. Such a scene would have been imprinted indelibly upon the imaginations of those who witnessed it. In this there may be evidence of a real historical event of Roman times metamorphosized into a procession of marching ghosts.

Was there, one wonders, a real historical basis for the well-known story of the haunting of the Old Ferry Inn at Horning by the mournful spectre of a girl? According to a long-established belief in the locality the girl was raped and murdered here well over four centuries ago by the monks of St Benet's Abbey. Now it is said a beautiful wraith with an ashen face glides slowly to the river bank and sinks beneath the waters.

Norfolk, like other counties, can boast the occasional eccentric ghost, in this case Angry Armine of Hunstanton Hall who expressed the dying wish that her favourite carpet should be kept intact. Instead it was cut up, which led to the return of Armine's ghost, its face convulsed with rage. Not until the carpet had been stitched together again was the ghost at all mollified. Even now there are occasional reports that it has been seen striding wrathfully through the grounds.

The cultural climate of Suffolk is particularly favourable to supernatural occurrences. Included in the county's folklore both legendary and topical there is the ubiquitous demon dog Black Shuck, a mysterious marine monster with quasi-human attributes and of course the regular ghosts of stately homes and cottages. There is also a suggestion of a race of elemental sprites from Fairyland, for Ipswich, the county town, can actually boast a road called Sprites Lane.

Suffolk has suffered constant erosion from the sea and there are consequently many fascinating stories there of drowned villages betrayed by the tolling of church bells, which is usually regarded as an indication of forthcoming storms.

The lost bells of Dunwich, a town largely submerged by the inundation of 1328, are still heard occasionally; and among other echoes from the past are the bells of Greyfriars Priory, Bungay, now a melancholy ruin, which resounds at night to the chanting of long dead monks.

A house named Grey Friars at Bungay became a haunted place long ago as the outcome of a disastrous love affair between a young nobleman and a female servant. Denied access to his sweetheart, the man pined away and died of a broken heart. His ghost occasionally returns to haunt the scene of his melancholy end.

Sudbury, near the Essex border, is famous for St Gregory's, its mother church. Here the visitor will see the coat of arms of Simon of Sudbury set in the central roof boss of the ceiling above the north aisle.

Simon, Archbishop of Canterbury, was beheaded by Wat Tyler's rebels in the Peasants' Revolt of 1381, and his head later removed to the sanctuary of St Gregory's where it is still preserved, 'dried up and shrivelled as to be almost indistinguishable from a skull'. His ghost occasionally returns to the church where footsteps have been sometimes heard at dusk by the bell ringers, some of whom believe that the decapitated archbishop whose body is buried at Canterbury seeks to be reunited with his head at Sudbury.

Kentwell Hall, a magnificent sixteenth-century mansion at Long Melford, was once haunted according to its gardening staff by the ghost of the wife of a former owner who, unable to escape from the din of an eighteenth-century wild party, flung herself from a bedroom window to an icy death in the moat.

One of Lowestoft's most hallowed ghosts haunted Oulton High

House at Oulton Broad. Here during the eighteenth century occurred a number of macabre murders of a most mysterious character. The first to die was the householder who, having discovered his wife in the arms of her lover, was killed by him on the spot. The other murders took place many years afterwards when the errant wife returned with a band of thugs to collect her now grown-up daughter. The girl happened to be sitting with her lover whom the intruders immediately murdered, thereby enabling the mother to decamp with her daughter whom she later murdered herself.

It is firmly believed in that part of Suffolk that the murderous mother, robed in white, often wanders at night through Oulton High House, the scene of her crimes, accompanied by a mysterious stranger (presumably Satan) and escorted by a pack of demon dogs.

Until recently one could visit Great Bealings House near Woodbridge and hear from the lips of the housekeeper the awesome story of Bealings Bells. However, a change of tenancy has rendered this famous house less accessible to the inquiring ghost hunter.

It was here for nearly two months from February to March, 1834, that the house bells extending to the kitchen rang almost continuously being operated, it was assumed, by hands from beyond the grave. Despite extensive investigations at the time and even more speculation later the mystery surrounding this affair has never been elucidated. It has been classed, therefore, as one of the most inexplicable poltergeist happenings in the annals of English hauntings.

As a matter of additional interest, one of the earliest recorded instances of poltergeist activity occurred at 'Dagworth', also in Suffolk, in the twelfth century where a mysterious voice was heard disclosing the secret doings of members of the household. Like the Bealings poltergeist, the Dagworth phenomena has never been properly explained.

A somewhat more tangible phantom haunts Thorington Hall, a National Trust property at Stoke-by-Nayland, which was built in the sixteenth century. The ghost in occupation has been described as a girl in a brown dress whose footsteps are occasionally heard in the upper part of the Hall. During renovations a woman's shoe of the Elizabethan period was discovered behind the chimney, this being a well-known charm to keep ghosts from the house.

Some American tourists were alarmed on viewing the property several years ago when a human pelvis fell from a cupboard onto the floor. Although the present occupants have never been troubled by the ghost there remains a considerable aversion in the locality to passing Thorington Hall after dark.

There is obviously an extremely high concentration of supernatural activity centred around Roos Hall on the River Waveney not far from Beccles, for here one ghost perambulates the gardens, another wanders through the guest room, and a phantom coach pulled by the usual complement of headless horses arrives at the front door each Christmas Eve. To add further to the supernatural amenities of the establishment the imprint of the Devil's hoof is to be seen on a wall, and there is a tree in the garden, once the local gibbet, around which one can dance at the midnight hour and see the Devil.

If the foregoing is at all representative of contemporary Suffolk beliefs it would seem that there has been little real change of attitude towards the supernatural over the last three-quarters of a century, the only real difference being, possibly, the departure from the scene of the traditional village wizards and 'Cunning Folk'.

According to William Dutt's *Highways and Byways in East Anglia*, written just before the turn of the present century,

> Belief in the supernatural wisdom of 'wise women' and 'cunning men' is not yet quite dead in East Anglia; but fear of exciting ridicule makes the rustics shy of admitting it. ... The horseshoe still hangs over every stable door in East Anglia. The atmosphere of East Anglia seems to favour the survival of these old beliefs.

Black Shuck, the East Anglian devil dog, seems to have felt particularly at home in Suffolk where he is considered fairly harmless as long as no one attempts to stroke him. He is usually invisible but late travellers occasionally report having felt, or sensed, his body brushing against them in the darkness. Not everyone views his presence with equanimity however, for it is still living history that his unexpected arrival at Bungay Church in 1577 during a violent thunderstorm created carnage among the worshippers, some of whom were afterwards found to 'shrink up as it were a piece of leather scorched in a hot fire'. It is little wonder that M. R. James, the pioneer of the horrific ghost story, should have found East Anglia an ideal setting for his macabre tales; for even today there is a profound belief along the salt marshes that demons and devil dogs haunt the coast at dusk.

The ruins of Bungay Castle are one of Old Shuck's headquarters. Incidentally if any visitor chooses to dance seven times, anti-clockwise, around an old tomb in Bungay churchyard the Devil will materialize and politely ask him his business.

There is a fundamental rule of ghost lore that a soul can sometimes remain earthbound for centuries, unable to leave this vale of tears because of some terrible crime committed against a fellow human being in the distant past. Such is the case at Hintlesham Hall, between Ipswich and Hadleigh, the ancient home of the Lloyds one of whose ancestors, a woman, starved her stepson to death. Following her own death the murderess has paid the price of her crime; for her spirit is often seen standing in a tragic pose at the head of the stairs.

In so many ghost stories one glimpses an aspect of life as it was lived hundreds of years ago. Old tragedies which have been by-passed by historians are frequently preserved as localized legends which represent a veritable treasure trove to the investigator in pursuit of neglected history.

Black Toby, the Negro drummer, for example, who haunts the roads near Walberswick as a penance for murdering a girl in 1750, reminds us that at the beginning of the eighteenth century the British Army began to employ Negroes to play the cymbal and the drum. In Major T. J. Edwards' *Military Customs* Negro bandsmen are described as wearing 'brilliant coats and trousers of contrasting colours with tall turbans festooned with an abundance of tinsel'.

Black Toby has evidently received post-mortem promotion for in his latest manifestation his ghost has been seen driving a phantom coach pulled by headless horses past Toby's Walk, where he was hanged some two and a half centuries ago.

Another mobile phantom well known to racegoers is the ghost of Fred Archer, the famous jockey who died in 1886, who sometimes alarms his fellow jockeys by thundering down the course at Newmarket. Another ghost closely linked with this famous racecourse is the gipsy boy who lies buried in a roadside grave at Kentford some three and a half miles away. The boy, who is said to have committed suicide over a century and a half ago after being falsely accused of sheep stealing, is still supposed to haunt the site. Passers-by have sometimes detected an uncanny chill emanating from his grave and cyclists have been compelled by some powerful supernatural force to dismount from their machines. The grave has become something of a shrine in recent times for flowers, sea shells and even coins are deposited there by unknown hands. Coach drivers and other motorists leave coins among the flowers as an insurance against road accidents, and even racegoers have become involved in the cult.

According to the latest superstition, if flowers are placed on the grave by a Newmarket man, on the day of the big race, a horse trained at Newmarket provided it is ridden by a Newmarket jockey, will be the winner.

Another wayside grave with mysterious and tragic associations is that of Dobbs, the suicide who is buried at a crossroads at Kesgrave near Great Bealings. The site is marked by several stones.

Maria Marten, the famous victim of the Murder in the Red Barn, is buried in Polstead churchyard where her grave is a place of pilgrimage. The skull of William Corder, her murderer, was long preserved in private hands until the suspicion arose that it brought its holder bad luck. Corder's skin, however, can still be seen as the binding of a book describing the trial exhibited in Bury St Edmunds museum. Incidentally the village pond at Polstead has other sinister associations for it is still remembered locally as having been used for ducking the witches. A great many Suffolk ponds were dedicated in the past to this purpose, and witch-ducking remained a popular rural pastime until well into the last century.

In 1825 a pedlar of Wickham Skeith was accused of bewitching a cobbler's stock in trade with the result that 'his wax would neither melt nor work properly'. In order to restore his good name the pedlar voluntarily underwent the water ordeal and was thrown into the village pond to discover whether he would sink or swim. The experiment was brought to a summary end by the arrival of the outraged parson who commanded everyone to go home immediately.

Stowmarket became involved in the witch-hunting mania when the seventeenth-century Witch Finder General, Matthew Hopkins, descended upon the county with the promise of a fee of twenty shillings from every town he purged of its witches. Hopkins, who succeeded in bringing about the executions of some sixty witches in the county, earned about twenty-eight pounds in the Stowmarket area alone. One Suffolk victim was old John Lowes, the octagenarian parson of Brandeston who was sentenced to death for bewitching a ship at sea, although subsequent enquiries indicated that no such ship had ever existed. When the witch finder departed from the scene in search of sorcery elsewhere hundreds of his victims still languished in Suffolk jails.

The fantasies of witchcraft are in reality no more remarkable than the midsummer-night dreams of Titania and her fairy kingdom, and as one would expect of Suffolk old tales of fairy folk were even popular there. In Hollingworth's *History of Stowmarket* we read of fairies seen dancing in moonlight near the Bury Road. There were, said the man who saw them, 'a dozen all told, the biggest about 3 feet high, the small ones like dolls'. This particular witness who hurried off home as fast as possible, explained later, it is hoped unnecessarily: 'I was quite sober at the time'.

Considerably less sober, however, were the minute fairies seen by bystanders in Tavern Street, Stowmarket, for they are said to have behaved 'in an exceedingly frolicsome fashion'.

A curious legend associates the village of Woolpit with a fairy visitation. One autumn day long ago two very strange children emerged from the old wolf pits from which the village takes its name. Their skins were green, the language they spoke unknown, but once they had acquired a knowledge of English the two disclosed that they had previously lived in the sunless Land of St Martin but on hearing the bells of St Edmundsbury had lost consciousness only to awaken in a field of Suffolk corn. In time the boy died but the girl married a young man from King's Lynn and there the story ends.

From Suffolk fairies to monstrous marine creatures is but a step in credulity or, alternatively, a variation of mood in mythology, depending upon one's attitude towards the dream world of the past.

A few miles south of Aldeburgh lies the ancient town of Orford, with its Norman castle of which only the keep now remains. It was here, according to Ralph, Abbot of Coggleshall writing in the thirteenth century that a semi-human monster was netted by fishermen and brought ashore for inspection. The creature, although bearded, was completely bald and incapable of expressing itself in speech. So tame did it become that it was permitted to accompany the fishermen on their expeditions and always returned with them. However, wearying of its captivity, the 'monster' swam out to sea and was never seen again.

In recent years interest has been aroused by the many curious traditions of a supernatural character associated with East Anglian farming life. In Suffolk for example there long existed a secret society of horse-workers who were reputed to have magical power over their animals. Rumour had it that the secret lay in the possession of a toad's bone concealed in the labourer's pocket; on the other hand there were whispers of curious rites and magical powders reminiscent of the witchcraft of ancient times.

The following recipe for acquiring power over horses was found by the author in a MS which had once been the property of an East Anglian 'cunning man'—in fact an English style witch doctor. A living toad had to be buried in an ant-heap until the flesh had been completely eaten away. The bones were then dropped into a south-running stream and carefully watched as they drifted with the current. Any bone which floated upstream was presumed to have magical properties, and was ground into a fine powder which when sprinkled close to a horse's nostrils was supposed to immobilize the animal. A curious little charm this—but one which enabled the horse-worker to exploit the superstitious fears of his master by threatening to bring the entire work of the farm to a halt if his demands for increased wages were not met.

Folklorists and lovers of ancient magic have deplored the passing of the traditional harvest rites, and with them the last vestiges of the worship of the corn spirit in the form of the corn dolly. All these customs became inevitable casualties of the agricultural technical revolution of the last century. The last to go was the harvest supper, or 'horkey' as it was known in Suffolk; its departure coinciding with the introduction of the official agricultural minimum wage during World War I, although it could well have lingered on here and there until the 1930s.

With the passing of the horkey most of the harvest songs,

some of them very old, were gradually forgotten. Other relics of the age of magic continue to overawe the imagination among these the curious five-ton boulder known as the Blaxhall Stone standing in the yard of Stone Farm, Blaxhall, which is supposed to increase in size every year. Certainly it was a tale that grew with the telling and if only a fraction of what has been said of the stone were true it must have begun as a very small pebble indeed. There are even those in the district who are certain that in the days of their forefathers the Blaxhall Stone was no larger than an ordinary loaf of bread—of such is the kingdom of magic in the Suffolk peasant mind.

Reculver Church and Roman Fort, Kent

The Avebury Stone Circle, Wiltshire

Sandford Orcas Manor House, Dorset

5

Horror in the Home Counties

The county of Bedfordshire has acquired an unenviable reputation in recent years for black magic of a most sinister character. Cemeteries have been invaded by amateur Satanists who have left grisly souvenirs in the shape of sheep's hearts stuck with pins on gravestones. The police have frequently been withdrawn from their normal duties to deal with these seemingly irrational activities, which included attacks on Christmas cribs in churches all of which were brought to a summary end by the law.

There is now every reason for believing that a group of necromancers has been operating in the area of Clophill for a considerable number of years. A pamphlet issued in the locality over sixty years ago hints at such sinister occurrences in the old parish churchyard without actually elaborating upon them. Research carried out by the author of this book indicates that the people of the district believe their ruined church—or Black Magic church as it is sometimes called—to have been a focal point for similar incidents for a very long time.

It was in March 1963 that Clophill received nationwide Press and television coverage following the destruction of a number of graves and the disinterment of the skeleton of Jenny Humberstone, an apothecary's wife who died in the eighteenth century. Her skull was actually discovered in the church porch impaled on an upright post, standing in the centre of a 'magic circle' consisting of human bones. Curious symbols were painted on the surrounding walls in white, several of them representing the human eye. The atmosphere of the churchyard was disturbingly sinister. Some of those participating in a subsequent television reconstruction of the incident admitted to having become aware of a sense of evil.

No satisfactory explanation for the Clophill affair has yet been put forward despite certain statements to the Press that it involved a black mass in which the body of a nude girl had been utilized in place of an altar. It is far more likely, however, that it was a ritual for communicating with the spirits, using a skeleton as a mediumistic force.

There could also be another explanation. Occasionally magicians of past times impregnated human bones with magical power and pointed these at their enemies with the avowed object of killing them. Similar rites are carried out by Australian aboriginals to this day.

The desecrations in Clophill churchyard continue. On a recent visit the author discovered that even more graves had been disturbed by unknown ghouls.

Also at Clophill is the Gilbertine Priory of Chicksands which falls into the traditional pattern of supernatural England. The priory which is perhaps better known for its associations with Dorothy Osborne in the seventeenth century, is haunted by two mournful spectres, a monk and a nun, who were executed after being caught in an amorous intrigue. The ghost of the nun usually appears on the seventeenth of the month, which is presumably the anniversary of her death.

This county lays claim to one of the most famous haunted houses in the British Isles, Woburn Abbey, the stately home of the Russells, standing near the Buckinghamshire border. The abbey was founded in the twelfth century by Hugh de Bolebec to accommodate monks of the Cistercian order. At the Dissolution Robert Hobs, its last abbot, was hanged in the grounds for refusing to accept the royal supremacy. Another former owner, Lord William Russell, was executed after becoming implicated in the Rye House Plot. There seems to have been no clear cut evidence that either of these tragic figures has ever returned to haunt their ancient home although Woburn has two ghosts, one an indefinable emanation and the other an enigmatic figure in an old-fashioned top hat. It is possible of course that one of these is the ghost of an earlier duke who took his own life.

The writer on folklore Miss Christina Hole mentions in her book *Haunted England* a horrifying female apparition which haunts the roads immediately to the north of Bedford. The ghost was seen gliding along a grass verge between the villages of Willesdon and Ravensden wearing funereal black and having what was described as 'a fiendish expression'. For years there has been considerable speculation as to the ghost's identity but she is generally assumed to have been a witch. This could well be the case for Mother Sutton, who lived not far from here, was hanged with her daughter for witchcraft in 1612. Mother Sutton had performed her tasks as municipal hog-keeper in a perfectly satisfactory manner until, following a quarrel with a local man, his pigs began 'to rend each other's guts' and for this, the old woman and her daughter were held responsible.

The ghosts of Bedfordshire not only succeeded in preserving an active 'life' for centuries but every now and then managed to capture the newspaper headlines. For years there were Press reports of the mysterious White Lady of the motorway, a ghost who caused a great deal of anguish to drivers since they were forced to swerve suddenly to avoid hitting her. More recently there have been stories of a phantom car careering wildly along the Bedfordshire highways at fantastic speed, usually on the wrong side of the road.

Another of Bedfordshire's highway ghosts is the late-lamented Dick Turpin who has made his mark on the occult scene by riding furiously down a lane in the neighbourhood of Apsley Guise (north of Woburn), apparently intent on quenching his thirst in the cellars of the old manor where long ago in real life he drank his fill, in secret, from the vats.

All manner of supernatural events have occurred in Bedfordshire over the centuries and entered popular legend. During the eighteenth century a steeplejack accidentally toppled from the tower of Keysoe parish church but remembering to recite a prayer whilst falling landed on *terra firma* uninjured.

Christian prayers seem to have had a far more profound effect in this county than elsewhere and it is therefore not surprising to discover in the Reverend Thistleton Dyer's *English Folklore* written more than a century ago, the following local example of bee lore: 'In Bedfordshire it is by no means uncommon for the peasantry to sing a psalm in front of hives in which the bees are not doing well as afterwards they are sure to thrive.'

The perpetual conflict between the forces of good and evil assumed melodramatic characteristics in the Bedfordshire countryside where the forces of the Devil were known to have made sporadic raids from time to time. In 1492 a vast horde of devils 'garbed in divers colours' was reported running wild in the Biggleswade area but all had discreetly vanished by the time a party of exorcists had arrived to banish them, aided by bells, books and candles. During the Middle Ages the parish church of Odell on the River Ouse was attacked by Satan in person who shook the building almost to its foundations after one of his human dupes had refused to hand over his soul on the day stipulated. A number of curious scratches on the church door are mementoes of that terrifying assault.

The Devil was always on hand to exploit differences between neighbours hence the curious story of Goodwife Rose of the town of Bedford who sought his assistance in sending one plague of lice into a neighbour's house and another of maggots to attack his peas.

It was not merely the peasantry who hurled accusations of witchcraft against each other for we find an ancestral Duchess of Bedford complaining to the Privy Council in 1478 that she had been falsely charged with witchcraft by an enemy. It should not be forgotten either that it was a Duke of Bedford who complained to the King that the defeat of the English at the siege of Orleans had been due to a secret liaison between the witch Joan of Arc and the Devil.

As one travels southwards in the British Isles it becomes noticeable that the supernatural element becomes ever more strongly pronounced insofar as ghosts are concerned. Ancient earthworks and camps, the sites of temples dedicated to forgotten faiths are everywhere associated in the minds of local folk with the spirits of those who once used them. Sometimes, however, one discovers from a place name a link with the time when the name Wayland the Smith was famous throughout the land, for example in Wayland's Smithy a long barrow on the Berkshire Downs. We are told in a well known legend that any rider whose horse had cast its shoe had merely to tether his animal on this spot and could return later and find it re-shod. Wayland had an apprentice named Flibberty Gibbett who left the imprint of his heel on a nearby boulder.

The supernatural powers attributed to blacksmiths in the days of old were based to a considerable degree upon the mythology of Wayland, the mystical smith of antiquity. Countryfolk long held that any village blacksmith could calm the wildest horse with a secret word or incantation known only to himself. Even the water in which the horseshoes had been cooled was supposed to have valuable medicinal qualities and was much sought after for treating the sick. And who, one may ask, was this remarkable fellow Wayland? He was a figure straight from folk fantasy, his name being an Anglo-Saxon version of the Scandinavian Vollund, prince of the elves, the North European version of Vulcan, god of fire.

The mystery of the white horses cut into the chalk on a number of English hillsides is difficult to solve and there can be no certainty that any clear-cut explanation for their presence will ever be forthcoming, although in the case of the Uffington horse there has been speculation that it might be a stylized dragon commemorating the battle between St George and the dragon on nearby Dragon Hill.

The ancient Celts were horse worshippers, who venerated a horse goddess named Epona, and it was possibly this type of cult which became responsible for the well-known superstition that a white horse is always a luck-bringer. On seeing a white horse one must spit, then wish, and finally cross one's fingers, keeping them crossed until a dog is seen. As for the white horse of Uffington, Berkshire folk were once convinced that it had the supernatural power of movement. To quote an old writer—'The country people erroneously imagine that the Horse ... has got higher up the Hill than formerly.'

A recent newspaper article, in drawing attention to the crumbling of the contours of the animal's head, reminds its readers of the old superstition that 'it is lucky to stand on the head and eyes'.

Berkshire folk are strong upholders of superstitions, many of which are an inheritance from the remote past. Writing at the end of the last century the Reverend Thistleton Dyer referred to a ritual which indicated that even then moon worship was not entirely extinct. 'In Berkshire, at the first appearance of a new moon, young women go into the fields and while looking at it, say

> New moon, new moon I hail thee.
> By all the virtue in thy body
> Grant this night that I may see
> He who my true love is to be.'

They then returned home convinced that the identities of their future husbands would soon be revealed to them in a dream.

Another curious survival from Berkshire's past is the Hocktide ceremony held on the Tuesday following Easter week. At 8 a.m. precisely the Town Crier of Hungerford sounds his horn and the bellman begins to perambulate the town summoning the commoners of the manor to the Court House to answer to their names. Two Tuttimen or Tythingmen visit the homes of every commoner in turn demanding money from the men and a kiss from the women, each Tuttiman carrying a pole bedecked with ribbons and surmounted by a nosegay and an orange. An 'orange scrambler' then tosses the fruit to the hordes of shrieking children who follow them on their rounds. The ceremony could well be a vestige of some ancient springtime fertility rite.

There is a long and interesting history of witchcraft in Berkshire where several of the cases were considered sensational enough to be published as pamphlets. The curious story of the Witch of Newbury which was 'credibly related by gentlemen, commanders, captains of the Earl of Essex' during the English Civil War in a pamphlet of 1643, describes the arrest of an old woman who had been observed crossing the river at Newbury on a plank instead of a boat. The superstitious Parliamentary soldiers must have decided that she was walking on water for they prepared to shoot her on the spot. However, the witch with remarkable adroitness 'caught the bullets with her hand and chewed them'. It was then proposed to tear her forehead so that the blood flowed, this being the traditional method of neutralizing a witch's power. She cried out: 'And is it come to pass that I shall die indeed.' A pistol was discharged at her head and 'she straight sunk down and died leaving her legacy of a detested carcase to the worms'.

Windsor deserves an entire chapter to itself in view of the many supernatural occurrences, including witchcraft, which are associated with this important town. On 26th February 1579, Elizabeth Stile, Mother Dutton, Mother Devell and Mother Margaret, four notorious witches, were executed for a series of crimes which would make sensational reading even today. Between them they had bewitched to death the Mayor of Windsor, a local farmer, two butchers and a housemaid by making waxen images which they pierced with a hawthorn 'prike'. Another victim was so incapacitated by black magic spells that she had to be wheeled into the courtroom in a barrow.

However, to the average reader Windsor's occultism means little more than the phantom Herne the Hunter, the central figure in a number of legends which are so very ancient that their origins are now untraceable. Herne who has been described as a 'wood-spirit metamorphosed into a ghost' is mentioned by Shakespeare in *The Merry Wives of Windsor*.

> There is an old tale goes that Herne the Hunter
> Sometime a keeper here in Windsor Forest
> Doth all the winter-time at still midnight
> Walk round about an oak with great ragged horns;
> And there he blasts the tree, and takes the cattle
> And makes milch kine yield blood and shakes a chain
> In a most hideous and dreadful manner.

In one version of the legend Rycharde Herne was a forest warden whose body was found hanging from a tree in Windsor Great Forest in the days of King Henry VIII. This tree was blown down in the great storm of 1863 but the Herne tradition lives on independently. Herne's ghost which is supposed to appear whenever the royal family or nation comes under threat of disaster was seen in 1931 immediately before the economic crisis and more recently in 1976. The ghost has also been observed in the Long Walk where oddly enough a guardsman committed suicide some years ago and now a second ghost has returned to haunt the site and, like Herne's, its arrival is said to herald serious problems for the royal family and country.

The true identity of Herne the Hunter is unlikely to be discovered at this late date, although John Harries reminds the readers of his *Ghost Hunters Road Book* that Cernunnos the Celtic god who was worshipped in pre-Roman Britain, wore antlers similar to Herne's.

Although Windsor has existed as a domain and as a royal castle from Saxon times, it only entered the mainstream of history in the days of Edward I. The ghost of the architect of the present building, William of Wykeham, is still supposed to keep a watching brief over the structure, his favourite 'walk' being the Round Tower which in life was his particular pride and joy.

Other historical ghosts have been seen in the castle from time to time.

In the winter of 1897 a mysterious woman garbed in black and wearing a sable mantilla was observed gliding through the Queen's Library where she vanished. This has been identified as the ghost of Queen Elizabeth I who spent endless hours among the books.

The spectre of Elizabeth's father, Henry VIII, is rumoured to walk in the Deanery where his majestic footsteps have been heard.

A later royal ghost is the sad but, apparently, far from mad George III who like Elizabeth I haunted the library when alive and is unable to leave it although dead. It is here that much of his memorabilia is carefully preserved.

One of the most mysterious of the supernatural stories associated with Windsor Castle is often presented as established fact. In the days of King William III a soldier who had been accused of sleeping on guard duty submitted, in his defence, that he had actually heard the clock of St Pauls in London chime thirteen times at midnight. The claim was investigated and he was acquitted. Apparently it was Great Tom of Westminster, not St Pauls as he thought, which struck thirteen times that very night.

Cumnor Hall retains a tenacious hold upon our imaginations, even though the ancient house is no more. The very utterance of its name brings to the mind the tragic story of Amy Robsart who died by her own hand or was more likely murdered, in 1560. Neglected by Dudley her husband, she removed to Cumnor Place not far from Oxford where on 8th September 1560, she was discovered with her neck broken at the foot of the stairs. History has gone hard with Dudley's memory over the Robsart affair and to this day many believe that he contrived her death. Tradition tells of the atmosphere of tension which prevailed at the funeral service when the clergyman inadvertently used the words 'pitifully murdered' instead of as he had intended 'pitifully slain'. Time and time again Amy's ghost appeared on that fatal staircase from which it was finally exorcized by twelve clergymen. In another venerable tale her ghost materialized in Leicester's bedchamber immediately before his death.

The story of Amy Robsart found lasting expression in an old ballad relating to the days when Cumnor was still pointed out as a home of ghosts.

And in that manor now no more
Is cheerful feast and sprightly ball
For ever since that dreary hour
Have spirits haunted Cumnor Hall.

The wayfarer in Berkshire, finding himself in Bisham church, will see the tragic effigy of Lady Hoby, a fitting memorial to a mother condemned by an incredible crime to remain earthbound for ever. At some time during the last century workmen taking down old window shutters at Bisham Abbey, the ancient seat of the Hoby family, discovered a number of copy books belonging to the Elizabethan period. The exercises were ill-written and, it is said, defaced with tears as if their owner had wept bitterly whilst compiling them. The finders were at once reminded of the tradition relating to the Hoby boy William, first son of Lady Hoby, wife of the ambassador to France, who was said to have been cruelly beaten by his mother because of his lack of scholarship. A number of old accounts describe the sufferings which resulted in his death. In one, the boy died from his injuries, and in another he was locked in a closet where he was later found dead.

Whatever might be the precise circumstances of his death, most of those who were aware of the facts held his mother responsible. The ghost began to walk her old home immediately after her own death garbed 'in antique widow's weeds', attempting unsuccessfully to wash invisible bloodstains from its hands.

Readers of Dr Lee's masterpiece of Gothic ghostliness *Glimpses in the Twylight* will probably be aware of the curious story of the Sandringham Horror, a headless spectre which once haunted the Bracknell Road creating such terror to those who met it that they would run with ashen faces into the nearest house for refuge.

This ghost as it happens, has now vanished from the scene but another equally horrific has taken its place, walking the same road although much closer to Ascot than its predecessor. Here the mutilated features of a phantom police officer have been seen by terrified motorists and pedestrians alike. History seems to have taken a number of liberties with one of Berkshire's more famous ghosts, Hamilton (or Hampton) Pye of Farringdon, who in one version of the story is described as an officer in Cromwell's army, and in another as a naval officer whose head was blown from his body at sea. In either case it might be advisable to keep a safe distance from old Farringdon churchyard when darkness falls, for the mystical Pye is certain to be standing nearby with his severed head clutched firmly in his hands.

Inevitably the Devil enters the story of supernatural Berkshire, in this case in the legend of Aldworth church which is better known perhaps for its La Beche memorials, or Aldworth Giants. Beneath one of the arches lies the body of an ancient member of the La Beche family who trusted that this particular mode of burial would protect him from being dragged down to Hell.

Berkshire ghosts are many and varied and universally gloomy. Glancing through the accounts of the county's occult lore one discovers melodious spectres like the sonorous singing nuns of Coombe Manor near Newbury. Another ecclesiastical site Ladye Place at Hurley was troubled by phantom monks just as long as excavations were carried out on the site. Once these had been completed the grumblings of the ghosts ceased.

There is in my possession an old print depicting an Oxford scholar performing a strange ritual. He stands within the protection of a magic circle, wand in hand, and with an air of intense concentration upon his face. Before him rises a spirit but whether angel or devil is difficult to determine without penetrating the secrets of that scholar's mind.

For centuries earnest Christians regarded the term Oxford scholar as almost synonymous with devil worshipper for it implied the sorcerer's apprentice who attempted to unlock mysteries intentionally concealed by the Deity from the prying eyes of men. In the year 1532, for example, an Oxford wizard named Richard Jones undertook to manufacture gold and silver for the royal treasury by the secret art of alchemy but his rooms when searched were found to contain all the paraphernalia necessary for raising devils.

Conventional university men were sometimes astounded at the devilry which went on around them. Thomas Cooper, who later became a clerk in Holy Orders, declared in a curious work *The Mystery of Witchcraft* that in his time (*circa* 1600) the magical arts were rife in the university. Another Oxford scholar left on record his opinion that devils infested not only the university but had overflowed into England as a whole. The authorities were understandably averse to taking proceedings against these knowledgeable accomplices of Satan bearing in mind the trial of a wizard in sixteenth-century Oxford when the judge and jury and most of the lawyers were suddenly struck down by a plague which had been brought about by their prisoner lighting a magic candle.

In Oxfordshire devilry of one kind or another seems to have established a permanent foothold among all classes of the population. It is traditional that at least two churches, Bloxham and Adderbury, owe their completion to the work of an itinerant workman who, on closer inspection, was found to have cloven hooves in lieu of feet. At Checkendon Satan must have been a constant thorn in the side of the regular incumbent for there is a field there known as the Devil's Churchyard.

Satan displayed a passion for popular sports which is rarely found among the brimstone and lechery brigade, when he took part, uninvited, in a game of cricket at Northleigh, sending the wickets flying one after another, thereby demonstrating to the startled players that a demon bowler could exist in fact as well as fancy.

Visitors to the small Oxfordshire village of Stanton Harcourt will be aware of its three upright stone pillars which archaeologists attribute to prehistoric times and which are known as the Devil's Coits. The ancient earthworks which stood nearby was destroyed by vandals long ago. Yet another, but infinitely more famous, group of stones stands on the Oxfordshire hill overlooking the village of Long Compton. These are the Rollrights which are associated with many curious legends.

There are, all told, about sixty of these stones within the Oxfordshire border while a short distance away (in Warwickshire) stands another known as the Kingstone. To the south-east there are five more, called the Whispering Knights. In the legend associated with the Rollright Stones we are told of a king who planned to conquer the land, but on climbing to the summit of the hill above Long Compton was confronted by a witch who declared

> Seven long strides shalt thou take
> And if Long Compton then can'st see
> King of England thou shalt be.

Metrical verse being the conventional media of conversation of those days, the King replied:

> Stick, stock, stone
> As King of England I shall be known.

He then took seven strides forwards only to find his view obstructed by a huge mound, presumably a prehistoric burial chamber. The witch, chortling at his discomfiture, began chanting shrilly

> As Long Compton thou can'st not see
> King of England thou shalt not be
> Rise up stick, stand still stone
> For King of England there shall be none.
> Thou and thy men hoar stones shall be
> And I, myself, an elder tree.

The hilarious verbal exchange having reached its climax the witch began to suit the deed to the words; the warriors were turned to stone, the king becoming the Kingstone, while the witch was transformed into an elder.

There is a firmly established tradition in this locality that if a knife is plunged into one of the nearby elders blood will flow from the tree, while it is prophesied that at some unknown date in the future an armed warrior will emerge from the Kingstone and conquer all England.

It is supposed to be impossible to count the Rollright Stones accurately since one always moves out of sight while the count is taking place. In a well-known legend a baker placed a small loaf on each of the stones and then counted the loaves but even this failed to produce an agreed total. The most recent attempt at solving this mathematical mystery gives seventy-two as the correct number, but apparently this makes no allowance for the stone that got away.

A number of fascinating legends are associated with the five large stones known as the Whispering Knights. According to one story two armies were camped nearby on the eve of battle. Five knights belonging to one side left the camp secretly at night with the intention of betraying their cause to the enemy, but were turned to stone by a wizard as a punishment for treachery.

There is another old story describing how a farmer removed the Whispering Knights from their sites with the intention of building a bridge. The stones, however, refused to settle and he wisely restored them to their original positions. The Whispering Knights are far from immobile however: they have been seen on more than one occasion moving sedately downhill to a stream in order to drink.

The origins of these mysterious stones are still unclear, but on one point there can be reasonable certainty: their preservation has been largely due to the awe with which they have been regarded over the centuries. It is still considered bad luck to remove or damage them in any way. And there is yet another well entrenched superstition held locally that the King's Men, as they are called, will one day be restored to human shape.

In a curious fashion this now seems to be taking place for at Hallowe'en strange figures have been discerned at the Rollrights performing weird dances. These are of course the followers of Wicca, the modern witchcraft cult, who regard the Rollrights as one of their more important shrines. To the onlooker unversed in modern witchery it would indeed appear that on the night of Hallowe'en the stones had come to life.

Oxfordshire country folk are aware that the county contains shrines of minor magic. Not far from Shipton-under-Wychwood stands the decayed trunk of an ancient oak into which the passer-by must cast his coin or ill-luck will dog his day. Another tree, an elm, is said to have remained permanently stunted because it was once used as a gallows.

While Oxfordshire children continue to draw water from the Lady's Well in Wychwood Forest each Palm Sunday it cannot be truly said that the ancient cult of well-worship is quite extinct. Similarly while their elders retain the belief that the underground Assanden spring will always surface immediately prior to the outbreak of war, it has to be conceded that faith in the power of prophetic waters has never died.

Old-style weather prophecies have a permanent niche in Oxfordshire rural philosophy. Country folk insist that a thundery winter is a harbinger of a wet summer and occasionally one hears repeated the old superstition that a storm out of season portends the death of a national leader, in accordance with the old belief that any departure from the norm in nature is a warning from the supernatural powers of great troubles ahead.

The cult of the dead seems to be strongly established in Oxfordshire, in view of the innumerable hauntings which are reported there. A ghoulish legend is associated with Minster Lovell Hall, a ruined mansion near Witney, which is supposed by local folk to have provided the setting for the sad old legend of the Mistletoe Bough. But Minster Lovell is now far better known for its ghost, the wretched Lord Lovell who died there in the most miserable circumstances.

It was at Minster Lovell, following the defeat of the army of the usurper Lambert Simnel in the reign of Henry VII, that the Lord Lovell took refuge from the King's avenging host. He arrived home at dead of night and, with the connivance of a faithful servant, concealed himself in a secret chamber to which the servant alone had the key. At the King's command the house was largely pulled down and the occupants dispersed, leaving the wretched Lord Lovell to perish from hunger and thirst in his secret hiding-place.

Two centuries later, during further demolition at the hall, the corpse was discovered still in a perfect state of preservation seated in a chair with a prayer book before it. Once the air reached the body it crumbled to dust. The picturesque ruins of Minster Lovell Hall on the banks of the Windrush are haunted by the ghost of the unfortunate Lord Lovell even today.

The well-known tradition that a suicide cannot rest until it has been properly exorcized provides the basis for the sad tale of the haunting of Courtiers House, Clifton Hampden, by the ghost of Sarah Fletcher, an over-sensitive unhappy wife who hanged herself more than two centuries ago. Her beautiful tragic figure is occasionally seen wandering miserably from room to room of her old home. On her tomb in Dorchester Church one may read her epitaph: 'She sunk and died a martyr to excessive sensibility.'

Burford Priory in the Cotswolds, a restored Elizabethan mansion once the home of Speaker Lenthall of the Commonwealth Parliament, retains links with its former monastic owners by providing facilities for the phantom monk who haunts the grounds and who in recent years has been joined by a poltergeist. The town of Burford had witnessed many tragic events during the

Civil War, particularly when Cromwell had a number of mutineers shot in the churchyard. This possibly explains the sinister black shadow which has been observed hovering above the rooftops prior to any serious disaster affecting the townspeople.

The annals of Oxfordshire occultism incorporate the remarkable story of the 'crisis apparition' of Queen's College the details of which were discovered posthumously among the papers of the Reverend More of Leyton in Essex. On Sunday, 18th November 1750, at noon precisely, Mr More, who was then a tutor, saw standing before him John Bonnell, one of the commoners with whom he was slightly acquainted. Bonnell's features were distorted in a hideous and frightening manner and the experience was so disturbing that Mr More remarked upon it to others and was informed that he must have been mistaken as Bonnell was lying in his chambers at the point of death; in fact he died the following day. It was established after further enquiries that the 'spectre' had been seen by several others at the university at about the time of the death.

Phantoms of the dying are among the most frequently recorded cases in the annals of psychical research, although they are usually seen by those linked with the dying person by ties of blood.

Another clerical anecdote relates to the ancient palace of Woodstock which was demolished at the beginning of the eighteenth century. With it has vanished the scene of one of the most remarkable hauntings in the annals of British ghosts.

It was here during the Civil War that a party of Parliamentary commissioners arrived under orders to survey the park with a view to felling and removing its timber which had been confiscated by the state. During their brief tenure the visitors seem to have come under violent attack from hordes of the most nerveracking ghosts ever known in England and they finally decamped, convinced that devils haunted the house. The full story of the hauntings was found in the diary of the then Rector of Woodstock, Thomas Widdows, and published under the title *The Just Devil of Woodstock or a True Account of the Several Apparitions, the Frights and Punishments Inflicted upon the Rumpish Commissioners sent thither to survey Manors and Houses belonging to his Majesty*. It appears that a dedicated Royalist named Joseph Collins had been unknowingly appointed as secretary to the commissioners and had ensured that they were not merely scared out of their wits but out of the house as well. This enterprising anti-Republican 'spook' has gone down to history under the nickname 'Funny Joe'.

It is somewhat remarkable that Hertfordshire, a county which is credited, like Cambridgeshire, with having been 'the original home' of the innocent hot-cross bun should have acquired a reputation for some very grim ghosts. A possible explanation for the large number of hauntings there could be the close proximity of Cambridge to London, providing easier access and greater scope for the army of ghost hunters which every now and again descends upon the home counties in quest of the unearthly.

Hertfordshire is also a county much favoured by legendary devils the survivors, no doubt, of the hordes of evil spirits which once dominated the whole country, most of whom over the centuries have gradually given way to the more popular ghosts.

No less than six prehistoric earthworks near Stevenage, which are also known as the Six Hills of Old Hertfordshire, are supposed to have been constructed by Satan in person. At Aldbury, which is best known for its stocks and whipping post, the Devil seems to have favoured scientific pursuits for he acted as assistant to the alchemical experiments carried out by the local lord, Sir Guy de Gravarde, and with tragic consequences for the castle blew up with a tremendous bang after which neither the Devil's disciple nor his deputy were ever seen again.

The Great Bed of Ware, eleven feet one inch long by ten feet eight and a half inches wide, a national heirloom now housed in the Victoria and Albert Museum, has a reputation for ghosts more frightening perhaps than any other bed in the British Isles. It has had a long and curious history dating from the fifteenth century when it was especially constructed by Jonas Fosbrooke for King Edward IV. After the murder of the King's son the bed became part of the furnishings of various inns in Ware and was frequently used during town festivals when there was a shortage of accommodation for visitors.

Apparently the spirit of Fosbrooke became ever more restive, for having intended the Bed of Ware for the exclusive use of royalty its maker greatly resented its use by *hoi polloi*. The ghost disturbed anyone who attempted to sleep in it by the most un-

Berry Pomeroy Castle, Devon

Chysauster prehistoric village, Cornwall

pleasant pinchings and scratchings. Even Harrison Saxby, King Henry VIII's Master of Horse, was severely bruised while sleeping in it. In the past the Bed of Ware was often exhibited at the Crown Inn where the visitors were expected to drink a toast, not only to the bed but to its ghost.

Knebworth House, the family home of the Lyttons and the more famous Bulwer-Lytton, the nineteenth-century novelist and occultist, was long haunted, according to the people of the neighbourhood, by Jenny Spinner, who was described in an old pamphlet as 'a ghostly housewife' who disturbed sleepers with the sound of her spinning-wheel. The spinning-wheel seems to have been removed from the house at the beginning of the last century, much to the relief of the Lytton family who regarded its nocturnal whirring as a warning of forthcoming death.

The City of St Albans is supposed to be haunted by a number of men-at-arms who died in the famous battles of 1455 and 1461 during the Wars of the Roses. On each anniversary of these conflicts phantom warriors return and make the nights hideous with the clash of steel and horrific groans.

Cassiobury near Watford, once the family seat of the Earl of Essex, was haunted by the ghost of a headless man, Arthur, Lord Capel, once described as the most zealous and highly esteemed of the Royalist nobility. With Sir Charles Lucas and the Earl of Norwich he fortified Colchester during the Civil Wars but finally surrendered to the Parliamentary General Fairfax in expectation of receiving honourable quarter. Two of the Royalist commanders were executed by a firing squad but Capel might have saved his own life had he not said sardonically, 'They should do well to finish their work and execute the same rigour to the rest.'

His enemies were many and remorseless. He was beheaded in 1649 the same year as his king, a martyr to the cause he loved. His ghost continues to walk Cassiobury Park.

Apart from headless men, there are occasional reports of headless horses haunting the highways and byways of rural Hertfordshire. A number of these have been seen galloping wildly at dusk in the neighbourhood of Burnham Green near Welwyn, where a bloody battle was fought with the Danes about a thousand years ago. Another headless horse which has been noted at Datchworth is supposed to be the ghost of a charger which was decapitated by a group of half-witted Roundheads.

One of the most interesting and at the same time attractive of Hertfordshire stately homes is Salisbury Hall at London Colney not far from St Albans, which stands on the site of a much older building and possibly a battlefield since a number of human bones and spurs have been found nearby.

Among its former occupants was Nell Gwynn, whose spectre has been seen on the stairs.

A second ghost is a phantom cavalier known as the Captain, who committed suicide with his own rapier to prevent certain secrets entrusted to him by his king from falling into enemy hands.

Despite these manifestations Salisbury Hall is a pleasant home to visit, being open to the public at times detailed on the notice board which stands outside. Several years ago when a series of ghost hunts were carried out in the building two entirely new spectres were reported by some of the visitors, a knight in armour and a sinister black hound.

Still on the sombre, and at the same time enjoyable, theme of Hertfordshire ghosts one turns to the now inevitable phantom highwayman who rides through the night intent upon holding to ransom some long dead traveller seated comfortably in a phantom coach. However, Clibbon, the highwayman of Bulls Green is a ghost with a difference. Long ago in the eighteenth century he was literally beaten to death by a posse of irate farmers. Now, whoever happens to be on the road at the right time of night can hear his dying groans and see his ghost.

The village of Abbots Langley received national Press coverage several years ago when the parochial church council proposed to tidy up the graveyard which involved uprooting the gravestone of Mary Treble or Maid Mary as she was known, the village ghost. Mary is sometimes seen leaving the parsonage *en route* to her tomb garbed in a ghastly white shroud. According to local legend she was a vicar's daughter who committed suicide with a pair of scissors.

In another version of the same story Mary was a former servant at the vicarage who was suddenly taken ill. The unfeeling wife of the then vicar accused her of malingering, and not only refused to let her rest, but gave her a severe shaking. Half an hour later poor Mary was found dead in bed.

The ancient village of Sarratt, near Watford, is renowned for a curious incident in the bedroom of a house which the President of the Ghost Club, Peter Underwood, has identified as Rose Hall.

Here a house guest declared to his hosts after a somewhat restless night:

'I saw the figure of a well-dressed man in the act of stooping, and supporting himself, in so doing by the bed-clothes. He had on a blue coat with bright gilt buttons, but I saw no head ...'

He was then informed that a man, so attired, had been found decapitated in that very room many years before.

An interesting story is associated with Sarratt Church which dates from the eleventh century, for here the Devil demonstrated his usual hostility to ecclesiastical edifices by removing every stone as fast as it was laid down. The builders finally gave him best and erected the building in the position where it stands today. Minsden Chapel, an ancient ruin near Hitchin, is haunted by the figure of a white-robed monk who thoughtfully chooses Hallowe'en for his visits. He seems aware that since the calendar change of 1752 Hallowe'en occurs eleven days earlier than formerly.

Hertfordshire's occult lore covers an immense range of psychic phenomena, much of it involving churches and churchyards. The county's many infusions of population seems to have had little or no effect upon local superstitions.

Visitors to Tewin churchyard will be shown the grave of Lady Anne Grimston, an early eighteenth-century heretic who audaciously denied the Resurrection of Jesus Christ. She was adamant to the end, declaring to the priest who sought to administer the last rites that if the Bible was the Word of God then seven trees would sprout from her grave. Religious-minded visitors to Tewin churchyard will be delighted, and irreligious ones confounded, by the fact that Lady Anne's prophecy came true.

J. S. Thompson observed in his *Mystery and Lore of Apparitions* published nearly half a century ago, that 'Hertfordshire appears to be particularly rich in legends and traditions of apparitions and ghosts'. He cited such examples as the headless apparition in black in Ashwell churchyard, the 'gleaming presence' of Bovington and the phantom coach which enters Hatfield House via the main entrance and after mounting the staircase dissolves into thin air. All of these ghosts appear to maintain an undiminished vigour for they are frequently seen today, as well as another famous ghost discussed at length by

Thompson *The Wicked Lady Ferrars of Markyate Cell.*

Markyate Cell was originally a priory but its grounds are haunted not, as one might imagine, by monks but by the seventeenth-century Diana Ferrars who became a 'highwaywoman' for the sheer pleasure of terrorizing and dominating those she encountered on the road. Dressed as a man she would fling herself onto the backs of travellers from the overhanging branches of the trees bordering the estate. Fate caught up with the lady when one of her intended victims put up a fight and shot her. She was discovered dead in Markyate Cell close to the entrance to her secret hiding-place. Shocked by her escapades the new owners of the house bricked up the secret chamber and it remained undisturbed for the next one hundred and fifty years.

On more than one occasion Markyate Cell has caught fire, all of which has been blamed on Lady Ferrars' ghost, or the Wicked Lady as she is called. In the fire of 1840 a woman in black was actually seen descending from a sycamore tree, and even today the restless spirit of the Wicked Lady is very much 'alive', for she has been observed, pistol in hand, crouching expectantly among the branches of the same ancient tree or, according to a more recent report, 'flying over Markyate Cell'.

Like the adjoining county of Essex, Hertfordshire has a macabre history of witchcraft extending from the sixteenth century right down to the present day.

It was at Royston in 1606 that Alice and Christiana Stokes, who were described in the records as spinsters, but who seem to have been mother and daughter, were found to have in their possession a chest containing two complete skeletons, a quantity of human hair and a large sheet of parchment inscribed with magical symbols. Under interrogation the two admitted that with the aid of their spirits plus the hair, bones and parchment, they were able to torture human beings and cattle by remote control. The two women were found guilty and sentenced to death by hanging, the execution being carried out at Hertford on 4th August the same year.

A pamphlet of 1669 *Hertfordshire Wonders* described a series of alarming bewitchments suffered by Jane Stretton of Ware who had unintentionally given offence to a witch. Her bed was 'haunted' with toads, coloured flames spumed from her mouth and her body became distended like a balloon.

The most important of all the trials for witchcraft in Hertfordshire and one which shook all England at the time was held at Hertford Lent Sessions and General Gaol Delivery in 1712. The accused was Jane Wenham, the Wise Woman of Walkern, a village lying between Stevenage and Buntingford, in what is a somewhat isolated area even today. Jane, having fallen out with her neighbours, was accused by them of a miscellany of offences derived from the belief that she had become an agent of Satan. It was noticed that cattle in the district had died of unknown diseases, while a sheep had been seen standing on its head. Furthermore, following a quarrel with a farmer, Jane had bewitched his young labourer so that he ran about like a madman with a bunch of straw stuck in his shirt. The parson's servant, a young girl, was discovered in a half demented condition after a cat with the face of Jane Wenham entered her room.

Jane was sent for trial on the charge of 'feloniously entertaining and feeding a certain evil spirit in the likeness of a cat' and found guilty despite the protests of the judge who had no option but to pass sentence of death. She was pardoned but this failed to mollify the mob and from fear of their violence she remained an exile from her own village until the day of her death. The trial of Jane Wenham was one of the main reasons for the repeal of the law against witches in 1736.

Jane is still remembered in Walkern where her old cottage is pointed out to strangers with a certain degree of pride. Nevertheless there are a number of villagers who prefer not to walk in its vicinity after nightfall, and there have been whispers that her ghost has been seen standing near the church.

A crossroads at Long Marston near Tring is supposed to be haunted at night by a huge black dog, described as the incarnation of Thomas Colley who was hanged there in 1751 for complicity in the murder of two old country folk named Osborne who were believed by their neighbours to have cast evil spells upon a herd of cows.

The story is a very sad one and typical of mid-eighteenth-century barbarism when superstitious fears continued to rule much of rural Hertfordshire life. The Osbornes had first aroused hostility by their open support of the Young Pretender during the rebellion of 1745 and were branded witches after a farmer named Butterfield had discovered his cows dying. A mob of villagers led by Thomas Colley proceeded to the Osbornes' cottage with the intention of ducking them in a stream at Long Marston to determine whether or not they were witches. The old couple took refuge in the workhouse which came under attack from the mob until the superintendent, out of sheer terror, revealed where the two had concealed themselves. They were stripped naked and thrown into the water where they suffered a series of murderous assaults from which they later died. Thomas Colley as ringleader, was arrested on a charge of wilful murder. He was sentenced to death and following the execution his body was suspended in chains at the crossroads where the phantom dog now walks.

In recent years there has been a considerable revival of witchcraft in Hertfordshire where a number of covens of modern witches have been reported in the St Albans district and more especially near Bricket Wood. However these are, in the main, the whitest of white practitioners of the magical arts, being supporters of Wicca, the modern witchcraft religion founded by Dr Gerald Gardner who lived for a short while in Hertfordshire after the Second World War.

Those who feel a stronger interest in the type of magic based on the supernatural links between man and nature, are referred to the famous Womere Brook at Redbourne near Harpenden which is expected to overflow whenever some national disaster looms ahead, and particularly when famine is about to stalk the land.

A recent investigation into some of the surviving ghost lore in the county brought to light clear evidence that most of the older phantoms are still with us and remarkably active.

William Jarman, the suicide, continues to haunt the old manor house at Little Gaddesden although the pond in which he took his life has long since disappeared. This was one of those rare cases in which a man died from unrequited love and remained earthbound to suffer an eternity of regrets. Jarman is a placid enough fellow, however, whose only preoccupation seems to be in switching on the electric lights. Recent visitors to the manor have been shown the rectangular stone 'coffin', attached to a lightning conductor on the roof, which 'encloses the suicide's remains'.

Boxmoor Common near Hemel Hempstead offers the wayfarer

the grave of Robert Snooks, the last highwayman to hang in England, whose body was removed from the crossroads to its present site by the Quakers. According to the latest account, if anyone cares to prance round the grave twelve times at midnight the highwayman will join them in the dance.

The English Civil Wars of the seventeenth century left an ineradicable scar upon the history of that age at an extremely deep psychological level; hence, perhaps, the profusion of ghost stories relating to that tragic epoch.

The mystery of the Verney ghost is a case in point for even after a lapse of more than three centuries the haunting of Claydon House at Middle Claydon, Buckinghamshire, by Sir Edmund Verney has a stirring effect upon the imagination. Although the present Claydon House dates from the eighteenth century it occupies the site of a much older building, the stately home of the Verneys, a family actively involved in, and divided by, the conflict between Parliament and King.

Sir Edmund Verney fought for the Crown and his son and successor, Sir Ralph Verney, supported the Parliament, with the inevitable emotional and traumatic effects upon the family. Finally word was received that the father had died at Edgehill, his hand having been found grasping the staff of the Royal Standard with such rigidity that it had to be severed at the wrist. The body was never recovered but there were persistent stories that the ghost sought to reunite itself with the hand which was interred in the family vault at Claydon. Old servants would tell, with a certain amount of fear, of seeing a cloaked figure in seventeenth-century dress standing on the stairs. One retired housekeeper distinctly recalled the night when terrified housemaids barricaded themselves in a bedroom after loud footsteps had been heard in a corridor. Visitors to Claydon, which is perhaps more famous as the old home of Florence Nightingale, will see in the chancel of All Saints Church the fine memorial erected to the memory of Sir Edmund by his son.

Many Buckinghamshire hauntings have a distinctly ecclesiastical character, for even in life its clerics were restless, wayward souls. The unquiet ghost of Henry Burghersh, a Bishop of Lincoln in the fourteenth century, has been seen in the garb of a forester in a wood near Fingest in the Chilterns, where he undergoes a perpetual penance imposed upon him by God, oddly enough for enclosing the lands of the people for the church. The story hints at an affinity with the better known Windsor legend of Herne the Hunter; there seems to be a slight overlapping of traditions in this curious tale.

A more orthodox phantom haunts Missenden Abbey, the remains of a twelfth-century Augustine foundation at Great Missenden which is now a centre for adult education. In the part of the original building that survives, a mysterious figure in a grey habit has been seen on a stairway and on at least one occasion to the author's knowledge, a chilling presence has been sensed in one of the bedrooms. In another similar case a sleeper had the terrifying experience of feeling himself clutched by unseen hands and pulled backwards over his bed. There are valid grounds for a haunting at Great Missenden since a girl committed suicide in the building many centuries ago. In addition the monks of Great Missenden were a particularly unsavoury crew who by all accounts deserved to be earthbound to the end of time.

Hughenden Manor is haunted by the ghost of Benjamin Disraeli, Earl of Beaconsfield, the famous statesman who died at Curzon Street in 1881 and who was buried in accordance with his will at Hughenden which had been his home for the previous thirty years.

Creslow Manor House near Whitchurch is haunted by the ghost of Rosamond Clifford, who favours one particular room for her materializations and in the old records we read of the rustling of a silk dress at night accompanied by a woman's footsteps. The haunting was reported in some detail by a gentleman who slept in the fatal chamber. Hearing strange noises he sprang out of bed and darted to the place from which the sound originated and tried to grasp the intruder. 'My arms met but enclosed nothing. The elusive lady had escaped yet again.' Ruminating upon the experience afterwards he soliloquized.

> Doubtless there are no ghosts
> Yet it is better not to move
> Lest cold hands seize upon us from behind.

A road near Haddenham is haunted by the ghost of a farmer

who was murdered there by a footpad in a particularly horrible fashion over a century ago. At the moment of his death the farmer's spirit materialized before his shocked wife with his ribs smashed as if by a heavy implement. In another account of the same haunting the farmer appeared holding a hammer in one hand while he clutched at his chest with the other. Since 1848, the year of the murder, there have been constant reports of a ghost having been seen at the site of the killing.

Gib Lane at Calverton has another roadside ghost, this time a woman who was murdered and robbed there over three centuries ago. The murderer was executed and hanged on a gibbet on the spot where his victim died.

The village of Hambleden is best known as a shrine of rural charm. It possesses a seventeenth-century manor house, a Georgian rectory, and an ancient mill. Hambleden, however, continues to be associated in the minds of many people with that strange murderess 'the unfortunate Mary Blandy' who was sentenced to death and hanged after killing her father with minute doses of arsenic which she insisted to her accusers was a magic potion which would render him favourably disposed towards her marriage. The potion, which had been obtained from a Scottish wisewoman, was well within the tradition of love magic, a craft which has been practised from time immemorial. Paracelsus the alchemist had laid down a doctrine which was still current in Mary's time: 'Poison is everything, there is nothing without poison. The dosage makes it either a poison or a remedy.' So they hanged poor Mary and her ghost has been seen in the neighbourhood of her old home ever since, on one occasion riding a white horse as she watched the rehearsal of a play based on her own tragedy.

Until the eighteenth century, Buckinghamshire seems to have been low on the list of witch afflicted counties but this could well be because of the inadequacy of the records.

Only two cases were noted by the writer Ewen in his authoritative work on witchcraft based on many years of research. However one of the charms used by Buckingham witches has been preserved. It was employed by lovesick maidens to compel indifferent males to submit to their wiles when all other inducements had failed. The girl would light a candle at midnight and after inserting a number of pins into it would chant:

It's not this candle I would stick,
But ....'s heart I mean to prick.
Whether he's asleep or awake
I'll have him come to me and speak.

It is not altogether clear whether the lover was intended to appear in spectral form or in the flesh, but in either case the experience must have been extremely unnerving for both parties.

The Devil acquired a certain prominence in the county's affairs, when he was exorcized by the famous magician-cum-exorcist 'John Shorn gentleman born' who was rector of North Marston from about 1290 to 1314. The exorcist won nationwide fame when he succeeded in luring the Devil into a boot instead of a bottle, which was the more common procedure.

John Shorn's Well, which is still in existence, had marvellous healing properties and was visited by pilgrims from all over the British Isles in search of a miraculous cure for gout.

Not far from Aylesbury is Hang Hill St Leonards where public executions were carried out in the gruesome past. No malefactors' spectres haunt the site—instead black boars have been seen and heard at dusk making the most disgusting sounds.

Boars, pigs and similar noisome animals were often selected by Satan in the old days as disguises when he visited mankind. The proper method of dealing with an evil presence of this kind, according to Cornelius Agrippa, was to confront it boldly and say very firmly: 'Away accursed beast.'

It is perfectly understandable that modern occultists should display a far greater interest in Satanism and the black mass than in the more conventional type of witchcraft based on the peasant life of past ages. The black mass has been defined as a blasphemous parody of the Catholic Mass involving grotesque sexual profanities of a most obscene character. It is frequently accompanied by the sacrifice of animals and, more rarely, by the murder of infants. Under threat of torture or more often during its application, incredible confessions were extracted from suspects during the trials of the Middle Ages, including copulation with Satan, the consecration of the host over the bodies of nude girls and the use of urine in lieu of sacramental wine.

Many modern authorities now regard Satanism as a largely spurious folklore of the Church which was invented to justify heresy-hunting, the blood sport of the clergy. Dr Robbins, author of the informative *Encyclopedia of Witchcraft and Demonology*, believed it to be virtually a literary creation—an invention of magically-minded scholars belonging to the post-witchcraft era.

The closest England seems to have approached to the fantasies of continental diabolism lay in the curious antics of the Hell Fire Club which scandalized not only Buckinghamshire but also all Britain in the eighteenth century. The age was in many ways one of sophisticated vice, when the rich and powerful seemed bent on rejecting in the most flamboyant manner most of the moral precepts of their ancestors.

The Hell Fire Club, or to give its proper title, the Order of the Friars of Medmenham, was a mystical society in which the interests of the members were divided impartially between the defiance of orthodox religion and the pleasures of the flesh. The founder was Sir Francis Dashwood, a decadent aristocrat, and it was managed by twelve Apostles of Vice whose role needs no further definition. The membership included such prominent members of society as the Earl of Bute, the Earl of Sandwich, Bubb Doddington 'a bullfrog with a lascivious face' who supplied the women, and John Wilkes, the famous advocate of political liberty. Benjamin Franklin and Thomas Potter, a son of the Archbishop of Canterbury were also members.

The abbey, which was first established at Marlow on the Thames, was embellished with blasphemous statues and erotic frescoes. Above its porch was the club's motto 'Do what thou wilt'; within, the monks with their nuns, performed their offices at night under the benevolent eyes of the degenerate Sir Francis. These pitiful obscenities were supplemented by devil worship and parodies of the Christian Mass over which the club secretary, Paul Whitehead, officiated as sexton.

It was at Medmenham Abbey that the famous black mass took place which provided the only amusing aspect of an otherwise absurd affair. A ceremony had been organized for the express purpose of summoning Satan to appear in person; black candles had been lit, the normal rites of the church reversed, and the celebrants were on their knees invoking the master of hell. It was then that a waggish member of the club suddenly let loose an ape which he had previously concealed in a box beneath the altar. The animal, which was dressed as a devil complete with horns and forked tail, sprang out of the box and the horrified devil worshippers either ran for their lives or leapt out of the windows.

When the club was transferred to West Wycombe for greater privacy it left behind the ghost of a lady in blue and a phantom maid. The new premises, which are now famous for the Hell Fire Caves, were haunted for a time by the sad spectre of Paul Whitehead, the club secretary, who probably found hell somewhat tepid after the excitements of the Hell Fire Club.

It is not easy to recognize in modern London, with its soulless towers of glass and its roaring traffic, a shrine of occult mysteries, a realm of ghosts and romantic fantasy. Early Londoners were vaguely aware of curious myths surrounding the origins of their city: London was to them a city founded by Brut, great-grandson of Aeneas, one of whose descendants was Lud, a monarch from whom Ludgate obtained its name. Those two magnificent effigies Gog and Magog in Guildhall traditionally represented the giant Gogmagog who died in battle warring with the Trojans. Whatever the validity of these ancient legends, they certainly justify the description of the metropolis as a centre of mystery. They also help to explain the fascination felt for their mother city by generations of antiquarians, folklorists and lovers of tradition.

Set in its iron cradle opposite Cannon Street railway station is London Stone, one of the visible enigmas of the London scene. Originally built into the wall of St Swithin's Church, this fragment of the 'great stone called London stone', to quote the historian John Stowe, is traditionally associated with the rebel Jack Cade who struck it with his sword to indicate his mastery over the city. In earlier times the citizens of London seem to have chosen the site of the stone for important declarations. They also regarded it with superstitious awe, believing that so long as it remained *in situ* the welfare of the city was secure.

Father Thames, London's river, has been venerated for so many centuries that it is often forgotten that in Britain's pagan past, offerings were made to its tutelary River Spirit. This possibly explains the discovery of large numbers of Roman coins on the bed of the Thames off Botolph Stairs.

It is almost certain that St Pauls stands on what was originally a pagan site. Camden, the antiquary, witnessed, as a boy, the head of a stag carried on a spear into St Pauls by the clergy accompanied by the blowing of horns, which suggests the survival of a pre-Christian ritual in sixteenth-century England.

There can be little doubt that sacrifices of animals were carried out on this site in pre-Christian times for a deposit of their bones, including those of oxen, was discovered buried there. It is a curious fact that as late as the 1920s barren women touched the pillar closest to the west door of the cathedral in order to acquire fertility.

A vast amount of folklore, ghost lore, magic and mystery is associated with the Tower of London which has been described, somewhat oddly, as 'the cradle of the English race'. More apt perhaps is the quotation from Bridgett's *Life of The Blessed John Fisher*: 'There is no place in England so crowded with memories of every kind as the Tower of London, memories of strife and triumph, of glory and misery, of crime and sanctity'. To attempt a chronicle of the imprisonments, tortures and executions which have taken place within those grim walls would be an exhausting task. The Tower has witnessed the judicial murders of queens, princes, lords and ladies; it incarcerated the adherants of Rome and Protestantism alike and dispatched them in batches to bloody execution in turn. The cruelties perpetrated in the Tower cry out to Heaven for redress and some of the victims still relive their age-old sufferings as ghosts.

The Bloody Tower, scene of the cruel murders of the two boy princes, subsequently witnessed the return of their unquiet spirits, while from the Council Chamber of the Lieutenant's lodgings in the Tower dreadful groans have been heard on the anniversary of Guy Fawkes' interrogation under torture by the Council of State. Guy was racked terribly to extort a complete confession from his agonized lips which would reveal the secrets of the conspiracy and the names of those involved. However, according to a very strong belief current at the time, the supernatural played no small part in its detection.

The antiquarian, John Timbs, refers in his *Garland of the Year*, to a curious story which was told to account for the miraculous discovery of the Gunpowder Plot. According to some old writers the conspiracy had been first brought to light by the famous astrologer, Dr John Dee, to whom it had been revealed in his showstone, or magic mirror (now in the British Museum). Most old time sorcerers employed such mirrors in lieu of the crystal balls now in fashion. It was as the direct outcome of this discovery that many Londoners then adopted tiny mirrors as dress ornaments or wore them in their hats.

Anne Boleyn is among the more illustrious ghosts who have been reported in the Tower at one time or another. She has been seen in the White Tower and at the place of her execution. A guard at the Tower, once fainted dead away after meeting a headless figure on his rounds and would have been severely punished for dereliction of duty had not two officers come forward with evidence that they also had seen a mysterious phantom in the Tower that night.

Another martyr to the persecution mania of the age, the Countess of Salisbury, suffered a terrible death in the Tower in 1541, being chased round the block by the headsman and finally brought to the ground by repeated blows of his axe. Her bloodstained ghost has been seen on more than one occasion—still screaming and with the headsman still in pursuit.

The ghost of Sir Walter Raleigh has been reported in the Tower and also the tragic spectre of poor Lady Jane Grey, although she, for some obscure reason, failed to put in an appearance until the four hundred and third anniversary of her execution.

Among living relics of the past are those strange birds, the Tower ravens, who indicate the state of London and the nation, if one is to believe the ancient superstition: 'If ever the Tower ravens fly away the White Tower is doomed to fall'. It is no doubt with the capital's security in mind that the authorities ensure that their wings are kept regularly clipped. It is said that misfortunes of the most tragic kind will befall anyone who dares to kill one of these remarkable birds.

No Roman ghost has as yet come forward to confirm the old tradition that Westminster Abbey stands on the site of a Roman building, but there are several other ghosts in residence, according to the latest reports: the spectres of the Unknown Warrior who is buried in the abbey, John Bradshaw the regicide who walks the deanery, and Father Benedictus, a monk of pre-Reformation vintage of whom nothing else seems to be known.

One of the more enjoyable features of the London tourist season is watching tardy visitors being hustled from the abbey at closing time with the friendly warning, 'Hurry up, ladies and gentlemen, don't get caught by the ghost'.

St Bartholomew the Great, Smithfield, the ancient priory established by the ecclesiastic-cum-jester Rahere, is haunted by its founder whose footsteps are occasionally heard in the ambulatory. Rahere's post-mortem supernatural manifestations are regarded with far greater seriousness than the miracles he is said to have performed in his lifetime, when he was denounced as an impostor by some of his fellow monks.

During the seventeenth century Smithfield provided the setting for a haunting by one of the most remarkable spectres ever recorded. This was the mysterious figure with horns and hooked toes who was seen hopping, skipping and jumping among the butchers' stalls, seemingly unperturbed by the hail of knives and cleavers with which he was assailed from every quarter and which passed through his body without inflicting the slightest injury. The spectre then proceeded to Eastcheap and Whitechapel Market, creating similar sensations before disappearing from London's history for ever.

Moving slowly through the wards of St Thomas' Hospital at night there is a woman in grey who has long been regarded as the ghost of the founder of the nursing profession, the great Florence Nightingale. She carries her lamp as she did when alive, but alas no longer symbolizes a mission of hope, for over the years the story has been given a savage twist and the children of the locality are now convinced that when the lady of the lamp is seen, a death will occur in the ward which she walks.

The antiquary William Andrews described a curious case in his *Curiosities of Law and Lawyers*, in which a London murder mystery was solved as the result of an occult dream. A Grub Street tradesman had been found murdered by some persons unknown and the case proved insoluble until a Mrs Greenwood, the dead man's neighbour, revealed to the authorities a vivid dream in which the corpse had led her to the home of a man named Maynard and told her that he was one of the murderers. Maynard was arrested and during interrogation disclosed the identity of his confederates. All were tried, condemned to death and executed, and afterwards the murdered man reappeared in another of Mrs Greenwood's dreams and thanked her profusely.

Another old London tragedy with supernatural implications has gone down in history as the case of the Bank Nun. During the first twenty-five years of the last century the black-garbed figure of a woman, with rouged lips, was often seen wandering morosely in the vicinity of the Bank of England. Her appearance was most striking: in the words of one who saw her 'her cheeks disclose the ruddy glow of uninterrupted health. Is it that her looks belie her garb or her garb belies her looks'. The woman was Sarah Whitehead whose sanity had given way after the execution of her brother for forgery, under the harsh property laws then prevailing. Miss Whitehead was obsessed with the idea that she was owed an immense fortune in stocks, bonds and bank deposits amounting to hundreds of thousands of pounds, besides leaseholds, copyholds, freeholds and annuities, including the entire value of the Muswell Hill estate. On one occasion she approached Baron Rothschild on the steps of the Stock Exchange and accused him of defrauding her of her fortune. Tactfully Rothschild presented her with a half-crown on account and she cheerfully proceeded on her way.

Sarah was last seen, living, in the 1860s but her ghost has since returned to haunt the City of London, a strange figure in old-fashioned black wandering sadly along Threadneedle Street.

Some of the more horrific aspects of London's old-time executions continue to echo down the centuries in the shrieks of ghosts. Anthony Babington, who was convicted of high treason following the failure of the Babington Plot and was hanged, drawn and quartered in 1586 with refinements designed to protract his agonies as long as possible, long haunted the scene of his execution, which later became Lincolns Inn Fields.

London theatres are famous for a number of thespian ghosts who seem never to tire of returning to the scenes of their past triumphs and tragedies, where they take their bows before audiences who never knew them in life. The ghost of William Terris who was stabbed to death by an insane fellow-actor at the entrance to the Adelphi Theatre in 1907, has been seen on a number of occasions and the hauntings include a somewhat unexpected materialization on the platform of Covent Garden Underground station.

Dan Leno, the comedian, has been seen, posthumously, at the Theatre Royal, Drury Lane. Another Theatre Royal ghost, a figure in grey, could well be connected with the discovery of a dead body in a sealed room of the theatre many years ago.

A spectral, John Buckstone, the nineteenth-century actor-manager, is always a welcome figure at the Haymarket Theatre since his arrival is a sign that the current production will be a success. His ghost was first seen in 1880 about a year after his death, seated in Queen Victoria's box, which is not surprising since he was one of her favourite actors. He now stands outside dressing-room doors awaiting the invitation to enter, which is usually in the form of 'Come in, love'.

Mummified remains of one kind or another have contributed to the macabre aspects of London occultism over the years. The mummy cover listed as Exhibit No. 22542 in the second Egyptian Room of the British Museum, has an extraordinarily macabre potency for evil if only half the stories told about it are true. W. T. Stead, the famous spiritualist, declared in 1889 that 'the expression on the face was that of a soul in living torment'. Strange stories continue to circulate about the mummy case although they are somewhat less sensational than those of the past. One is that the presence of the sarcophagus in the Museum has caused physical disturbances, and another that the mummy was in some mysterious fashion responsible for the sinking of the *Titanic*. When it first arrived in the Museum many visitors laid bunches of flowers on the floor in front of the mummy case to propitiate the restless spirit of the long-dead Princess of Thebes who once occupied it.

St James, Garlickhill, is a rare example of a city church which can boast a medieval mummy among its antiquities. The mummy was discovered when the vaults were closed in 1839 and at one time the more frolicsome choir boys 'used to take the mummy for a run round the church'. A notice on its case takes the form of the well-known obituary:

> Stop stranger, stop as you pass by.
> As you are now so once was I,
> As I am now you soon will be,
> So pray, prepare to follow me.

Occasionally a tall spectre in a white sheet, who is presumed to be the mummy, has alarmed unsuspecting tourists. Fortunately the mummy has a retiring disposition and once detected immediately takes refuge in its case.

A third London 'mummy' is the skilfully disguised skeleton of the philosopher Jeremy Bentham, which is on view near the entrance hall of University College, London. Under the terms of Bentham's will his body was dissected and the bones wired together. Jeremy's features were modelled from a portrait of the famous philosopher who still presides in spirit over the proceedings of the Council. Jeremy is supposed to leave his case occasionally and has been seen wandering dreamily down a corridor in the general direction of the library.

The annals of the Royal College of Surgeons include the remarkable story of a corpse coming to life and committing manslaughter. In 1803, during an experiment with electricity, a dead body was suddenly re-animated. It sat up, flexed its muscles and punched one of the experimenters on the jaw with the result that the poor man collapsed and died of shock.

Before undertaking a brief survey of London's haunted suburbs, it is necessary to discuss a curious discovery made at Lauderdale House at Highgate about fifteen years ago. During the restoration of this sixteenth-century building by the local authority the following strange objects came to light secreted in a recess built into the hearth: the foot of a goblet, a cork-soled shoe and fragment of a second shoe, part of a candlestick, four mummified chickens two of which had been strangled, and the remains of a builder's sling. The objects had been deliberately placed in the recess by the builder's workmen in the days of Elizabeth I and were apparently very late survivals of the ancient ritual of foundation sacrifice which had lingered in the form of a luck-bringing superstition until about the year 1600. Symbolically the shoes represented a human life, the candlesticks the spirit of life, the goblet blood, and the chickens living flesh. In pre-Christian times a human being would have been sacrificed during a foundation ceremony.

Among other occult survivals in North London, but of a less tangible character, is the spectral coach of Enfield which is usually seen during the Christmas season floating several feet above terra firma *en route* to the River Lea where it plunges noiselessly beneath the water.

On the night of each 3rd November, Bruce Castle, Tottenham now a museum but once the home of the seventeenth-century Lady Constancia Coleraine, echoes to the frenzied screams of her ghost. This is the anniversary of the dreadful events of 1680 when she flung herself to death from the battlements onto the flagstones below after being imprisoned in a room of the castle by her jealous husband.

The London Borough of Waltham Forest possesses some extremely interesting ghosts, including a spectral workhouse mistress who haunts the Vestry Museum, originally the parish workhouse. There is also a haunted grave at the entrance to St Mary's, the parish church, and another at its rear where the ghost only puts in an appearance if a coin is placed on the headstone.

In the adjoining parish of Wanstead where a horrific skeleton trundles the coffin cart through the graveyard at night in quest of its wife, a phantom woman in white leaps out of her tomb and clasps her bony husband in passionate embrace.

The grounds of Old Wanstead House, now a public park and golf course, are sometimes patrolled by a phantom coach containing the ghost of Queen Elizabeth I who continues to revisit the estate of her long-dead favourite, the Earl of Leicester.

Closer to London, on the north side of the Thames and facing the Royal Naval College, Greenwich, is that gloomy dockland area, the Isle of Dogs, once known as Stepney Marsh. Its name has been attributed to the presence there of the royal kennels or alternately to the wild ducks which were once common on these marshes. From the supernatural standpoint, however, the Isle makes a useful contribution to the folklore of London for there is a locally held legend that a demon huntsman and his phantom hounds are sometimes seen flying at night through the sky above the island.

Crossing to Greenwich one is once more in the very heart of the occult, although there are few witchcraft legends in the Borough, despite the fact that several of the Lancashire witches were brought to the Ship Tavern in the town for examination in 1634. So vast is the population of ghosts recorded in the Royal Borough that it is possible to mention only the most unusual: Greenwich Park is haunted by a monster 'part-human part-animal' which walks sideways like a crab, while in a house near Woolwich Common a grandmotherly figure occasionally leans over the beds of young children and attempts to strangle them. Blackheath Library, once the rectory, is visited by the ghost of

Elsie Marshall, a missionary who was murdered in China at the close of the last century. The most intriguing of all the ghosts of Greenwich, however, is the seventeenth-century libertine William Langhorne 'the hot blooded phantom of Charlton House' who in life left no chambermaid unturned, and who is believed even now to lay in wait on the stairs for unsuspecting females.

Turning to West London one finds there a fascinating heritage of ghost lore, both new and old. It includes that classic ghost story involving the lecherous Lord Lyttleton who was haunted at his home in Hill Street by the recently dead Mrs Amphlet whose two daughters he had callously seduced. The phantom suddenly appeared at Lord Lyttleton's bedside and uttered the awesome words, 'Prepare to die, my lord—Within three days you will be in the state of the departed'. Precisely three midnights later Lord Lyttleton collapsed and died in the arms of his servant.

The Grenadier public house, Wilton Row, is haunted by yet another defaulter the ghost of an army officer who was murdered long ago by his companions after he had been detected cheating at cards.

Moving further westwards we arrive at Holland House, once a home of the nobility but now a youth hostel, which has been haunted ever since the seventeenth century by the ghost of its former owner, Henry Rich, first Earl of Holland, who was beheaded in Palace Yard, Westminster, in 1649, in the same year as his royal master Charles I. Holland House was also the home of Lady Diana Rich who, after seeing her double approaching her in the grounds, decided that this was an omen of death and did in fact die of smallpox within a matter of months. It is one of the oldest and most gruesome of superstitions that to see one's double is fatal. There have been other reports of psychic doubles at Holland House but whether these heralded some kind of tragedy is unknown.

For a regal ghost with a continuing interest in his country's welfare one must go to Kensington Palace where the late-lamented King George II has been seen with his nose pressed against a window patiently awaiting the outcome of the Seven Years War.

Nineteenth-century London seems an unlikely setting for a ghost-laying ceremony and even less for the impaling of vampires, but it was here that the barbaric custom of burying suicides at the crossroads with a stake through the heart was last performed in 1823. It took place at the crossroads between Grosvenor Place and the Kings Road. As the result of public indignation an Act of Parliament was passed decreeing that henceforth in cases of *felo de se* the remains were to be interred 'without any stake being driven through the body of such a person'. As has been indicated earlier in the book, this macabre rite had been introduced with the object of preventing the ghost of the suicide from escaping from its grave.

London suburbs can boast few ecclesiastical ghosts although a procession of monks has been seen from time to time passing through Acton churchyard.

For further regal ghosts we have to go much further afield, to Middlesex, now largely swallowed up by the metropolis, where the ear-shattering shrieks of Henry VIII's errant Queen Catherine Howard have echoed along the corridors of Hampton Court Palace for the past four hundred years. It was here that Catherine received the dread news that she was to be put on trial for adultery, and as with so many others who fell by the wayside in those bloody days she ended her life on the block. Her paramour Francis Dereham was also beheaded but his ghost now haunts West Dereham, in Norfolk, where his body lies.

Henry VIII has put in an occasional appearance at Hampton Court as a ghost; he was actually seen there some ten years ago, and also the ghost of his fallen favourite Cardinal Wolsey who returns to survey the scene of his past glories in the palace that was once his own.

Mistress Penn, wet-nurse to the infant King Edward VI, haunts Hampton Church where her memorial can be seen, and her grey-garbed shape has also been detected gliding through Hampton Court Palace, where the whirring of her spinning-wheel is sometimes heard.

There is a popular misconception that witchcraft, magic and occultism are more popular in rural areas than in the towns, but in view of the vast number of occult books on sale in London this is obviously far from the truth. London has on tap an infinite variety of supernatural specialists, clairvoyants, psychic healers and Tarot tutors, not to mention palmists, psychometrists and phrenologists, and it has witches who are nicely settled in the covens they established about twenty years ago.

This is completely in accordance with the tradition of a city where even in the days of the witch hunts, magical rites could be carried out with relatively few risks provided the practitioner was well-to-do. There have always been mishaps, of course, as when the renowned seventeenth-century astrologer-herbalist Nicholas Culpeper was accused by the courts of bewitching a client who died of a wasting disease after placing his medical affairs in Culpeper's hands.

Most physicians of that day were prepared to ascribe the ills they could not cure to the black arts. When Elizabeth Jackson of Upper Thames Street was accused of bewitching her neighbour, the doctors came forward to declare that the latter's illness had been caused by supernatural agency. A doctor who demurred was silenced by the judge, who informed him that he was personally confident that the woman had been bewitched.

Magic had its part to play in love matters, as in 1591 when a London wizard who had exercised his devilish arts on behalf of a client who coveted another woman's husband, was imprisoned for a year.

The art of necromancy also had its adherents, and corpses were exhumed from churchyards and utilized for the manufacture of grisly charms. Little has changed apparently over the centuries for the London police still find they have their work cut out to protect graves from modern magicians who carry out macabre ceremonies in ancient vaults. Highgate Cemetery in North London which is usually associated with the high-priest of materialism, Karl Marx, who was buried there in 1883 has recently become a focal point for a revival of medieval necromancy on a grand scale. Tombs were repeatedly opened and the corpses stolen, and skulls had to be rescued by the authorities from the homes of eccentrics who found they made admirable book-ends. A half-burned body was discovered by its grave after being utilized in some obscure black magic rite. The sombre saga only came to an end following drastic police action and now Highgate Cemetery has happily been restored to its original role as the shrine of mid-Victorian posthumous respectability. There is, however, much talk of two spectres there—a ghostly woman who wanders among the tombs and a vampire with a passion for human blood who is suspected of being more living than dead.

Although London has become a centre of operations for a wide variety of mystical cults, only one of these, Wicca appears to have avowed openly a belief in magic; Wicca the creation of the late Gerald Gardner, is a semi-secret society dedicated to white witchcraft, to which reference has been made previously. Much more is known about this movement than formerly because of the uninhibited desire of its adherents to discuss the mysteries of their craft on the television screen. From such revelations and from the many books now available on the subject we learn that witches worship secret gods whose names must never be divulged, and are organized in closely knit groups called covens where they perform ceremonies reminiscent of ancient magic and modern folk dancing. They have as their 'bible' a handbook of occult philosophy called *The Book of Shadows*. From the witches one meets it is obvious that they sincerely believe they have the power to cast spells, but these fortunately, are usually of the benign or helpful kind.

In a typical Hallowe'en rite when the author was present, a slow dance was performed by naked middle-aged matrons and their stouter spouses, followed by an invocation to the 'Dread Lord of the Shadows' and a supper of cakes and ale. Despite the neurotic anxieties of many of our clergy there seems precious little cause for concern in the frolics of modern witches, if the London covens are representative of the movement as a whole.

If witchcraft has any serious impact today then it is in the techniques used to intimidate others by rituals which strike at the emotions at a deep psychological level. Towards the end of April 1976 a curious box found beneath a bridge spanning a waterway at the Royal Albert Docks, London was carefully opened and the following objects revealed: a white dove, still living, with its wings and tail feathers clipped and its legs and beak tied with silk ribbon, a tuft of human hair and several joss sticks. This, according to the secret laws of witchcraft, was a spell designed to bring death to some person unknown. Black Magic never dies; it is perpetually renewed from the well of hatred deep in the human mind.

6

The Sinister South

The well-known distinction between a Man of Kent, that is, one born east of the River Medway, and a Kentish Man, one born in West Kent, can be attributed to the Norman Conquest when the Men of Kent came to terms with the invader and were permitted to preserve most of their customs intact.

As a result of this compromise Kent escaped much of the devastation suffered by other parts of Britain, (particularly Yorkshire) and its traditions remained in consequence relatively unchanged for centuries. The same applied to occult lore in the county, some of which is clearly traceable to the Roman occupation, a classic example being the case of the phantom baby of Reculver.

The Roman fort at Reculver on the Thames dates from the third century A.D., and obviously any object discovered in its foundations must be at least sixteen hundred years old. Over a considerable period of time no less than eleven skeletons of infants, all only a few weeks old, have been brought to light here during archaeological digs. One was found at the centre of a wall, another beneath it, and yet another in one of the corners. Strange to say, long before the dig had even commenced there a story circulated in the district to the effect that the site was haunted by a baby who had been buried alive by the Romans. It is possible of course that the folk memory of the sacrifice had been kept alive in the locality for some sixteen hundred years. Alternatively could it have been a genuine case of a phantom baby haunting the scene of its murder?

Similar infant skeletons have been discovered in the foundations of the Roman town of Springhead, while Richborough, another Roman site, is supposed to be haunted by a column of phantom Roman legionnaires led by a centurion who march towards the sea. Other spectral Roman soldiers have been reported in the same district fighting on the beaches to the considerable amazement of all beholders.

One of the most interesting of Kentish folk tales concerns a hidden treasure, some say a golden idol, which is supposed to be buried in the parish of Ash near Woodnesborough, a place with obvious associations with the Norse god Woden or Odin. Over the centuries many treasure hunters have sought it in vain.

Many of the castles of Kent are reputedly haunted, perhaps more so than elsewhere in eastern England. Hever, built and rebuilt in the reign of Henry VI by Sir Geoffrey Boleyn, is haunted by his tragic descendant, Anne Boleyn who materializes at Christmas time. Canon Pakenham Walsh described in his *Tudor Story* a séance he attended at the castle in which communication was actually made with her ghost.

Lympne, where the traditional ghosts are seven Saxons and a Roman sentry, has more recently been haunted by a baby whose crying was heard in one of the towers.

Rochester's ghost is the lady of Ralph de Copo, killed when the castle was laid under siege during the Baron's Wars. Charles Dickens has recently returned to haunt his favourite town.

A number of curious superstitions continue to be associated with both the castles and stately homes of the county. At Chillham it is unlucky if a species of birds bearing 'the same name as the owner' settle in the castle estate. It is still remembered how, after a flight of herons had nested in the grounds in the nineteenth century, the family in occupation, whose name happened to be Heron, soon gave up their occupation.

A very macabre story is associated with Ightham Mote, once the home of Dorothy Selby whose cryptic letter to Lord Monteagle was responsible for the disclosure of the Gunpowder Treason of 1605. There is a well-known tradition in the locality that her companions in revenge walled her up alive in the building, which is no doubt the reason for the presence of her restless ghost at Ightham Mote.

Dover Castle, which stands on a 400-foot cliff overlooking the sea, is one of the principal bastions of England and has in consequence suffered constant attacks over the centuries. The castle was strange to say captured from the Royalists in 1642 by a Parliament man named Drake with only twelve followers. After the Civil War the fortress dropped out of history until the outbreak of the French Revolution when it was considerably strengthened and altered to accommodate two thousand soldiers, one of whom a drummer boy was found murdered under circumstances which remain a mystery to this day. His ghost, which is for some inexplicable reason headless, continues to make the rounds of Dover Castle.

Lesnes Abbey near Abbey Wood is haunted, perhaps inevitably, by a monk, Cranbrooks' ghost is Bloody Baker, a multiple wife murderer, while Smarden's phantom in residence is Satan himself. Far less dramatic is the dignified ghost of the Black Prince who haunts Hall Place where he once spent the night.

Pluckley, to the south-west of Charing, which has been described as the most haunted of Kentish villages, has twelve ghosts covering a wide range of Kentish history. An elemental spirit in the shape of a white lady haunts the site of the old Manor House, while a red lady patrols the churchyard. The medieval period is represented by a spectral monk and the eighteenth century by a highwayman and a phantom coach and four. Among other wayfarers' delights offered by hospitable Pluckley are a series of unearthly screams emanating from the man who died many years ago in a flooded quarry. A ghostly gipsy woman is also occasionally seen. This lady was burned to death long ago in the mill, the ruins of which are haunted by a spectral miller.

Although Kent seems to have escaped the worst excesses of the witch-hunting era there were a number of tragic occurrences which sullied the county's reputation in this respect. In 1652 several women were tried at Maidstone with a variety of crimes including murdering their neighbours by witchcraft, and were sentenced to death and hanged before a vast crowd.

For later manifestations of witchcraft in the county we are largely indebted to the researches of Sir Charles Igglesden which he published in his book *Those Superstitions* about half a century ago. Sir Charles described the miracles worked by old Granny Burton, the 'witch fortune teller' of Bethersden, who possessed a number of healing charms written in crabbed writing on pieces of paper which were 'brown with age'. One charm, obviously of pre-Reformation vintage, called upon the Angels in Heaven to heal burns and scalds. To the author's own knowledge there was also a Kentish healer, known as the 'Sorceress of Sevenoaks', with a vast clientele, who was renowned for a magical recipe for arthritis, a weird brew of stewed nettles, reinforced by slowly chanted incantations. The sorceress with a companion attempted to break a drought by untying a rain rope, a series of knots in a length of cord. However, at the first clap of thunder they lost their nerve and retreated into their houses in terror.

The superstitions of Kent have never been far from the surface and a number originally mentioned by Sir Charles Igglesden continue to have an undiminished vitality today. Among the shepherds on Romney Marsh it was lucky if a farmer saw the first lamb of the season with its head towards him, but unlucky if it greeted him with its hindquarters and tail. A black lamb, incidentally, always brought good fortune to the flock. Among superstitious objects he mentions, was the witch ball, an ornament once seen in cottage windows which was supposed, like the horseshoe, to keep witches from the home. Belief in the restless dead must have received considerable reinforcement in the Pembury area a hundred and seventy odd years ago following the funeral of Anne West of Great Bayhall Manor. Like so many of her generation she suffered from a morbid fear of being buried alive and arranged for a bell to be placed in her tomb so that she could if necessary sound the alarm. Following her death in 1803 the bell rang continuously for night after night and, more frightening still, her corpse was reported strolling slowly down the village street *en route* to Bayhall Manor, her old home, which remained haunted for years until finally abandoned to the ghost. In time the building ceased to attract ghost-hunters, and since then, one is happy to say, Anne West's soul has been at rest.

The people of Kent have long memories and the sites of spectacular deaths which occurred centuries ago are still pointed out to visitors.

There is a lonely spot on Romney Marsh, by the roadside, where in the eighteenth century the body of a highwayman was hanged in chains and later buried at the foot of the gibbet. The place is still regarded as accursed and shunned even in daylight. Even more sinister is the site of the gibbet on the Canterbury Road where cars have a tendency to crash. Some supernatural power overwhelms the drivers preventing them from applying the brakes.

One visible testimony to old-time Kentish beliefs is Satan's hoof-print at Newington church. The Devil was so irritated by the ringing of the church bells that he climbed the tower with the intention of spiriting them away but lost his balance and crashed to the ground, leaving as a sign of his presence a hoof-mark on a stone by the gate.

The Devil or at least his adherents have not yet abandoned the habit of vandalizing Kentish churches to judge by the curious occurrences at Shoreham, the attractive North Downs village on the River Darent. Here in 1970 crosses were smashed in the churchyard and bodies removed from graves. However, the culprits could possibly have been treasure-hunters since there is a well-known tradition in the locality that members of the Mildmay family who are buried here left instructions for their armour and jewellery to be placed in their tombs.

The Kentish coast has always been ideal territory for both smugglers and smugglers' ghosts, and although the curious flashing lights which once shone at night from the cliffs are seen no more, a spectral exciseman named Gill continues to battle with a long-dead smuggler on the edge of Reculver cliff.

Chatham's maritime traditions have been reinforced in recent years by the presence in the Naval Barracks of a sailor's ghost with a wooden leg. The man was murdered, it is believed, by French prisoners during the Napoleonic Wars.

Apart from the vast array of historical ghosts the county has to offer, there are later ones making their bow upon the occult scene. Biggin Hill, the World War II airfield, is haunted by a wartime Spitfire performing its victory roll, reminding us that this was one of the vital centres of the Battle of Britain in 1940, while throbbing engines have also been heard over Hawkinge. Closer to London a phantom enemy plane occasionally crashes to a watery end near Erith marshes.

Modern forms of transport seem to be greatly favoured by the ghosts of Kent for a phantom limousine has been noted on a road near Lamberhurst, and there are a large number of crossroads where that most ubiquitous of ghosts, the phantom hitchhiker, vainly attempts to thumb a lift from passing cars.

Surrey provides an ideal hunting ground for those, particularly Londoners, intending to investigate the folklore of the occult. Its population ranges from the truly rural to the sophisticated, from the cottager to the denizens of the stockbroker belt; yet social class has very little influence upon prevailing attitudes towards the supernatural.

One of the best-known examples of Surrey's modern psychic phenomena is the phantom motorist who continues to race along the old Brooklands track completely oblivious of the fact that it no longer exists, having long since been overwhelmed by housing estates and factories. It was in one of the latter that engineers were petrified by the sight of a phantom car careering madly through the works.

Few of us recognize that in psychic terms it is a mere step backwards in time from the age of screaming Alpha-Romeos and Bentleys to that of the old-fashioned spectral coach, one of which haunts the roads near the Hop Bag Inn at Farnham, while another has been noted at Riddlesdown, complete with coachman, proceeding at a steady pace along the track of a long vanished country road.

English ghosts possess an inherent conservatism which ensures that they are invariably seen where expected. They can also be guaranteed to repeat the tragic series of events which led to their becoming earthbound in the first place. This is particularly evident in Surrey hauntings which, when presented chronologically, portray an intriguing panorama of the county's psychic past.

A beast reminiscent of the kelpies of Scotland (the loch monsters of the ancient Celts) once haunted a stream near the village of Buckland to the west of Reigate. It was known as the Buckland Shag and terrorized the neighbourhood until thrust back into the Celtic twilight by the ministrations of an exorcist priest.

We are reminded of a strange medieval tragedy when we pass the sinister Silent Pool in its lonely setting at Shere under the North Downs. It was in these waters in the thirteenth century that a maiden chose to drown herself rather than fall into the rapacious clutches of the villainous Prince John (later of Magna Carta fame). As one would anticipate following such a tragedy her restless spirit continues to haunt the pool over which broods an atmosphere of intense tragedy and despair.

The medieval period made a powerful contribution to Surrey folklore with a number of ecclesiastical hauntings and stories of graveyard ghosts. The ruins of thirteenth-century Newark Priory on the River Wey are haunted by a phantom monk who has been seen standing in the water-meadows, no doubt regretting the pleasures of monasticism which he is no longer able to enjoy. In their time the monks of Newark acquired a county-wide reputation for irreligious behaviour, good food and amorous exploits, hence the old ode:

> The monks of the Wey seldom sang any psalms
> And little they thought of religious qualms
> And they could not swim, so fat were they ....
> Those oily amorous monks of the Wey.

After years of sensual bouts with like-minded nuns the monks were all drowned in the river ... a just retribution, one might say.

> Oh churchmen beware of the lures of the flesh.
> The net of the devil hath many a mesh
> And remember whenever you're tempted to stray
> The fate that befell the poor monks of the Wey.

Phantoms and buried treasure are associated with the ruins of Waverley Abbey, the first of the English Cistercian houses which was also built on the banks of the Wey. There are old traditions still current in the neighbourhood relating to images of the twelve apostles which were concealed there in order to secure them from the ravages of the Protestant Reformers. On various occasions visitors claim to have seen spectral apostles standing amid the ruins, only to vanish a moment later. A great treasure belonging to the monastery is also believed to be buried here.

The same tragic period which witnessed the dissolution and destruction of the monasteries saw also the legal murder of many who sought to uphold the old way of life. Following the execution of Sir Thomas More in 1535, the martyr's head was rescued from London Bridge where it had been exhibited, and taken to Baynards Hall for safe custody. Although the head is now buried in the family vault at Canterbury, Sir Thomas' ghost has been reported at Baynards Park.

The Tudor period is particularly important from the standpoint of the supernatural since it witnessed an ever-growing terror of ghosts—which is obvious from a study of Shakespeare's plays. Prior to the Reformation the unquiet dead seem to have been easily exorcized by the old priests, but now the expulsion of ghosts was a thing of the past.

The spectre of Queen Elizabeth I haunts Richmond Palace where she died in 1603 after seeing her psychic double 'pallid shrivelled and wan'—a well-known omen of death. The Fetch, or psychic double, which was expected to appear whenever death was at hand, was similar to the Norse 'fylgja', the spirit follower who accompanied every man and woman through life and died with them.

Moving forward to the tales of the turbulent seventeenth century and its civil wars one discovers a Cromwellian judge still haunting the old Manor House at Walton-on-Thames. This ghost has been identified as that of John Bradshaw, the regicide who passed sentence of death on King Charles I, and whose body was disinterred at the Restoration and gibbeted with the bodies of Cromwell and Ireton. Oddly enough, his ghost has been noted in two other places, Westminster Deanery where he signed Charles' death warrant, and Red Lion Square where he walks arm in arm with his fellow regicides, seemingly untroubled by the traffic hazards of what were once Red Lion Fields.

Ham House, Petersham, an annexe of the Victoria and Albert Museum, was long renowned for the Restoration orgies which took place there during the general reaction against the austerities of the Puritan regime. The district is haunted by one of the roisterers, a mad cavalier who, having tippled too well, toppled into the Thames and drowned. His cloak figure, still staggering, is occasionally seen on the towpath hastening to keep a seventeenth-century rendezvous with death.

The Devil was as lively in Surrey as elsewhere, and during the ages of faith his activities in the county were commemorated in a number of sites which bear his name. A series of mounds near Frensham Ponds known as the Devil's Jumps are not only dedicated to his memory but considered unlucky to disturb in any way. This old fear received considerable reinforcement during the late nineteenth century when an intrepid astronomer set up his telescope on the middle Devil's Jump and shortly afterwards went mad and murdered his wife. A comment made at the time reflects the local attitude to astronomy: 'Education and ability used for the devil's work are certain to arouse distaste.'

Belief in the Devil as such has largely vanished from our folk vocabulary but a number of even older beliefs still linger on among the cottagers of the Surrey Hills.

Well worship is not yet quite extinct if we consider the case of the Surrey housewife who dropped a pebble into a well each evening to protect herself from ill luck. Was this, one wonders, the source of the modern ritual of tossing pennies into wishing-wells? This custom would have been condemned as downright heretical up to a couple of hundred years ago when the fear of witchcraft still lingered in rural Surrey.

One is reminded of the strange world of the past when viewing Mother Ludlam's 'cauldron' or 'kettle' in Frensham church. Old Mother Ludlam the witch lived near Waverley Abbey where she was long remembered for the indolent habits of her dog. The saying 'as lazy as Mother Ludlam's dog' sums up the general attitude towards this perpetually tired animal, which had been known to lean against a wall in order to summon up the energy to bark.

The Surrey witch I like best was old Jane Butts, the sorceress of Ewell who dispatched poltergeists to attack those who offended her, with instructions to shower them with stones. Acting on the advice of the village white wizard her victims buried bottles of urine in their back gardens and set fire to their clothing in order to break the spells she cast upon them. Finally, wearying of her curses they took her to court where a good-humoured magistrate acquitted her of all devilish practices and sent her home without a stain on her character.

A mystical quality pervades the Sussex downlands, suggesting secrets as old as time which will be revealed only to the initiated. One cult centre, Chanctonbury Ring, situated a few miles from Worthing, attracts large numbers of visitors who often declare that it is a focal point for supernatural forces of stupendous power.

Within a grove of trees is an Iron Age earthworks and a Romano-Celtic temple. There is an eerie quality overhanging this site which is difficult to describe—a stillness unbroken by bird song, a place where one is never free of the uncanny sense of being watched. Local traditions associate Chanctonbury with both the Devil and the Druids, either of whom are ready to materialize if one is prepared to visit the site at midnight and circumnavigate it seven times.

As with the Rollright Stones in Oxfordshire, it is supposed to be impossible to count the trees at Chanctonbury with accuracy, some supernatural power invariably inhibiting the operation. Rarely have so many venerable legends attached themselves to a single site. It was from here, according to one old tale, that Satan leaped from the earth leaving behind him a hoofprint clearly visible in the soil. In another tradition we learn that if we remain pure in heart we shall see the fairies of Chanctonbury dancing in a ring. Not even the advent of scientific materialism has managed to modify the miraculous reputation of this strange place, for it has now become a viewing site, not only for flying devils, but for flying saucers, several of which have been observed from the hilltop in recent years.

Alfriston, that delightful village on the River Cuckmere, is another place of mystery which has attracted to itself an interesting legend. Its church, which is often described as the 'Cathedral of the South Downs', was only erected after constant harassment from the spirits who apparently removed the stones to another site as fast as the builders laid them down. Then someone had a vision in which there appeared four white oxen recumbent and cruciform in a field and it was decided that this must be the place intended for the church. It was in fact erected on a pagan site, which suggests a decisive victory for the other side.

Over the ages the tale has been told many times to visitors, but not even the wildest stretch of imagination could have produced a folklore half as macabre as that which has become associated with Alfriston in modern times. Satanists have conducted their own pilgrimages to the village, desecrating the tombs in the churchyard and have then moved on to Jevington and St Nicholas at Bramber, where they painted cabalistic symbols on the doors.

The Long Man of Wilmington, a huge human figure cut into the chalk of Wendover Hill some five miles from Eastbourne, is yet another shrine of mystery, the origins of which continue to be a matter of debate among archaeologists. However, the site has now been adopted as their cult centre by the Sussex witches who stand naked upon the summit on Midsummer morn to greet the rising sun.

The attractive town of Mayfield has an established position in Sussex folklore as the place where St Dunstan met the Devil and put him to rout. Satan, disguised as a voluptuous maiden, crept into the saint's cell with the intention of seducing him or at the very least tarnishing his reputation for celibacy, however, St Dunstan penetrating the disguise seized a pair of red hot pincers which happened to be handy and . . .

> pulled the devil by the nose
> With red hot tongs that made him roar
> That he was heard three miles or more.

There is a long standing superstition in the area of Beachy Head that the cliff tops are haunted by a sinister presence who lures walkers to the edge, where they are overcome by vertigo and plunge to a dreadful death on the rocks below. Such cliffs have been associated with horrors of all kinds from time immemorial. In pre-Christian ages human sacrifices were carried out at similar places, and later, in the days of the Anglo-Saxons, it was customary to hurl criminals from high cliffs into the sea. One theory which has been advanced to account for the Beachy Head phenomena is the presence there of the earthbound spirit of someone who either committed suicide or was executed on this spot many centuries ago.

The Sussex coast has been associated with some curious events over the centuries but, possibly, none quite as eccentric as the encounter of a ship's captain with the Sea Witch of Pevensey.

In the Calendar of State Papers there is an entry dated 1st September 1656, in which Captain Adam Smythson complained to the Navy Commissioners in London that an evil-tongued woman of Pevensey, with a reputation for witchcraft, had cast a spell upon his ship which was likely to prevent him from leaving port for the following three months.

The fear of the black arts must have reached unheard of proportions in Rye to judge from the chronicles of 1558 when 'the parochyans of Rye' accused their curate of involvement in the black arts after discovering that he had prescribed libations of holy water for the treatment of bronchial catarrh.

The castles and mansions of Sussex, like those of Kent, are

notorious for uncanny hauntings. Arundel, the ancient home of the Howards, is haunted by a girl who committed suicide by throwing herself from one of the towers because of unrequited love, while the ruins of Knepp Castle have an unusual spectre; a phantom doe, which is supposed to be the spirit of a girl who was transformed into animal shape by a witch many centuries ago.

It is generally agreed by the people of Hastings that their castle is haunted by the ghost of St Thomas à Becket who conducted religious services in its Chapel about the year 1157.

Herstmonceaux Castle (the name means the 'Wood of the Monceaux') situated some seven miles south-east of Battle, is best known in occult circles for its nine-feet tall phantom drummer who beats fiendish tattoos to commemorate his personal participation in the Battle of Agincourt. A phantom woman of melancholy appearance is sometimes seen near the moat.

The Battle of Hastings, fought in 1066, is commemorated by Battle Abbey, the magnificent monastic foundation which William the Conqueror erected on the site. William, who like most warriors and tyrants, was extremely superstitious, on being told that a sanguelac, (or bloody fountain,) had sprung up on the battlefield as a sign of heavenly anger at the shedding of so much Christian blood, decided to make his peace with God; the Abbey he built must therefore be seen as a symbol of atonement as well as of victory. On more than one occasion the ghost of the defeated King Harold has been seen on the battlefield, saturated with blood caused by the arrow which tradition insists pierced his eye.

The mysterious hand of God was detected in yet another strange event, this time at Bosham where the coast once lay under constant harassment from marauding Danes. A group of raiders sacked the town, murdering the people and carrying off vast quantities of loot. They then removed the church bells and carried them aboard their ships which lay in Bosham Creek. Suddenly the skies darkened, the day becoming as black as night and when the sun shone again the raiders were nowhere to be seen, having sunk to the sea bottom. The bodies were never found, but according to an ancient tradition the silver-toned bells of Bosham have been heard ringing from the depths of the waters on saints' days and festivals, in synchronization with the church bells of the entire county of Sussex.

Brede Place, that ancient Tudor mansion, once housed a human ogre who revelled in eating the flesh of babies. Justice caught up with him in the end for he was sawn asunder by an army of avenging children. All Brede's ghosts are of the melodramatic kind—a priest haunts the chapel, a murdered girl haunts the grounds, and a third spectre, wanders about minus his head.

Sherrington Manor at Selmeston, has a ghost story which the author investigated personally about ten years ago. Re-reading the notes made at the time one finds reference to mysterious footsteps, the turning of door knobs, fleeting glimpses of human shapes, and a strange man in a cloak seen standing in the drive. One of the gardeners at Sherrington was certain that he was often watched by hostile eyes when working in a particular corner of the grounds, an area shunned by domestic animals and birds.

Before moving on to the macabre mysteries of Hampshire a passing reference should be made to St Leonard's Forest which is the habitat of that rare species of fauna, the Sussex Dragon, as well as an arboreal devil which creeps from tree to tree, and a ghost who leaps onto the backs of those who have the temerity to leave the beaten track.

Describing the countryside he knew over a century ago, that delightful pagan Richard Jefferies said of Hampshire: 'There is a frontier line to every civilization in this country yet, and not far outside its great centres we come quickly now on the borderland with nature.' Alas, much has changed since those words were written and the rural scenes beloved by Jefferies have been ravaged in ways that he would not have believed possible. Whatever frontiers now exist belong to the realms of imagination, those ill-explored areas of human experience bordering the supernatural. Jefferies wrote of the dying fragments of a peasant mythology with its faint whispers of witches and shadowy ghosts; strange that these occult images should have been resuscitated in our own times when the social environment which fostered them has virtually passed away.

Hampshire offers the imaginative mind an occult feast, with a well-balanced menu of dragons and grampians, Druids and devils, treasure-guarding spirits and walled-up nuns. We are reminded of an old tragedy at Moyles Court at Ellingham near Ringwood, for it was long haunted by the unquiet ghost of Dame Alice Lisle, the victim of a cruel legal murder perpetrated by bloody Judge Jeffreys following the failure of the Monmouth Rebellion in 1685.

Dame Lisle, an ancient lady who had survived the darkest period of the Civil War and Commonwealth, misguidedly sheltered several refugees from the ferocious soldiers of James II and in doing so rendered herself technically guilty of high treason. She was tried by Judge Jeffreys who sentenced her to be burned at the stake, which was later commuted to beheading. Despite a national outcry she died on the block, but her body escaped the ignominy of a felon's burial and lies peacefully in Ellingham churchyard. For several centuries Dame Alice's pathetic ghost haunted her old home but must finally have found rest for it has not been seen there for many years.

Apart from crumbling ruins little survives of the ancient Cistercian abbey of Netley, on Southampton Water. It has a solitary guardian in the somewhat menacing monk who has been seen on the site after midnight and who is considered by local people to be a harbinger of disaster.

Early in the eighteenth century while the chapel was under demolition a carpenter purchased the old timbers and arrived to take them away. Suddenly the spectral monk of Netley appeared, warning him of terrible consequences should he carry out his intentions, and shortly afterwards a huge lump of stone crashed down on his head, killing him on the spot.

Among other stories associated with Netley is the legend of a treasure which is supposed to lie secreted in the ruins. In view of the fate of the carpenter, however, the hoard is unlikely to be disturbed.

Beaulieu Abbey, also a Cistercian foundation, is supposed to resound at night to the chanting of long-dead monks. Since the abbey was originally a sanctuary, the ghosts are always benign.

Alas, the same cannot be said of Chilbolton Rectory which was built on the site of a thirteenth-century convent where a novice was bricked up alive for some disciplinary offence. Her spectre, which has been occasionally mistaken for a nurse, has been seen in one of the rooms.

Crondall to the north-west of Farnham has a long tradition of hauntings and here for some forgotten reason the hooves of phantom sheep have been heard clopping along the road at night, although the animals themselves are usually invisible. Apart from horses and dogs, spectral animals are something of a rarity in England, for our ancestors in refusing to admit that animals had souls virtually excluded the possibility of their returning as ghosts.

Crondall's night life is surprisingly active for so remote a district, for it includes a ghostly soldier who was murdered by a footpad, and a platoon of Cromwell's Ironsides galloping along the road towards the Norman church. From these and other ghostly souvenirs of the great Civil War we can assess something of the traumatic effect of the Cromwellian era upon the minds of those intimately involved in the struggle. It has been said, that it was a relatively unbloody conflict, but in view of the haunting memories it has produced one wonders if this is true.

Civil War memories are revived by what remains of Basing House, the sixteenth-century mansion at Basing which was stormed by Cromwell's forces in 1645 and then blown up after a siege lasting nearly three years. The ghost of Old Noll, which has been seen here from time to time, is probably searching for the Paulet family plate which is believed to lie hidden somewhere on the site.

The New Forest has a royal ghost, William Rufus, who was accidentally killed with an arrow while hunting in the forest. His ghost has been seen on 2nd August, the anniversary of his death, near the place where he died, which is marked by an obelisk known as the Rufus Stone.

For more than eight hundred years the foresters are supposed to have passed down the true circumstances of the death, as a closely guarded secret. Perhaps we have here a hint of some other explanation for the tragedy—that Rufus was murdered in order to make way for his successor. The King had hardly been buried more than a few hours when his younger brother Henry hurried off to London to take over the throne.

There are prehistoric sites in Hampshire associated with fairy haunting of a type not usually found so far south in the British Isles. Even in Shakespeare's day the fairy kingdom was fast fading from memory, and at an earlier period still the subject was discussed in the past tense, as we read in Chaucer's *Wife of Bath*:

> In olde days of King Arthur
> Of whom that Britons spoken great honour
> All was this land fulfilled of fayrie.

A number of Hampshire ghost stories are in reality disguised legends of the fairy kingdom as we may see from the following example:

Along the lanes near Liphook the spirit of a fair-haired boy has been seen and more often heard, playing his flute to guide lost travellers to a haven of safety. While it is possible that we have here a half-forgotten account of a kind-hearted shepherd's boy, the tale is also reminiscent of an old fairy tradition and should not be dismissed as yet another Hampshire haunting. In ancient times when the woods and forests were supposed to be peopled by members of the fairy race, their pipes were often heard for, as Louis Spence says, 'fairy music may often be heard at certain spots and like the fairies themselves be of exquisite beauty'. There are grave risks, however, for those who allow themselves to be bewitched by fairy pipes. Those who enter Fairyland must remain its prisoners until the end of time.

Also belonging to the arcana of the past are the fabulous monsters associated with Hampshire's pagan sites. At Burley they tell the tale of a dragon who after being promised a living sacrifice in the shape of sheep was fobbed off with milk. A gallant knight put in an appearance at the psychological moment and destroyed the beast. The dragon-slayer is one of the most popular characters in English folklore and represents the spirit of holiness who overcomes paganism and sin.

The lake at Highclere is today more familiar for its tench than aquatic monsters, yet if legend be true it was once the chosen habitat of a grampus 'a blunt headed dolphin-like cetacean' which spouted huge columns of water as it wallowed in the mud. By perching on a tree near the church the grampus attracted the attention of the parson, who exorcized it on the spot and it was never seen again.

Poor eyesight plus inadequate or non-existent street lighting seem to have been responsible for some remarkable psychic manifestations over the years, although grotesque animals, whether real or fictional, have an honoured place in folklore for they belong to that mysterious world of oral tradition in which fantasy is pleasingly intermingled with fact.

Hampshire witchcraft seems curiously devoid of the animal familiar one finds in other parts of the British Isles, although the witches were nonetheless regarded with awe. There were references in the records of an old trial of 1652 to a Hampshire man who possessed a witch's book of charms containing 'the names of witches who had listed themselves under the Devil's command'.

Twenty-two years later, in 1674, two Winchester witches, John and Agnes Guppie, were accused of 'feloniously laming a neighbour' by black magic. Fortunately the evidence against them was inconclusive and they were set free.

Perhaps the most interesting of these cases occurred a generation later in 1689 when three women, whose names have not been preserved, were thrown into Winchester jail charged with casting spells on the daughter of Goodman Alexander of Basingstoke, giving her attacks of fits. Since the disorder lay well beyond the capacity of the local physician, an astrologer was called in and finally succeeded in effecting a cure with the aid of distilled water and prayers. A devil then escaped from the patient's body in a sudden burst of wind, after which she appeared much relieved. Later however she suffered a relapse and abandoned her normal food for a diet of pins.

Witchcraft is far from extinct in the county for a well-known coven still meets at Ringwood in the New Forest, and on Hampshire hilltops at Hallowe'en huge bonfires glow red in the night as the weird sisters, with their even weirder brothers, dance naked at the celebration of Samhain on the eve of the Celtic New Year.

In common with islands generally the Isle of Wight possesses distinctive characteristics of its own and the same rule is applicable to its supernatural heritage. Brading, that veritable folk museum of ancient history, with its bull-baiting ring and carefully preserved stocks and whipping post in the Town Hall was once associated with Druidic sacrifices in which criminals were burned alive in huge wicker cages to aid the fertility of the soil. Julius Caesar referred to this ancient British custom with disgust for, despite their many cruelties, the Romans regarded the sacrifice of human beings as utterly barbaric. On another site on the Isle of Wight which is associated with the Druids are the stones of Mottistone Downs where white bulls were sacrificed to the gods. It goes without saying, however, that the stones are far older than the Druidic priesthood who no doubt utilized them for their ceremonies.

Puck is a somewhat unexpected character for the twentieth century, but he is still associated in the minds of old residents, with Puckpool near Ryde for it was here that the mischievous sprite lured the guileless Father Martin into a quagmire by imitating a woman's voice. Puck was endowed with the remarkable power to change his sex, at will.

This is the vintage Puck of traditional mythology unchanged by time who found nothing so enjoyable as flashing his magical lantern to lure lost travellers into trackless wastes. The poet Drayton knew him well as he who:

> Leading makes us stray
>   long winter's nights out of the way
> And when we stick in mire or clay
>   he doth with laughter leave us.

Puck crops up elsewhere under other names: Will o' the Wisp, Jack O'Lantern and Robin Goodfellow.

The Isle of Wight preserves some delightful stories and one can always refresh the detective instincts when inspiration runs dry by partaking of a magical potion drawn from the famous wishing well on St Boniface Down.

The Dorset countryside has attracted the attention of folklorists and ghost hunters for decades, largely because of the wide range of its occult phenomena. There are haunted prehistoric barrows, a phantom Roman legionary, and even a screaming skull among the county's supernatural treasures, and one of the earliest descriptions of the stock-in-trade of an English wizard emanates from Dorset.

In 1566 John Walsh, a sorcerer of Netherbury, a small village on the River Brit, was interrogated by a commission set up by the Bishop of Exeter to investigate the prevalence of witchcraft and allied beliefs in his diocese.

Walsh seems to have openly avowed his involvement in the black arts; nevertheless, for some reason which is not made clear he was afterwards set free. During his examination he produced his grimoire, or black magic handbook, complete with spells and mystic symbols, and admitted that he owned a familiar or evil spirit which he fed with blood, and that he sacrificed 'two living things a year' to a creature with cloven hooves. Walsh came forward with some surprising revelations about fairies of which he knew three kinds—the white, the green and the black, the latter being the most dangerous.

He also disclosed how one could destroy an enemy by magic, using clay mingled with earth from a new grave and the ashes of a human rib. This was shaped into a puppet and pricked with a thorn, and the human being so represented suffered accordingly. If the image was stabbed to the heart, the victim died within nine days.

Walsh agreed with his interrogators that the Devil was always impotent when confronted by those with implicit faith in Jesus Christ and it is possible that this avowal saved his life.

The fear of evil spirits has been known to take many strange forms but rarely perhaps quite so remarkable as the choice of a human skull as a talisman against ghosts and devils. Such a macabre symbol has become one of Dorset's most important heirlooms and is founded on a very curious story, the legend of the screaming skull of Bettiscombe Manor.

The tradition originated in 1685 with the defeat of the Monmouth Rebellion in which Azariah Pinney, the young heir of Bettiscombe Manor, participated and for which he was exiled to the West Indies. One of his descendants, John Frederick Pinney, returned to the ancestral home some sixty years later with a Negro servant to whom the promise was made that when he died he would not be buried in England, but in his original African home. This promise was not kept.

The servant, whose name has not been recorded, was buried

in Bettiscombe churchyard and shortly afterwards the manor came under supernatural assault when crops failed, farm stock died and the nights were made hideous by screams emanating from the Negro's tomb. Realizing that all these disasters were the awful consequences of breaking faith with the dead, the squire of Bettiscombe had the Negro's body disinterred and brought into the house. Now only the skull survives as a grisly memento of a remarkable Dorset folktale, but one in which, as an article on Dorset history puts it: 'The legend of the Bettiscombe skull, unlike most such traditions, has developed a sequel of a very interesting and romantic nature.'

The first clear-cut reference to the skull as a charm against ghosts was made in 1849 when a visitor to whom it was shown was informed, 'As long as the skull is in the building no ghost will ever haunt Bettiscombe House.' A number of other stories testify to the skull's grisly reputation.

A former squire of Bettiscombe threw the skull into a pond, but after this had been followed by a sudden thunder-clap accompanied by screams, it was speedily returned to its normal place—a niche in the brickwork of the attic.

Curious sounds heard overhead by a visitor at night some ten years ago were described by the housekeeper as the activities of 'ghosts playing skittles with the skull'.

An attempt was made to bury the skull in the garden but it succeeded in digging its way to the surface with its teeth, in three days precisely.

There is another venerable tradition locally: if the skull is ever taken out of doors the householder will die within the year, but to the best of the author's knowledge no squire of Bettiscombe has as yet been prepared to put this to the test.

The mystery of the screaming skull of Bettiscombe is not likely to be solved at this late date in history. Like similar tales in other counties, it remains one of the heirlooms of folklore, macabre, fascinating and curiously enjoyable.

It is a well-known fact that prehistoric sites often acquire a reputation for sinister hauntings, hence the apprehension with which they are regarded by those living in their locality. There seems to be a generally accepted belief that the original inhabitants of these sites resent the intrusion of the modern world, and although they might have been dead for thousands of years, their anger can occasionally be sensed by the twentieth-century trespasser.

A number of Dorset people have been frightened by the phantom Bronze Age horseman of Bottlebush Down who rides past the ancient barrow on the site. Those who have seen this ghost include an archaeologist who came upon a spectral horseman there about half a century ago; a cloaked figure riding without stirrups. Since stirrups were unknown until the fourth century A.D. the ghost belongs to a very early period of history—some regard its costume as that of a warrior chieftain of 1600 B.C.

A hint of the ancient rites of foundation sacrifice has been incorporated in the legend of the Batcombe wizard, Conjuror Mynterne, a sixteenth-century lord of the manor who sold his soul to the Devil and thereafter became an adept in the black arts. Mynterne is said to have flown through the air on horseback, sailing over the village and damaging one of the pinnacles of the church tower in the process. According to the people of Batcombe the spot where he landed is destined to remain barren forever.

Mynterne left directions to his heirs that to frustrate the Devil his body had to be buried 'half inside and half outside the church' —but as a compromise the corpse was interred beneath the walls. His tomb bears no inscription but others of his family lie peacefully there. From one of the wall tablets we read that the last of the mysterious Mynternes died in 1716.

The same remote hamlet has an interesting legend connected with the stone pillar known as the Cross in Hand which stands on Batcombe Hill. In some traditions it is described as the site of a miracle wrought in the Middle Ages. There is also a very old tale to the effect that it marks the spot where a man was executed for selling his soul to the Devil.

The prehistoric stone memorials of Dorset are eternal reminders of its very ancient past. The imagination is stirred by the Grey Mare and her Colts on Black Down, north of Portisham, and also by the mysterious Hele Stone, which relates to the northern European Hela, the monster appointed by Odin to preside over the realms of the dead. Similar guardian spirits protected the ancient earthworks known as the Washers Pit near the village of Ashmore until it was demolished by road builders about a century ago and the bones of the ancient dead transferred to the parish churchyard. Their shrill protests are still heard by those passing the place at night.

Dorset can offer a number of out of the way hauntings in which the ghost gourmet will find a source of unceasing delight. Althelhampton Hall near Puddletown, a building once described as 'the most picturesque in the county', was actually haunted by the ghost of a pet ape which was accidentally locked in a closet where it starved to death.

Worbarrow Bay, west of Kimmeridge, was very much smugglers' territory up to about one hundred and fifty years ago and it was here on the beach that a smuggler was murdered in the seventeenth century by a sadistic Revenue officer. The tragedy will never be forgotten locally for the dead man's dying screams are often heard from the sands at night.

The beautiful manor of Sandford Orcas is yet another ghost connoisseur's delight, for over a long period no less than fourteen phantoms have perambulated its ancient rooms. The army of ghosts has incorporated a monk, a farm hand, a red lady, a green lady and a spectral footman with a passion for chambermaids which is apparently undiminished by death; while for the musically inclined there is a ghost who plays the spinet at night.

The hauntings have been investigated in depth by many psychic experts. During one ghost hunt a phantom yokel materialized long enough to be photographed. Researches carried out by the Paraphysical Laboratory about ten years ago seem to have had inconclusive results for although curious noises were heard, nothing was actually seen. The sounds emanated, it has been suggested, from an ancestral ghost with creaking joints. In the face of a great deal of local cynicism Sandford Orcas has managed to retain its place at the top of the league of the most haunted houses in Dorset.

The ancient town of Lyme Regis which lies on a narrow ledge between the sea and the Downs might be renowned for the discovery nearby of huge bones of prehistoric reptiles. But Lyme was also the landing place for the tragic Monmouth and it was here that foolhardy countryfolk enrolled in the doomed conspiracy which was soon to drag so many down to a dreadful death.

Judge Jeffreys, the persecuting judge who hanged the rebels in batches, haunts the site of the Great House in Broad Street, where he dined whilst conducting his reign of terror over the townsfolk. Jeffreys is sometimes accompanied by a spectral hound, one of several demon dogs which traditionally haunt Lyme Regis.

Peter Underwood, that well-known collector of ghost stories, frequently brings to light unusual information, as in his account of the haunting of Eastbury House near Tarrant Gunville. The ghost in residence is that of a suicide named William Doggett who has been seen entering the house from a coach which halts at the door. A pistol shot then shatters the night as the suicide repeats the tragic act which brought about his death many years ago.

Beaminster School became the scene of a remarkable haunting towards the close of the eighteenth century and one which mystifies students of the occult even today. On Saturday, 22nd June 1728, four schoolboys heard curious sounds, followed by the singing of psalms in the church which was empty at the time. Within the schoolroom they saw a coffin lying on a bench and standing by it the ghost of one of their fellows who had died a short time previously. It was noticed that the ghost had a bandaged hand. Later, the woman who had prepared the body of the boy for burial, disclosed that when she had first seen the corpse its hand had been similarly bandaged.

Apparently the boy's death had occurred under the most mysterious circumstances, and although he had been found strangled in a field no effort had been made to bring the culprit to justice. The boy's mother had been told that her son had died from a fit. Was this, one wonders, yet another example of the traditional haunting in which a murdered person attempts to attract the attention of the living to the true circumstances of his death by returning as a ghost?

Wiltshire is one of those counties which creates in the mind a series of images of a most impressive kind. To the naturalist and geologist it appears as a huge ocean of chalk set in a basin of hills, while to the mystic it has an entirely different meaning, being a panoramic backcloth to an immense melodrama in which the ghosts of long-dead Britons re-enact religious life and tragedy as it was known thousands of years ago.

Wiltshire's greatest glory lies in its prehistoric temples which continually fascinate those who see them, however matter-of-fact their approach to the supernatural might be. Avebury, the largest stone circle of its type in Europe, and believed to be some three thousand years old suggests 'primeval forests emerging from chaos'. No one who observes for the first time, the columns of great stones rising like ghosts from the earth is ever likely to forget the strange emotions these can arouse. The temple builders may be unknown but their personalities live on in the stones. Dire misfortune threatens those who have the temerity to tamper with this shrine. During the Middle Ages orders were issued by the Church for the pillars to be cast down, presumably because the site was attracting too many pilgrims, but the consequences were calamitous for at least one of the desecrators, whose bones were discovered crushed beneath a fallen monolith when the site was excavated in 1938.

A similar sinister tradition is associated with several of the old stone cottages in Avebury village for it is considered extremely unlucky to live in a house built of Avebury stone. The author collected a curious tale in the locality which suggested that those who violated this taboo could expect to be troubled by an invisible presence known as 'the Haunt'. This horror from Avebury's forgotten past creates an atmosphere of such chilling intensity that no one can reside in the house for more than ten years. The whole area, as one would expect, is plentifully supplied with ghosts, Avebury Manor being haunted by a mysterious figure in white whom one assumes to be the long dead member of some ancient priesthood.

Silbury Hill, a man-made mountain one hundred and thirty feet high and the largest of its type in Europe, is yet another place of mystery, for even after extensive research its function remains unknown, notwithstanding the many ingenious legends which have been submitted to account for its presence. According to one tradition Silbury is the grave of a mysterious King Sil who lies within it mounted on his steed. From another and probably related legend we learn that the hill contains a human effigy made of solid gold. Excavation, however, has succeeded in bringing to light nothing more precious than the treasures of the imagination. It is a fact of history, however, that up to comparatively modern times local people made pilgrimages to the site and held some kind of festival. A further example of the romantic approach to history is apparent in the story that Silbury was accidentally created by the Devil. Satan was compelled by the priests of Avebury Circle to empty a sack of earth he was carrying and in doing so accidentally created Silbury Hill.

Next in order of importance among Wiltshire's mysterious sites is Stonehenge on Salisbury Plain which continues to mesmerize tourists, antiquarians and crypto Druids alike. During the eighteenth century this immense circle of grey stones fascinated the antiquary William Stukeley who published his own theories on the subject. However it is not the function of the folklorists to presume upon the possible origins of this relic of an unknown civilization but to record the legends which have become associated with it.

According to one legend the stones were originally brought from Africa to Ireland by a race of giants and then transported to Wiltshire by the wizard Merlin assisted by the Devil.

Geoffrey of Monmouth believed that the stones possessed a supernatural power to heal the sick. Lumps of Stonehenge were also abstracted by the more superstitious of the villagers to drop into their wells 'to drive away the toads'.

In comparatively recent times a cult of modern Druids has assumed the functions of the hypothetical temple priests of the past, arriving at dawn each May morn to greet the rising sun. However the true purpose of Stonehenge still eludes us although it could have been a prehistoric observatory. Perhaps if some latter-day necromancer were to communicate with the spirit of William Stukeley, who lies in an unmarked grave in East Ham, Essex, churchyard, further light might be thrown upon the enigma.

It is a mystery of history that Satan, the Christian devil, a comparatively late entrant into European mythology, should have intruded into so many English legends. He seems to have taken over the role originally allocated to the elves, those elemental spirits who were supposed by our ancestors to possess magical powers. Most of the latter were down-graded, in the late Middle Ages, to the status of witch's imp, but here and there some of the original breed can be found, for example in Wiltshire where one was once seen swinging his tiny legs from a tombstone in Corsham churchyard.

Satan also took over the role of poltergeist, as we find in the remarkable legend of the Devil of Tedworth whose exploits were noted by the distinguished demonologist Joseph Glanville in the seventeenth century. A vagrant drummer was hauled before a magistrate, Mr Mompession of Tedworth, who confiscated his drum. The drummer then took his revenge by sending a devil to beat an unholy and unceasing tattoo on Mr Mompession's rooftop. Even after the drum had been destroyed the uproar continued and on 5th November 1662, it was solemnly recorded, a plank came sailing round the Mompession living-room and an invisible spirit attempted to pluck the coat from a footman's back. Charles II, who had a passion for unravelling scientific mysteries, sent a commission to investigate the Tedworth Devil but it apparently drew a blank.

One of the most famous of all Wiltshire ghost stories concerns not a devil of the brimstone variety but Wild Will Darrell, a fiend in human shape, the setting being Littlecote House near Hungerford, in the year 1575. One dark rainy night in the month of November an old midwife was taken from her home to assist 'a person of rank'. She was told that the matter was of such great secrecy that she must be blindfolded, and her eyes were not uncovered until she was in the bedchamber of a lady who shortly afterwards gave birth to a fine boy. To the midwife's horror the baby was picked up by the man who had brought her and thrown on to a blazing fire. The midwife was paid, her eyes were bandaged and she was returned to her home. However she had marked the room of the murder by secretly cutting out a piece of bed curtain and had then sewn it in again, and she had also counted the stairs as she left Littlecote House. The midwife disclosed what had occurred to a magistrate and the dreadful murder was brought to the light of day. Darrell saved himself, however, by bribing the judge but died shortly afterwards in the hunting-field, the spot where he fell being known today as Darrell's Stile. Afterwards the ghost of a woman was seen in the bedchamber, while Darrell's ghost still walks at night at Darrell's Stile.

Longleat, the magnificent seat of the Marquis of Bath, was built on the site of an Augustinian priory, its name being derived from the long leat or conduit which conveyed water to the monastery. The ghosts here seem to belong to a much later period, the best known being the Green Lady whose lover was killed in a duel by her outraged husband some two hundred years ago. A skeleton presumed to be that of the lover was discovered beneath the floor of one of the cellars. The serious enquirer, however, may wonder why it is the lady rather than the gentleman who has returned to haunt Longleat. Among other occult occurrences we list the mysterious behaviour of the Longleat swans. According to an old legend, if the swans ever desert the estate the family in residence will become extinct.

A similar omen is associated with Salisbury Cathedral; if white birds are seen encircling the spire one of the clergy can expect to die.

Wiltshire's tragic history has given rise to many curious hauntings some, like the following, more than five hundred years old. The adherents of John Wycliffe, that ardent reformer of clerical corruption and religious abuses and one of the founders of the Reformation, are known to have suffered terribly for their convictions, being regarded as anarchists and enemies of the faith. One of them, Reginald de Cobham, is said to have been stripped naked and burnt alive before a frenzied mob at Langley Burrell, but even now his naked ghost occasionally materializes on the site of the execution. Could there be some confusion here with the execution of Sir John Oldcastle, the 'good lord Cobham' in 1417.

Witches and their curses have a prominent role in the history of the ancient town of Devizes where an obelisk in the market place commemorates a famous malediction which came home to roost. In 1753 a market woman named Ruth Pierce was accused of cheating her partners and took a solemn oath that God should strike her dead if that were true. She immediately collapsed and died on the spot, the money which she had concealed from her partners being afterwards found clutched in her hand.

One of the most feared of all Wiltshire witches was Anne Bodenham, a fortune-teller-cum-clairvoyant who lived at Fisherton Anger in the middle of the seventeenth century. Accused by one of her clients of trafficking with the devil she was sentenced to death at Salisbury Assizes and hurried off to execution. When the hangman asked her, as was then customary, for forgiveness for what he was obliged to do she cursed him in the following terms: 'Forgive thee, a pox on thee' and died unrepentant.

Even hard-headed Wiltshire folk sometimes find it difficult to dismiss out of this world phenomena and these includes those starry-eyed adherents of pseudo-scientific mysticism who have selected Warminster as a vantage point for the sighting of flying saucers. It was about ten years ago that the attention of the entire U.F.O. cult was concentrated upon this pleasant old town after a flotilla of cigar-shaped monsters from outer space had been seen speeding across the skies accompanied by saucers of every variety. It is not so much the seeing eye as the creative imagination of Wiltshire folk which ensures that in this remarkable county magic and mystery have an enduring life.

7

Ghouls of the Golden West

Almost inevitably, the first thought coming to mind in response to the key-word Somerset is cider, and on that note the county's psychic story begins. For centuries the curious custom of blessing the cider apple trees has been observed in the West Country, and in Somerset is regularly carried out at Dunkeswell near Honiton each 12th January otherwise old Twelfth Night.

Wassailing the apple trees, as it is known, was originally a magical ritual for ensuring a plentiful fruit harvest. A libation of cider is drunk and guns fired through the bare branches of the apple trees to drive away the devils of infertility. The litany which is chanted on such occasions is in reality a magical incantation addressed to the spirit of the tree. One version typical of the whole West Country goes as follows:

> Here's to thee, old apple tree
> Whence, thou mayst bud and whence thou mayst blow.
> And whence thou mayst bear apples enow.
> Hats full. Caps full.
> Bushel-bushel-sacks full
> And to my pockets full too
> Huzza! Huzza! Huzza!

Another West Country tree ritual which was at one time observed throughout the British Isles, involved passing a child suffering from rupture or rickets through a split ash sapling, the split being afterwards tightly bound. According to popular belief the child would recover at the same rate as the tree healed. It was usually stripped naked for the ceremony, which had to be performed three times at sunrise. The ritual is known elsewhere in Europe, particularly Germany and Scandinavia, where the tree chosen is usually the oak.

The legend of the Glastonbury thorn despite its links with Christianity, is in reality yet another expression of the superstitious reverence for sacred trees. According to the six hundred-year-old legend St Joseph of Arimathea and his disciples, whilst journeying to evangelize Britain, rested awhile one Christmas morning on Weary-all Hill near the town of Glastonbury. The saint stuck his hawthorn staff into the ground and it began to flower, and continued to do so from that time forth on the birthday of Christ.

The present hawthorn at Glastonbury was taken from a cutting from the original tree after it had been cut down by a Puritan bigot in the seventeenth century. In defiance of local feeling the iconoclast raised his axe to lop off one of the branches and to everyone's delight knocked out one of his eyes.

The hawthorn is a sacred tree in many legends both Christian and pagan. The blossom, however, is regarded as dangerous to health if brought into the house. The supernatural awe which once surrounded the tree found expression in a number of curious legends, in one of which, a woodcutter, whilst felling a hawthorn, saw blood spouting from the injured trunk.

Somerset superstitions are wide-ranging and frequently pagan; there are occasional reports even today of rheumatic sufferers using font water to ease their aching joints, a practice which was condemned as heretical by a Church ordinance in the Middle Ages.

It is only fair to admit that a great many of our surviving customs, including some of the most interesting, are either revivals of lapsed rites or even where there is evidence of historical continuity have little real meaning for those who observe them. The Minehead Hobby Horse ritual, however, is not so easy to categorize since it is almost certainly influenced by some primitive Maytime ritual, and is observed with a degree of fervour.

The Hobby Horse, in reality a nine-foot frame decorated with ribbons within which a dancer prances, creates considerable amusement among the large numbers of visitors who crowd into the town at the beginning of May to witness the event. Local tradition insists that the custom originated in a real historical occurrence during the ninth century when a band of raiding Vikings were driven off by a man-made dragon or sea monster, the ancestor of the present 'Horse'. Whatever the ultimate source of the Minehead Hobby Horse ritual it is not a localized tradition for Padstow in Cornwall has a similar animal which performs on May Day.

Once in the West Country we are in Celtic territory where the worship of the spirits of the water originally held sway. Today's relics of this ancient Druidic cult include wishing-wells and occasionally pin wells into which a pin is dropped in return for the favour asked.

There once existed two kinds of well: the wishing-well and the cursing-well. There is one of the latter at Bishops Lydeard west of the Quantocks and here the malevolent pilgrim can drop his pin into the water and whisper his malediction trusting that some terrible blight will fall upon his enemy. Cursing wells were not uncommon up to the early years of the last century, but most were filled in after being condemned as unsavoury relics of pagan superstition. An inscribed curse in Latin which was found on the Roman well at Bath when translated reads:

> 'May he who carried off
> Vilbia waste away'.

At Stanton Drew, near the River Drew, one can see a prehistoric stone monument with stone avenues and a standing stone, now supine, called Hautvilles' Quoit. The circle which is believed to be about three thousand five hundred years old was long known in the locality as the 'Evil Wedding' but is now usually referred to in the guide-books as the 'Devil's Wedding', because it was the site selected, for Satan's wedding feast. An associated legend described the misadventures of a wedding party who offended the deity by extending their revels beyond Saturday midnight into the Sabbath. To add to their sacrilege they unknowingly employed as their musician a stranger who turned out to be the Devil in disguise. As a punishment they were all turned to stone and must remain in this state until the Devil returns and plays to them again.

It should be mentioned that many Somerset barrows are supposed to be guarded by malevolent spirits, some of whom have a passion for drinking human blood. To build a house on such a site is an open invitation for the devils to move in.

The kingdom of hobgoblins is well represented in Somerset folklore, and occasionally a chimney goblin appears in the hearth as he is supposed to have done at an inn near Blagden.

Similar elemental spirits are recognizable in the phantom white ladies who have been seen standing guard over bridges or trackways. The White Lady of Wellow seems to be in the true banshee tradition since her rare appearances are supposed to herald a death in the Hungerford family. Jane Beech, the folklorist, points out in a recent study how the White Lady, 'her deified heritage forgotten has been sucked into the quicksands of modern ghost lore'.

Somerset folklore has preserved some old tales of English dragons, one of which, the Shervage Wood Worm, was cut to pieces by a woodman's axe. Another dragon must have been blessed with a cast-iron digestion since it swallowed a boy with one gulp, neither beast nor boy being ever seen again. Yet a third dragon was ridden by Satan from one end of the Inferno to the other.

The old-fashioned devil complete with horns, hooves and forked tail is no stranger to the Somerset scene, although he favours a variety of disguises the better to deceive his dupes as we find in the witchcraft records of 1584 when Margaret Cooper of Ditcheat was suddenly assaulted by a devil disguised as a headless bear without a tail which tickled her feet and rolled her up and down her bedchamber.

Comic demons apart, the wretched women who submitted to Satan's blandishments and adopted witchcraft as a profession, invariably regretted their lapse from faith. One of these, Jane Brooks of Shepton Mallet, bewitched a twelve-year-old boy by offering him a bite of a magical apple. The boy immediately became airborne and sailed off through the skies finally crash-landing on a doorstep. Jane Brooks was found guilty of witchcraft and hanged at Chard, to the great relief of her more down to earth neighbours.

In 1680 a man was tried at Taunton Assizes for witchcraft and acquitted by a sympathetic judge. Suddenly an old woman cried out from the courtroom, 'God bless your Lordship! ... forty years ago they would have hanged me for a witch and they could not, and now they would have hanged my poor son.'

The town of Wells seems to have been greatly favoured by witches, several of whom were sentenced to punishments of one kind or another by the courts of the seventeenth century. As tourists are well aware, the black sisterhood is represented at Wells today by the Witch of Wookey Hole who is on view in her cavern with her bevy of petrified demons. Another active survivor from the age of enchantment is the famous witch of Priddy whose ghost has been seen staggering along the roads.

For fiends in human shape we must turn to the devil-dominated squire of Norton Fitzwarren who rides through the night skies with his hell-hounds while another demon rider, minus hounds and headless has been noted flying like the wind through Cannington Park.

Somerset seems to have a great many ghosts. Legg Collier and Perrott list more than twenty ghost stories in their *Ghosts of Dorset Devon and Somerset* which range from spectral coaches to phantom fiddlers and include a remarkable funeral *cortège* at Calcott consisting entirely of long-dead Quakers.

For the traveller determined to keep within the mainstream of English occult history a visit to haunted Sedgemoor is essential. On this tragic battlefield which witnessed the rout of Monmouth's luckless army in 1685, flickering lights have been seen at night and sometimes the voices of the long-dead contestants heard.

The pitiless Judge Jeffreys who has become one of Somerset's more restless ghosts haunts the Tudor Tavern in Taunton the town where he held the Bloody Assizes of 1685.

When we cross the borderland separating history from mythology we discover a phantom King Arthur leading his Knights of the Round Table along a lane near Cadbury, an area long associated with the Arthurian Camelot.

Curry Mallet, an ideal setting for the returning dead is now haunted by a woman whose silk skirt can be heard rustling as she makes her nocturnal rounds. And in the gardens ancient warriors re-enact some bloody conflict of long ago.

The power of ancient magic is evident in the celebration of 'Punkie Night' at the village of Hinton St George near Crewkerne every Halowe'en, the punkies being scooped-out turnips carved into devilish faces and illuminated from within by lighted candles. Like an army of minor devils children parade through the village singing a song which has the power to make the bravest villager blanch and bolt the doors. 'It's Punkie Night tonight. It's Punkie Night tonight.'

To conclude the Somerset saga upon an appropriately chilling note we must mention the skull of Chilton Cantelo which, like that at Bettiscombe, is unable to find rest. It is from the corpse of Theophilus Brome who was buried in Chilton Cantelo Church in 1670, his last request being that his skull should be kept inside the house. The skull owes its preservation largely to the awe which it inspires and also to the fact that it was utilized as a beer mug in days gone by.

The deeper one ventures into the West Country the more fascinating appears its legendary lore. For this situation the long isolation of the area is responsible. Separated from regions to their east by two vast stretches of moorland, Dartmoor and Bodmin, the former inhabitants of Devon and Cornwall lived culturally in a world apart from the remainder of the British Isles.

Until well into the last century the belief in elemental spirits which had all but died out elsewhere, was preserved in the form of strange tales of pixies, piskies and similar characters from mythology. Pixies are not unknown in modern Devon as we shall see from the superstitions which surround a lonely wayside grave near Hound Tor Inn on Dartmoor. Jane's Grave, as it is called, is the sole memorial to a girl who committed suicide many years ago and, being denied a church funeral, was interred at the crossroads. Flowers are left on the grave by unknown hands, possibly by gipsies but, according to some local people, by the pixie folk who have a sense of charity greater than human kind.

To be 'pixie led' is a term still current in Devon to describe the situation of being lured out of one's way by some mischievous member of the elfin tribe. In a typical legend we are told of a man who, finding himself lost on Whitchurch Down near Tavistock, turned his coat inside out and thereby released himself from pixie power, and was able to reach home safely.

While it would be incorrect to say that the belief in pixies as such retains any real hold on the imaginations of modern Devon folk, it cannot be denied that vestigial beliefs still exist. At least two types of pixie symbols, Jack O'Lantern and Joan the Wad, are popular lucky charms, hence the old rhyme:

> Jack O' Lantern, Joan the Wad
> Who tickled the maid and made her mad
> Light me home, the weather's bad.

One strange creature who surely belongs to the pixie order is the mysterious dwarf of Chudleigh Knighton who stands on perpetual guard over a hoard of hidden gold. Those who read their *Dracula* will remember the tiny flames seen in the fields at dusk which were supposed to indicate the sites of buried treasure. At Hennock in Devon a similar flame, which flickers over a lonely track, is regarded locally as the hiding-place of a hoard of gold and silver buried for safety during the Civil War.

Treasure lights should not be confused with the *ignis fatuus* or bog lights which are reported from all over the county. It is a common belief in the Dartmoor area that 'the bog lights will get you if you go out after dark on a misty night'.

According to a local tradition a mysterious monster known as Hairy Hands haunts the Moretonhampstead district where it seizes steering wheels causing dreadful road accidents. Hairy Hands must be one of Devon's oldest ghosts for it is remembered that in pre-automobile days it grabbed the manes of horses, sending their riders crashing to the ground.

The demon dogs of Dartmoor which race at night along the Abbots Way have been made familiar to readers and television viewers by Conan Doyle's masterpiece *The Hound of the Baskervilles*, one of the best-known horror stories of fiction. The Baskerville tale was actually based on a type of folklore which has long been current in Devon. In fact the Black Dog of Uplyme, a similar canine monster, has actually been reported within the last ten years. It is a general belief that the howls of the devil hounds are omens of bad luck and death.

The Reverend Sabine Baring Gould refers in his *Book of Folklore* to an extremely macabre haunting in the Okehampton district, the 'ghost' being the spirit of death who rides in a coach made of human bones. Preceding the phantom coach is a spectral dog with a single eye, which seems to suggest some connection with one-eyed Shuck, the devil dog of East Anglia.

In the same category of hauntings comes the ghostly Squire Cabell of Wallaford who is accompanied on his hell-bound journeys by a pack of demon hounds.

The ghost of Sir Francis Drake, the conqueror of the Spanish Armada, drives a hearse accompanied by a pack of hounds whose dismal howls bring death to all dogs within hearing distance.

Drake incurred the inevitable curse which falls upon those occupying usurped ecclesiastical properties when he came into possession of Buckland Abbey. During building work the forces of evil became very threatening, and as fast as the stones were laid down, a horde of demons carried them away again. The indomitable Drake, refusing to accept defeat, climbed into a tree where he kept an overnight watch for the enemy. When the devils arrived and began removing the stones he emitted a shrill cock-a-doodle-do. 'It's cockcrow,' said one devil to the next, 'we have to be home by dawn.' Drake then lit his pipe, illuminating the darkness with the glow of burning shag. 'Sun up,' said another devil and the whole band scurried off like rats to the darker recesses of Hell.

Devil's Point, to the west of Devonport, is popularly regarded as the place where Sir Francis in company with demons and witches conjured up the great storm which scattered and destroyed the Spanish Armada. As we have noticed previously, witches were credited with the supernatural power to control the elements, which was usually achieved by untying knots in a length of cord or by stirring a cauldron widdershins.

Like King Arthur, the hero Drake is believed to watch over England's welfare in readiness for any national calamity, when he will answer his country's call. It is then that Drake's drum will roll as it is said to have done at the outbreak of the First World War and at the time of the German air attack on Plymouth in the Second World War. The hero's statue continues to stand guard over Plymouth town on the spot where the traditional game of bowls was played almost four centuries ago.

A mysterious demon whose identity has never been discovered created great agitation in Devon in 1855. When following countywide falls of snow a single file of hoofprints, set about eight inches apart, was found to extend from Totnes to Littleham, a distance of about one hundred miles. The hoofprints were clearly definable on rooftops and at ground level, which suggests that the devil concerned might possibly have been of the winged variety, a type somewhat rare in the British Isles.

This was not the first time that Devon had suffered from incursions of this kind. On Easter Saturday, 1682, a Spreyton man was lifted into the air by a flying devil and tossed into a distant bog where his wig was later discovered suspended from the branches of a tree.

The assaults of Satan and his hordes created endless difficulties for churchmen in the early days of Christianity in this county. During the erection of St Michael's Church Brentor, Satan adopted one of his best-known harassing tactics, by stealing the stones and laying them on the summit of the tor. In the end the clergy gave him best and built the church on the site the Devil had selected.

All kinds of precautions against demons seem to have been taken by those early church builders, including human sacrifice. When Holsworthy church was under restoration in 1885 a male skeleton was discovered in the foundations. It was presumed at the time that the man had been buried alive as an offering to the earth spirits.

Precautions are taken, even today, to keep the devil away from the village of Shebbear in North Devon by the ceremony of turning over a boulder known as the Devil's Stone on the night of 5th November. The custom, which is based on the ancient Celtic rites of Samhain (now Hallowe'en), must be strictly observed or misfortune will descend upon the village during the ensuing twelve months.

The fear of witchcraft survived in the West of England much later than elsewhere. It is a matter of history that the last witch to be executed was hanged at Exeter in 1684. Precautions taken against witches included propping a besom against the front gate, in the Dartmoor area, and in the same district some old women believed that when a witch approached the house their toes began to curl upwards, giving them time to prepare their defences.

Among other supernatural signs of approaching disaster we must include the remarkable behaviour of the pond at North Tawton which, although normally dry, is always full of water prior to the death of the monarch.

Nature displays yet further signs of a mysterious if gruesome intelligence in the activities of the River Dart which demands the sacrifice by drowning of one human life every year, hence the old lines:

> River of Dart, River of Dart,
> Every year thou claimest a heart.

GHOULS OF THE GOLDEN WEST 189

The dead seem to have been much less at ease in the West Country than in most other counties. Among Devon's innumerable ghosts is Sir William de Tracy who sits on Woollacombe beach endlessly weaving ropes of sand as a penance for his involvement in the murder of Thomas à Becket at Canterbury.

Among ghosts of a less illustrious character is the spectre of Lew Trenchard church, burial place of Madame Gould, ancestor of the writer Sabine Baring Gould. When the lady's grave was opened during restoration work in the last century the corpse suddenly sat up in its coffin, creating great terror among those present.

Buckfastleigh is haunted by several monks who lived there prior to the Dissolution of the monasteries. These placid spirits do not seem to have troubled the present monks to the slightest degree.

One of the most interesting Devon hauntings involves Berry Pomeroy Castle near Torbay, now a ruin but once the stately home of the famous de Pomeroy family. The present condition of the building dates from the seventeenth century when it was gutted by a mysterious fire. Among the castle ghosts is Sir Berry de Pomeroy who has been seen plunging from the battlements on the back of a spectral horse, and the distraught spectre of a woman who murdered her baby and continually searches the ruins for its body, wringing her hands in despair. The role of this particular ghost is similar to that of the banshee for its presence is regarded as an omen of death by those who have the misfortune to see it.

Monkokehampton is a parish where the ghosts of the living can be seen by anyone who chooses to stand in the church porch at midnight on the Eve of St Marks. A tale is told in the village of a man who, greatly daring, stood in the porch at the witching hour and watched a procession of men and women who were yet living, passing before him into the church. One of the spectres he realized with horror was himself. He returned home overcome by terror and took to his bed and was dead within the month.

A clue to the well-known superstition that it is unlucky to open an umbrella indoors is provided by an entry in the parish accounts of St Andrews, Plymouth, for 1749 which mentions the expenditure of the sum of sixteen shillings on a parish umbrella 'for the use of the minister at burials'. Originally the only umbrellas known in England were those used by the parson on rainy days at funerals. One can now understand why it became an omen of death for an umbrella to be opened inside the house.

Tavistock folk, who are among the most superstitious in the British Isles, firmly believe it is unlucky to wash blankets in May, since this results in 'washing the head of the household away'. There are even families who extend the same superstition to interior decorations and in one case brought to the author's attention, a woman considered she had risked her husband's life by buying a toothbrush in May.

One concludes this all too brief survey of Devon lore with the mystery of Cranmere Pool on Dartmoor which is reputedly haunted by a seventeenth-century mayor of Okehampton, named Benjamin Gear. The ghost is occasionally invoked by adventurous schoolboys with the incantation 'Bengie Gear. Bengie Gear, If thou art near please do appear'.

The nineteenth-century folklorist Robert Hunt, in the introduction to his *Popular Romances of the West of England*, reminded his readers that Cornwall had, until a recent period, maintained a somewhat singular isolation, 'England, with many persons, appeared to terminate on the shores of the river Tamar'.

Due to this long isolation of the Cornish people from the mainstream of English life, many fascinating beliefs were preserved largely by a class of rural story-tellers who survived until the first half of the last century, when they were displaced by the newspapers. Ever welcome at the cottage hearth, the droll teller (as he was called) could be certain of hospitality as he wandered from village to village retailing gossip and keeping alive legends of giants, piskies, mermaids, monsters, ghosts and witches.

The Cornish people were not only strongly attracted by the supernatural but demanded legends of the most gruesome kind. Bloodthirsty monsters predominated in a rustic mythology which ascribed mountainous rocks whether the works of nature or of man, to a lost race of extremely unpleasant giants. Cormelian, one of the more ferocious, was supposed to have built St Michael's Mount with his own hands. Carn Brea Castle, near Land's End, was reputedly the burial place of another sub-human monster, while Land's End itself was generally known as the Land of the Giants.

That giants were supposed to be blood-drinkers is clearly

stated in an ancient work, Havilan's *Architrenium*:

> Raw hides they wore for clothes.
> Their drink was blood.
> Rocks were their dining rooms.
> Their prey their food.

The early missionaries in Cornwall succeeded in transforming many of the warring giants into invading devils, yet despite certain modifications in the older tales, a number of giant legends survived intact until the eighteenth century when a second wave of proselytes, the Methodists, seems to have given the *coup de grâce* to most superstitious survivals.

Robert Hunt found that even in his day, the first half of the nineteenth century, the giants were regarded as having had a real existence. At Trebegian, for example, some huge bones which were discovered in a forgotten vault were automatically attributed to the local giant Trebiggan who had the delightful habit of frying village children on a flat rock near his cave.

In the elfin creed of Cornwall we find every field and valley, tor and stream, tree and flower, dominated by diminutive sprites under such delightful names as small folk, spriggans, brownies, knockers and piskies. Piskies seem to have dominated much of the county's folklore, as we find in the following fragment culled from the *Gentleman's Magazine*, which underlines the capriciousness of elemental spirits:

> Not long ago before threshing machines were thought of, a farmer going to his barn one day was surprised by the extraordinary quantity of corn that had been threshed during the previous night, as well as puzzled to discover the mysterious agency by which it was effected.
>
> At night, when the moon was up he crept stealthily to the barn door, and looking through a chink saw a little fellow in a tattered suit of green flailing with such rapidity that the eye could not follow the motions. Feeling the obligation to reward his unpaid farm labourer the farmer left him a new suit of green cloth. The elf dressed himself in the new clothes and sang
>
> > 'Pisky new coat, pisky new hood,
> > Pisky now will do no more good'
>
> and immediately flew away.

There are many quaint tales in Cornish folklore based on the same theme for Cornish piskies seem to have been far less appreciative of human kindness than Devon pixies although they were regarded as relatively harmless to those who wore their coats inside out.

The knockers, or 'fairy miners' who lived in the bowels of the earth were often heard tapping away in the workings with their antler-picks, their presence being regarded as a favourable omen indicating a rich lode of ore in the mine. Whether the tradition originated with real miners of prehistoric ages is now impossible to say. Certainly picks constructed from stag antlers have been found in the old workings, suggesting that this might be the case. Charles Kingsley was told that the knockers were the ghosts 'of the old Jews that crucified our Lord and were sent for slaves by the Roman emperors to work the mines ...' and again 'And they say, that if a man will listen of a still night about these shafts he will hear the ghosts of them at work, knocking and picking as clear as if there was a man at work on the next level'.

Cromlechs or Druids' stones and similar monuments belonging to the forgotten past seem to have been regarded with a greater degree of awe and fascination in Cornwall than elsewhere in the British Isles. This attitude survived until the arrival of the Methodists which was frequently followed by the casting down of the stones as relics of devil worship.

Typical of the new spirit of intolerance or, alternatively, of indifference to the past was the destruction of the Great Tolmaen or Hole of Stone in the parish of Constantine in 1869, described by John Timbs as 'one vast oval pebble, placed on the points of two natural rocks'. It was blown up by a quarryman who seems to have been blissfully unaware of the curse he invoked upon himself, since the traditional penalty for damaging it was 'a terrible superhuman vengeance'.

One famous stone popularly associated with the Druids is now recognized as far older than that strange Aryan priesthood. This is the Men An Tol near Madren, which responds to questions if two pins are laid on its summit. The pins are expected to vibrate in a peculiar way.

A comparatively recent discovery, is the prehistoric village of Chysauster near Gulval some two thousand years old, which contains a subterranean chamber.

Some visitors claim to have seen here a number of 'small grey men' of rather frightening appearance. In the early part of the nineteenth century the Methodists held services on this spot, hence its local nickname the Chapels, but there has been no suggestion, that the little grey men resented the hymn-singing and the fiery denunciations of paganism which was the theme of so many West Country sermons.

Near Lamorna is a stone circle known as the Merry Maidens and, nearby, two granite pillars called the Pipers which represent a popular theme in folklore since they commemorate the ancient conflict between paganism and the church. The stones were once real maidens who danced there on the Sabbath whereupon a sheet of forked lightning shot out of Heaven and transformed them into pillars of stone.

Cornwall has produced a number of famous clerical exorcists whose services were in demand throughout the county and even beyond its boundaries. Richard Dodge, the most famous member of this now somewhat discredited profession, was Vicar of Talland about two hundred years ago, a time when the fear of ghosts and devils was uppermost in everyone's mind. Satan had long established himself in the parish, having attempted, when the church was first under construction, to abstract the building material, but he always met his match in Dodge, who had made his reputation by exorcizing a phantom coach on the public highway. On seeing his formidable adversary the headless coachman had screamed in horror, 'Dodge is come, I must be gone' and had vanished into thin air.

Another remarkable exorcist Parson Corker who lived near Lamorna was highly skilled in the magical arts. In order to drive out one obstinate evil spirit Corker fortified his nerves with strong liquor and, having drawn a sacred pentagram, began to pray with such intensity that 'the sweat boiled from his body'. A terrifying gale suddenly arose in the midst of which the devil could clearly be seen sailing away clinging to a black thunder cloud. During the same exorcism an earthbound spirit hurled a hammer at the parson's head before joining the devil on his flight through the skies.

Parson Woods of Ladock, an exorcist who combined magic with missionary work, carried a staff embossed with the signs of the zodiac by means of which he was able to transform evil spirits into animals, which he then punished with his whip. On one occasion a devil in the shape of a huge bird perched in the rafters of his church and interrupted his sermons with ribald squawks. This formidable creature seemed impervious to exorcisms but finally capitulated when twelve newly baptized babies were brought into the church. At the sight of such a high concentration of innocence it fled from the building without even a parting squawk.

The most awe-inspiring of all Cornish exorcists, however, was Parson Jago, Vicar of Wendron near Helston, who had only to strike the earth with his staff for a devil to appear and groom his horse. Jago was greatly feared by all defaulters since he had the supernatural power to perceive every wrongdoing in the district at the very moment it was committed. This created such terror among his parishioners that they usually confessed their sins immediately he hove in sight. No one, it seems, was able to withstand the penetrating power of what became known as Jago's Eye.

John Wesley, during one of his tours of Cornwall, was invited to a feast at St Agnes which he straight away suspected as having been organized by the Devil. To make absolutely certain Wesley asked permission to say Grace but hardly had he uttered the name 'Jesus' when all the revellers disappeared without trace.

Sometimes penalties of an extreme nature were imposed on a particularly recalcitrant ghost. A parson of Penzance condemned a ghost to sit on the beach and spin ropes of sand for the next thousand years. In the main, however, ghosts and evil spirits were packed into bottles and dispatched for safe custody to the Red Sea.

Witchcraft and magic are very strongly entrenched in Cornish folklore and history as we find in some interesting traditional stories which have been handed down in the west of the county.

Near Zennor is the Giant's Rock which one has to climb nine times at midnight in order to become endowed with the power of a witch. The belief was fairly general in nineteenth-century Cornwall that by touching any logan stone nine times one could acquire the ability to cast spells.

The rendezvous of all the witches of the West was said to be

Trewa between Nancledra Bottoms and Zennor, an area littered with huge boulders supposedly flung there by the giants. Here the weird sisterhood met at midnight to conspire against the community. The last true Zennor witch died in the eighteenth century and those who succeeded her were far less effective casters of spells.

Countering the nefarious activities of witches presented no fundamental problems in Cornwall since all the resources of white witchcraft were readily available, through the agency of a class of white witches known as Conjurors whose powers were usually hereditary. Their techniques were secret but it is obvious from recorded instances that they succeeded in relieving their clients' anxieties by a kind of rudimentary psychiatry combined with arrant trickery. The Wise Man of Illogan transferred an evil spell from his client by touching him with a holed pebble which he then cast into the sea.

The Cornish white wizards, who were invariably seventh sons of seventh sons, were morally responsible for a great deal of suffering since they directed the hostility of their clients towards old women of the villages who were supposed to have cast evil spells. As late as the nineteenth century these unfortunates were assaulted by their neighbours in the most barbarous manner since the accepted technique for removing a spell was to tear the forehead of the witch with the fingernails until the blood ran down her face.

The county suffered, as elsewhere, from the melancholy sport of witch hunting during the seventeenth century when the Puritan clergy had the upper hand and all forms of magic came under furious attack. Like witches in other parts of the country, those of Cornwall possessed animal familiars, as we gather from the *Calendar of State Papers* for 1670 which mentions the freeing of a number of suspects despite their familiarity with 'rats and cats and other things'.

Sometimes the clergy found great difficulty in distinguishing between the traditional Cornish fairy and the new fangled witch's imp, as in the case of Anne Jefferies who lived in the parish of St Teath. According to the account in William Turner's *Remarkable Providence* (1697) Anne admitted that she had been visited by six green clothed fairies from whom she had received the power to heal by the laying on of hands. The unfortunate woman came at once under suspicion of witchcraft and was confined in Bodmin jail, where she baffled her clerical inquisitors by insisting that her fairies were in fact angels. She then quoted from the Bible, 'Dearly beloved, believe not every spirit but try the spirits whether they are from God'. The strange healer was at last set free since the evidence against her was far from conclusive.

There is a museum of witchcraft in Boscastle which offers the morbidly inclined many strange delights including the skeleton of a genuine witch. Other Cornish museums display relics of old-time witchcraft including those curious glass spheres called witch balls which once kept witches from the home, and, in addition 'charm sticks' which are not so well known. The charm stick which was similar to a glass walking-stick and contained coloured sand and, sometimes, hair, was put in the chimney at night as a safeguard against illicit entry by witches, devils and ghosts. Known also as a 'witching stick' it is supposed to have originated in France.

Whole armies of demons must have launched assaults upon the Cornish population if the traditional tales are to be believed. These included such sacrilegious monsters as the 'flying spirit' which knocked down the spire of Ludgvan church at the height of a raging storm; and the demon horse which has been seen in the parish of St Blazey north-east of St Austell and which was once mistaken for a phantom bear. Roche Chapel is haunted by a tin miner who was done to death by a devil many centuries ago. Not surprisingly, perhaps, the villagers of St Cleer light a bonfire each Midsummer Eve to keep witches and evil spirits at bay.

The fishermen of Cornwall once believed in mermaids, those strange elemental spirits of the sea, consequently, mermaid legends still form a substantial part of Cornish mythology. Around about 1825 R. S. Hawker, the eccentric vicar of Morwenstowe, attempted to demolish the mermaid myths once and for all by sitting on an offshore rock wearing an oilskin fish tail and a wig of plaited seaweed, whilst holding a mirror in one hand and serenading the moon.

The entertainment continued for several evenings, attracting vast crowds from every part of Cornwall, most of whom became convinced that mermaids really existed. After several such displays Hawker brought the show to an end by singing the national anthem and taking a high dive off the rock into the sea.

The Reverend Hawkers' self-imposed ordeal was infinitely less onerous than the punishment imposed upon Tregegle, the unquiet spirit of the West who was condemned by fate to empty the bottomless Dosmory Pool with no other receptacle than a limpet shell. Another of Tregegle's hopeless tasks is the sweeping of sand from the beach at Porthcurno Cove. His deep sighs as he strives to complete this impossible chore have sometimes been mistaken for the moanings of the wind.

Among Cornwall's best known occult traditions are the legends of lost lands which were long ago overwhelmed by the sea. One of these, Lyonesse, lies beneath the waves between Land's End and the Scillies. From its 'buried churches' the bells have been heard solemnly ringing in times of storm.

It has long been customary to invest national heroes like Arthur with the qualities of demi-gods and bestial human beings with the attributes of devils. Into the second category comes Cruel Coppinger, a Dane who settled in seventeenth-century Cornwall to become one of the most terrible wreckers of the coast. Among Coppinger's more horrible exploits was the beating to death of a number of half-drowned seamen from a ship he had lured on to the rocks. Both Coppinger's arrival and extremely dramatic departure from the county are commemorated in the curious verse:

> Will you hear the tale of cruel Coppinger.
> He came from a foreign land.
> He was brought to us by the salt water.
> He was carried away by the wind.

Coppinger was in fact whirled into a storm cloud by the devil and borne screaming to the infernal regions.

By comparison the exit of the immortal father figure, King Arthur, pales into insignificance despite the dramatic journey to Avalon. Robert Hunt, the folklorist, noted the scarcity of Arthurian traditions 'in Cornwall where that King is said to have been born and where we believe him to have been killed,' and he goes on to say, 'All the rock markings or rock peculiarities which would in West Cornwall have been given to the giants are referred to King Arthur in the eastern districts.'

In the past it was often believed that Arthur lived on in the form of a raven, but today it is rather as the Cornish chough whose scarlet beak symbolizes the great king's violent end.

Death is a familiar theme among the Cornish fisher folk who say that the voices of drowned sailors have been heard crying above the storm winds calling the names of fishermen who are destined to die next.

Yet Cornwall is by no means as dedicated to deathly things as many of its traditions might suggest, for there is a great deal of gaiety in the county. At Helston every 8th May couples dressed as for a garden party dance to the Furry Dance song, a ceremony so ancient that no one is certain how it originated. Some say it was introduced to celebrate the end of a plague; others that it commemorates the departure of a menacing Devil; while antiquarians have suggested that it began as an act of homage to Flora, the Roman goddess of flowers.

There are many intriguing legends surrounding the lives of the Cornish saints St Leven, St Just and St Neot among others, not forgetting the miraculous St Piran, patron saint of the tin miners, who floated on a boulder all the way from Ireland to Cornwall and lived more than two hundred years.

Miraculous voyages seem to have essential ingredients of the Cornish scene. One includes in this category the ghost ship which was last seen sailing over dry land in the area of Porthcurno where it suddenly vanished from sight.

The deep feeling for the mysterious past which is strong in Celtic lands has found expression in modern times in the revival of many ancient ceremonies. The most interesting of these is the Cornish custom of lighting bonfires on hilltops on Midsummer Eve, when the Master of Ceremonies pronounces a blessing.

The ritual ends with words uttered with great solemnity:

'We do as our fathers did in days long past.'

And so the story ends.

Bibliography and Recommended Reading

Books marked with * are of particular interest

Addison, William, *Epping Forest*, Dent, 1945
* Andrews, William, *Ecclesiastical Curiosities*, Andrew's, 1899
Atkinson, Rev. J. C., *Forty Years in a Moorland Parish*, London, 1892
Aubrey, John, *Miscellanies Upon Various Subjects*, 1857
* Bardens, Dennis, *Ghosts and Hauntings*, London, 1965
* Barrett, W. H. and R. P. Garrod, *East Anglian Folklore*, Routledge & Kegan Paul, 1976
Benwell, Gwen and Arthur Waugh, *Sea Enchantress*, Hutchinson, 1961
Bett, Henry, *English Myths and Traditions*, Batsford, 1952
* Boase, Wendy, *The Folklore of Hampshire and The Isle of Wight*, Batsford, 1976
* Bord, Janet and Colin, *Mysterious Britain*, Paladin, 1974
Brand, John, *Observations on Popular Antiquities*, London, 1849
* Briggs, K. M., *The Anatomy of Puck*, Routledge & Kegan Paul, 1959
Briggs, K. M., *The Folklore of the Cotswolds*, Batsford, 1974
Brockie, J., *Legends and Superstitions of the County of Durham*, 1886
Chambers, R., *The Book of Days*, 2 Vols., Chambers, 1888
Chetwynd-Stapylton, M., *Discovering Wayside Graves and Memorial Stones*, Tring, 1969
Chisenhale-Marsh, V. B., *Folklore in Essex and Herts.*, Essex Review, Vol. 5, 1896
Cashen, W., *Manx Folklore*, 1912
Cox, M. R., *Introduction to The Study of Folk-Lore*, 1893
* Day, J. Wentworth, *A Ghost Hunter's Game Book*, London, 1958
* Deane, Tony and Tony Shaw, *The Folklore of Cornwall*, Batsford, 1975
Ditchfield, P. H., *Old English Customs*, Redway, London, 1896
Dyer, T. F. Thistleton, *Domestic Folklore*, Cassell Petter & Galpin, London, 1881
Dyer, T. F. Thistleton, *English Folklore*, Hardwicke & Bouge, 1878
Evans, G. Ewart, *The Horse in the Furrow*, Faber, 1960
* Ewen, C. l'Estrange, *Witchcraft and Demonianism*, Heath Cranton, 1933

Fletcher, H., *Herefordshire*, Robert Hale, 1948
Folklore Journal, Vol. 71, December 1960, *The Witches of Canewdon*, F.L. Soc. Publication
* *Folklore Myths and Legends of Britain*, Readers' Digest Assn. Ltd, 1973
Gomme, G. J., *Ethnology in Folklore*, 1892
* Green, Andrew, *Our Haunted Kingdom*, Wolfe Publishing Ltd, London, 1973
* Hallam, Jack, *The Haunted Inns of England*, Wolfe Publishing Co., 1972
Harries, John, *The Ghost Hunter's Road Book*, Muller, 1968
Heckthorn, C. W., *London Memories*, Chatto & Windus, 1900
* Hippesley Coxe, A. D., *Haunted Britain*, Pan, 1973
Hole, Christina, *English Customs and Usage*, Batsford, 1941
* Hole, Christina, *Haunted England*, Batsford, 1940
* Hole, Christina, *English Folklore*, Batsford, 1940
Hone, W., *Everyday Book*, Tegg, 1841
Hope, R. C., *The Legendary Lore of the Holy Wells of England*, Elliot Stock, 1893
Howard, Alexander, *Endless Cavalcade*, Arthur Barker, 1964
* Hunt, Robert, *Popular Romances of the West of England*, Chatto & Windus, 1881
Iggleson, Sir Charles, *Those Superstitions*, Jarrold, N.D.
* Ingram, J. H., *The Haunted Homes & Family Traditions of Great Britain*, Gibbings, 1897
* Johnson, W., *Byways in English Archaeology*, C.U.P., 1912
* Jones-Baker, Doris, *The Folklore of Hertfordshire*, Batsford, 1977
Jones, J., *Notes on Certain Superstitions Prevalent in the Vale of Gloucester*, N.D.
* Killip, Margaret, *The Folklore of the Isle of Man*, Batsford, 1975
* Kingsley, Palmer, *The Folklore of Somerset*, Batsford, 1976
* Legg, R., M. Collier and T. Perrott, *Ghosts of Dorset, Devon and Somerset*, Dorset Pub. Co., 1974
Lethbridge, T. C., *Gogmagog. The Buried Gods*, Routledge & Kegan Paul, 1957
Ludlam, Harry, *The Mummy of Birchen Bower*, Foulsham, 1966
* Macfarlane, Alan, *Witchcraft in Tudor and Stuart England*, Routledge & Kegan Paul, 1970
Maple, Eric, *The Dark World of Witches*, Robert Hale, 1962
* Maple, Eric, *The Realm of Ghosts*, Robert Hale, 1964
Maple, Eric, *Magic Medicine and Quackery*, Robert Hale, 1968
Mee, Arthur, *London*, Hodder & Stoughton, London, 1953
* Marlowe, Christopher, *Legends of the Fenland People*, Cecil Palmer, London, 1926

BIBLIOGRAPHY

* Mason, Mrs C., *Essex, Its Forest, Folk and Folklore*, Clarke, 1928
* Morris, Ernest, *Legends o' the Bells*, Sampson Low, N.D.

Norman, Diana, *The Stately Ghosts of England*, London, 1963

"*Notes and Queries*", *Choice Notes on Folklore*, Bell & Daldy, 1859

O'Donnell, Elliott, *The Screaming Skull and Other Ghost Stories*, London, 1964

Oxley, C. T., *More Ghost Tales of the North Country*, Dobson, N.D.

* Palmer, Ray, *The Folklore of Warwickshire*, Batsford, 1976

Parkinson, T., *Yorkshire Legends and Traditions*, 1889

* Porter, Enid, *The Folklore of East Anglia*, Batsford, 1974

Price, Harry, *The End of Borley Rectory*, Harrap, 1946

Radford, E. and H. A. (Ed. Christina Hole), *Encyclopedia of Superstitions*, Hutchinson, 1961

Read, Donald, *The English Provinces (1760-1960)*, Edward Arnold, 1964

* Rowling, Margaret, *The Folklore of the Lake District*, Batsford, 1976

Sikes, Wirt, *British Goblins*, London, 1880

* Simpson, Jaqueline, *The Folklore of Sussex*, Batsford, 1973
* Simpson, Jaqueline, *The Folklore of the Welsh Border*, Batsford, 1976

Spence, L., *The Fairy Tradition in Great Britain*, London, 1948

Suffolk Garland, The

* Thompson, C. J. S., *Mystery and Lore of Apparitions*, Shayler, London, 1930

Thorpe, B., *Northern Mythology*, 1851-2

* Timbs, John, *Abbeys, Castles and Ancient Halls of England and Wales*, London, c.1870

Udell, L. S., *Dorsetshire Folklore*, 1922

* Underwood, Peter, *A Gazetteer of British Ghosts*, Souvenir Press, London, 1971
* Vaux, Reverend J. E., *Church Folklore*, Griffiths Farran, 1894

Watkins, Alfred, *The Old Straight Track*, Garnstone Press, 1970

Whistler, L., *The English Festivals*, 1947

* Whitlock, Ralph, *The Folklore of Wiltshire*, Batsford, 1976

Index

Abbots Bromley (Staffs.), 42
Abbots Langley (Herts.), 130
Aconbury (Hereford.), 54
Alcocks Arbour (Warks.), 70, 72
Alconbury (Hunts.), 95–6
Aldbury (Herts.), 128
Alderley Edge (Ches.), 15–16
Aldworth (Berks.), 122
Alfriston (Sussex), 161
Anwick (Lincs.), 43
Arbor Low (Derby.), 31
Archer, Fred, 108
Arthur, King, 16, 184, 197–8
Arundel Castle (Sussex), 163
Ashingdon (Essex), 91–2
Ashmore (Dorset), 172–3
Athelhampton Hall (Dorset), 173
Avebury (Wilts.), 175–6
Aylmerton (Norfolk), 100–101

Babes in the Woods, the, 101
Babington, Anthony, 144
Ballona Bridge (Isle of Man), 19
Bamburgh (Northumberland), 22
Bambury Stones (Glos.), 48–9
Bank Nun, the, 143–4
Barguests, *see* DOGS, SPECTRAL
Barnack (Hunts.), 95
Basildon (Essex), 90
Basing House (Hants.), 166
Batcombe (Dorset), 172
Battle Abbey (Sussex), 163
Baynards Hall (Surrey), 158
Beachy Head (Sussex), 162
Beaminster School (Dorset), 174
Beaulieu Abbey (Hants.), 165
Bedfordshire cases, 113–16
Bees, folklore of, 16–17, 115
Bellister Castle (Northumberland), 23
Berkeley Castle (Glos.), 50–51
Berkshire cases, 116–22
Berry Dhones Pool (Isle of Man), 21
Berry Pomeroy Castle (Devon), 189
Bettiscombe Manor (Dorset), 170–1

Berry's Grave (Glos.), 50
Bilston (Staffs.), 40–41
Birdlip (Glos.), 48
Bisham Abbey (Berks.), 121
Bishops Lydeard (Somerset), 182
Black Heddon (Northumberland), 22
Black Mass, the, 138–9
Black Shuck, *see* DOGS, SPECTRAL
Black Toby, 108
Blandy, Mary, 137
Blaxhall (Suffolk), 112
Blenkinsop Castle (Northumberland), 23
Blickling Hall (Norfolk), 99
Bodenham, Anne, 178
Boleyn, Anne, *see* ROYAL GHOSTS
Bonfire rituals, 196, 198
Borley Rectory (Essex), 92–3
Bosham (Sussex), 163–4
Bostock, Bridget, 16
Bosworth Hall (Leics.), 59
Bottlebush Down (Dorset), 172
Bowland Hall (Yorks.), 29
Boxmoor Common (Herts.), 134–5
Brading (Isle of Wight), 169
Bradshaw, John, 142, 159
Brampton Bryan Castle (Hereford), 56
Brandeston (Suffolk), 110
Bransil Castle (Hereford.), 55
Brede Place (Sussex), 164
Brentor (Devon), 188
Brigg (Lincs.), 46–7
Brooke, Rupert, 81
Brooklands (Surrey), 157
Broughton (Northants.), 64
Bruce Castle (Tottenham), 146–7
Buckfastleigh (Devon), 189
Buckinghamshire Cases, 135–40
Buckland Abbey (Devon), 187
Buckland Shag, the, 157
Bugganes, *see* SPIRITS, ELEMENTAL
Bunbury (Cheshire), 17
Bungay (Suffolk), 105, 107–8
Burford (Oxon.), 126–7

INDEX

Burley (Hants.), 167
Burton Agnes Hall (Yorks.), 28–9
Byland Abbey (Yorks.), 29
Byron, Lord, family ghosts of, 34–5, 81

Cabell, Squire, 186
Cambridgeshire cases, 77–82
Cambridge University, 77–8
Canewdon (Essex), 57, 86–7, 92
Cassiobury (Herts.), 129
Castle Rising (Norfolk), 101
Castletown (Isle of Man), 20
'Cauld Lad', the, 25
Caxton Gibbet (Cambs.), 82
Chanctonbury Ring (Sussex), 160–1
Charm sticks, 196
Chartley Castle (Staffs.), 33
Chatham (Kent), 156
Cherrington (Glos.), 51
Cheshire cases, 15–18
Chesterfield (Derbys.), 32
Chicksands Priory (Beds.), 114
Chilbolton Rectory (Hants.), 165
Chilham Castle (Kent), 153
Chilton Cantelo (Somerset), 185
Chudleigh Knighton (Devon), 186
Church bells, 30, 37–8, 51, 55, 73, 81, 102–3, 105, 156, 163–4
Churches, Satanic assaults upon, 15, 21, 73, 85, 116, 131, 161, 188, 193
——, (superstitions surviving), 39–40, 55, 58–9, 88, 92, 147
Chysauster (Cornwall), 192–3
Claydon House (Bucks.), 135
Clibbon, lynching of, 130
Clifton Hampden (Oxon.), 126
Clophill (Beds.), 113–4
Coaches, spectral, 18, 26, 59, 67–8, 76, 92–3, 99–100, 107–8, 131, 146, 157, 174, 186, 193
Coggeshall (Essex), 90
Colley, Thomas, 133–4
Combermere Abbey (Cheshire), 17–18
Coppinger, Cruel, 197
Corby Castle (Cumb.), 9–10
Corder, William, 109
Cornish cases, 190–8
Cornwall, prehistoric stones of, 190, 192–4
Cottingley (Yorks.), 30
Cranmere Pool (Devon), 190
Creslow Manor House (Bucks.), 136
Cromwell, Oliver, 56, 96, 127, 166
Crondall (Hants.), 166
rowland Abbey (Lincs.), 47

Cumberland cases, 9–10
Cumnor Hall (Berks.), 120–1
Cunning Murrell, 88
Curry Mallet (Somerset), 184
Curses, 10–11, 17, 27, 47, 52, 60, 62, 75, 86, 98, 103–4, 116, 132, 162, 178, 182

Dagworth (Suffolk), 106
Danbury (Essex), 85
Darrell, John, 36, 60
Darrell, Wild Will, 177
Dart, River, 188
Datchworth (Herts.), 129
Dee, Dr John, 141–2
Deerhurst (Glos.), 50
de Marmion, Robert, 42
Derbyshire cases, 31–4
Devils, *see* individual entries
Devils Dyke (Cambs.), 80
Devils footprints (Devon), 187
Devil's Jumps (Surrey), 159–60
Devizes (Wilts.), 178
Devonshire cases, 185–90
Dewsbury (Yorks.), 30
Ditcheat (Somerset), 183
Dodge, Rev. Richard, 193
Dogs, spectral, 15, 20, 30, 57–8, 80, 102, 107–8, 174, 186
Donington Hall (Leics.), 59
Dorset cases, 169–74
Dover Castle (Kent), 153–4
Dragons, 22, 24, 25, 50, 72, 84–5, 117, 164, 167, 183
Drake, Sir Francis, 186–7
Dudley Castle (Worcs.), 72–3
Dun Cow, the, legends of, 65–6, 71–2
Dunwich (Suffolk), 105
Durham cases, 24–6

Edgehill (Warw.), 69–70
Elsdon (Northumberland), 23
Elves, *see* SPIRITS, ELEMENTAL
Endon (Staffs.), 42
Epping Forest (Essex), 82–4
Epworth (Lincs.), 46
Essex cases, 82–93
Ewell (Surrey), 160
Exorcism, 11, 18, 36, 41, 54, 57–8, 60, 68–9, 74, 88, 138, 157, 159, 167, 193–4

Fairies, *see* SPIRITS, ELEMENTAL
Farringdon (Berks.), 121–2
Faxton (Northants), 62
Featherstone Castle (Northumberland), 22

INDEX

Ferrars, Lady Diana, 132
Fingest (Bucks.), 135–6
Flixton (Yorks.), 30
Flower family, the, 45, 59–60
Flying Saucers, 29, 161, 179

Gardner, Dr Gerald, 20, 134, 151
Gaveston, Piers, 68
Ghosts, headless, 29, 47, 59, 99–100, 105, 121–2, 129, 131, 142, 154, 164, 193. See also individual locations
Giants, 11, 65, 80–1, 103, 140, 176, 190–1, 195
Glastonbury Thorn, 181
Gloucestershire cases, 48–53
Gloucester Jail (Glos.), 52–3
Goodrich Castle (Hereford.), 54
Gog Magog, 80–1, 140
Grantchester (Cambs.), 81
Grayrigg Hall (Westmorland), 11
Great Bealings (Suffolk), 106
Great Leighs (Essex), 86
Great Paxton (Hunts.), 96–7
Greenwich (London), 147–8
Griffith, Anne, 28–9
Grimes Graves (Norfolk), 103
Grimston Grave, the, 131
Guilsborough (Northants), 64

Haddenham (Bucks.), 136–7
Hadleigh (Essex), 88
Hairy Hands (ghost), 186
Hallaton (Leics.), 61
Hall Place (Kent), 154
Haltwhistle (Northumberland), 22–3
Hambleden (Bucks.), 137
Hampshire and Isle of Wight cases, 164–9
Hampton Court Palace (Middx.), 149
Hand of Glory, the, 27
Happisburgh (Norfolk), 102
Harvest customs, 111–12
Harvington Hall (Worcs.), 75
Hastings (Sussex), 163
Hatfield House (Herts.), 131
Hawker, Rev. R. S., 196–7
Healing, 16–17, 19, 26, 31, 41, 44–5, 49, 55–6, 66, 154–5, 162, 180–1, 195–6
Hedley Cow, the, 22
Hell Fire Club, the, 139–40
Helston (Cornwall), 198
Henham (Essex), 84
Herefordshire cases, 54–8
Herne the Hunter, 119

Herstmonceux Castle (Sussex), 163
Hertfordshire cases, 128–35
Hever Castle (Kent), 153
Hickling Broad (Norfolk), 100
Hicks, Mary, 75
Highclere (Hants.), 167
Highgate Cemetery (London), 150
Hill Hall (Essex), 89
Hilton Castle (Durham), 25
Hinckley (Leics.), 58–9
Hintlesham Hall (Suffolk), 108
Hinton St George (Somerset), 184
Hob of Hart Hall, 29
Hobgoblins, see SPIRITS, ELEMENTAL
Holbeach (Lincs.), 43–4
Holland House (London), 148
Holsworthy (Devon), 188
Holy Island (Northumberland), 23
Holywell (Hunts.), 94
Hopkins, Matthew, 86, 90, 97, 109–10
Horning (Norfolk), 104
Horseworkers and Blacksmiths (superstitions relating to), 61, 111, 116–17
Hoylake (Cheshire), 18
Hudson, Michael, Rev., 63
Hughenden Manor (Bucks.), 136
Hungerford (Berks.), 118
Hunstanton Hall (Norfolk), 104
Huntingdonshire cases, 93–8
Huntsmen, phantom, 23, 83, 147, 184

Ightham Mote (Kent), 153
Ilkeston (Derbys.), 32
Ilmington (Warks.), 67–8
Inkberrow (Worcs.), 73
Inns, haunted, 13, 28, 42, 63, 69, 75, 86, 94, 96, 104, 148
Izzard, Anne, 96–7

Jack o' Kent, 56–7
Jane's Grave, 185
Jeffreys, Judge, 165, 174, 184
Jesus Christ, legend relating to, 43
Jobling, William, 25–6
Kensington Palace (London), 148
Kent cases, 152–6
Kentford (Suffolk), 108–9
Kentwell Hall (Suffolk), 105
Keysoe (Beds.), 115
Kidderminster (Worcs.), 74–5
Kimbolton Castle (Hunts.), 93–4
Kinder Scout (Derbys.), 34
Kings Lynn (Norfolk), 103–4
Kington (Herefordshire), 57
Kirkby Lonsdale (Westmorland), **11**

INDEX

Knaresborough (Yorks.), 28
Knebworth House (Herts.), 129
Knepp Castle (Sussex), 163
Kynaston, Wild Humphrey, 37

Laidley Worm, see DRAGONS
Lambe, Dr John, 74–5
Lambton Worm, *see* DRAGONS
Lamorna (Cornwall), 193
Lancashire cases, 12–15
Langley Burrell (Wilts.), 178
Lauderdale House (Highgate), 146
Leicestershire cases, 58–61
Levens Hall (Westmorland), 10–11
Leverington (Cambs.), 80
Lewtrenchard (Devon), 189
Lilburne (Northants.), 65
Lilleshall Abbey (Salop), 40
Lincoln Imp, the, 45
Lincolnshire cases, 43–7
Liphook (Hants.), 167
Lisle, Dame Alice, 165
Little Baddow (Essex), 89
Little Comberton (Worcs.), 74
Littlecote (Wilts.), 177
Little Gaddesdon (Herts.), 134
Little Salkeld (Cumberland), 10
London and Middlesex cases, 140–151
London Stone, 140
Long Compton (Warks.), 67
Long Lawford (Warks.), 68
Longleat (Wilts.), 177–8
Long Marston (Herts.), 133–4
Long Meg and her Daughters, 10
Louth (Lincs.), 44–5
Love Charms, 137–8
Lower Quinton (Warks.), 67
Lowes, Rev. John, 110
Lowther Hall (Westmorland), 11
Ludlam, Mother, 160
Ludlow (Salop), 38–9
Lyme Regis (Dorset), 174
Lympne Castle (Kent), 153
Lyttleton, Lord, 148

Maidens' Garlands, 39
Maidstone (Kent), 154
Man cases, Isle of, 18–21
Marden (Hereford.), 55
Maria Marten, murder of, 109
Market Bosworth (Leics.), 59
Markyate Cell (Herts.), 132
May Day games, 49, 50
Mayfield (Sussex), 162
Mazes, 65

Medmenham Abbey, *see* HELL FIRE CLUB
Merlin, 15–16
Mermaids, 13, 34, 37, 55, 196–7
Mersea Island (Essex), 90
Minehead (Somerset), 181–2
Miners' superstitions, 33–4, 41, 192
Minster Lovel Hall (Oxon.), 126
Missenden Abbey (Bucks.), 136
Mongoose, the talking, 21
Moon superstitions, 117–18
More, Sir Thomas, 158
Mortimer, Regent, 35
Mottistone Downs (Isle of Wight), 169
Mummies, 145–6
Mynterne, Conjuror, 172

Netherbury (Dorset), 169–70
Netley Abbey (Hants.), 165
Neville Castle (County Durham), 25
Newark Priory (Surrey), 157–8
Newbury (Berks.), 118
Newchurch (Lancs.), 14–15
New Forest (Hants.), 166
Newington Church (Kent), 156
Newmarket (Suffolk), 108–9
Newstead Abbey (Notts.), 34–5
Nightingale, Florence, 143
Norfolk cases, 98–104
Northamptonshire cases, 62–6
North Tawton (Devon), 188
Northumberland cases, 21–4
Norton Fitzwarren (Somerset), 182
Nottinghamshire cases, 34–6
Nottingham Castle, 35

Oakham Castle (Rutland), 61
Okehampton (Devon), 186
Old Scarf, 102–3
Orford (Suffolk), 110–11
Osborne, Murders, the, 133–4
Oulton High House (Suffolk), 105–6
Oviedo, Leonora, 46
Oxfordshire cases, 122–8
Oxford University, 122–3, 127

Padstow (Cornwall), 182
Painswick (Glos.), 48
Peacock superstitions, 33
Peel (Isle of Man), 20–1
Peel Castle (Isle of Man), 20
Pembury (Kent), 155
Pendle Hill (Lancs.), 14–15
Penn, Sybill, 149
Petersham (Surrey), 159

INDEX

Pevensey (Sussex), 162
Pickingale, George, 87
Piskies and Pixies, see SPIRITS, ELEMENTAL
Pleshey Castle (Essex), 88
Pluckley (Kent), 154
Polstead (Suffolk), 109
Potter Heigham (Norfolk), 100
Prestbury (Glos.), 52
Prittlewell Priory (Essex), 89
Puck, see SPIRITS, ELEMENTAL
Puck Pool (Isle of Wight), 169
'Punkie Night', 184
Pye (Hamilton), 121–2

Quakers, 78–9
Quane, Margaret, 20
'Radiant Boy', the, 9–10
Raggedstone Hill (Worcs.), 75–6
Rahere, 143
Raynham Hall (Norfolk), 98–9
Reculver (Kent), 152
Redcap, Mother, 79
Rich, Lady Diana, 148
Rivers, springs and, streams, Supernatural, 13, 16–17, 21, 31, 35, 54–5, 134, 140, 188
Robin Hood, 35–6
Robsart, Amy, 120–1
Rochester (Kent), 153
Rochford Hall (Essex), 91
Rollright Stones (Oxon.), 67, 123–5
Roman Britain, ghosts of, 82, 104, 152, 153
Roos Hall (Suffolk), 107
Rothwell Church (Northants.), 63
Royal ghosts, 18, 35, 50–1, 82–3, 90, 93–4, 101, 120, 142, 148–9, 154, 159, 163, 166, 184
Royal College of Surgeons (London), 146
Rufford Abbey (Notts.), 35
Rye (Sussex), 162

St Albans (Herts.), 129
St Bartholomew the Great (London), 143
St Benets Abbey (Norfolk), 101, 104
St Cleer (Cornwall), 196
St Leonards Forest (Sussex), 164
St Mark's Eve, 189
St Michael's Mount (Cornwall), 190
St Osyth (Essex), 84, 86
St Paul's Cathedral, 140–1
Saints, 23, 42, 162, 198

Sacrifice, 10, 18, 23–4, 27, 29, 61, **141,** 146, 152, 162, 169–70, 188
Saffron Walden (Essex), 84
Salisbury Cathedral, 178
Salisbury, Countess of, 142
Salisbury Hall (Herts.), 130
Salmesbury (Lancs.), 12, 14
Samuel family, the, 97–8
Sandford Orcas (Dorset), 173
Sarratt (Herts.), 130–1
Sawston Hall (Cambs.), 82
Scarborough Castle (Yorks.), 68
Scot, Michael, 10
Sedgemoor (Somerset), 184
Sevenoaks (Kent), 155
Shebbear (Devon), 188
Shepton Mallet (Somerset), 183
Shere (Surrey), 157
Sherrington Manor (Sussex), **164**
Shipton, Mother, 27–8
Shipton-under-Wychwood (Oxon.), 125
Shocklach (Cheshire), 18
Shoreham (Kent), 156
Shorn, Sir John, 138
Shropshire cases, 37–40
Silbury Hill (Wilts.), 175–6
Silky, 22
Skendleby (Lincs.), 43
Skulls, 28–9, 32–3, 35, 59, 100, 170–**1**, 185
Smithfield (London), 143
Smithills Hall (Lancs.), 12–13
Smugglers, legends of, 90–1, 102, 156, 173
Somerset cases, 180–5
Soulby (Lincs.), 45
Southworth family, the, 12
Spinney Abbey (Cambs.), 81
Spirits, elemental, 19–21, 25, 29, 31, 36, 91, 105, 110, 161, 166–7, 169–70, 176–7, 182–3, 185–6, 191–2, 195–6
Spreyton (Devon), 187–8
Staffordshire cases, 40–3
Stanton Drew (Somerset), 182
Stanton Harcourt (Oxon.), 123
Staunton (Glos.), 49
Stiperstone Ridge (Salop), 37
Stonehenge (Wilts.), 176
Stowmarket (Suffolk), 109–10
Strafford, Earl of, 63
Sudbury (Suffolk), 105
Sudeley Castle (Glos.), 50
Suffolk cases, 104–112

INDEX

Suicides, cross-roads burial of, 148–9
Surrey cases, 156–60
Sussex cases, 160–4
Sutton, Mother, 114–15

Tamworth Castle (Staffs.), 42
Tardbigge (Worcs.), 74–5
Tarrant Gunville (Dorset), 174
Tavistock (Devon), 190
Tearle of Ballawhane, 19
Tedworth (Wilts.), 177
Tewin (Herts.), 131
Tewkesbury (Glos.), 52
Theatre ghosts, 144–5
Thorington Hall (Suffolk), 106–7
Thorpe Hall (Lincs.), 46
Three Choirs' Festival (Hereford), 58
Tilbury (Essex), 88–9
Tissington (Derbys.), 31
Toads, 87, 111
Tolleshunt Knights (Essex), 85
Tom Hickathrift, 80
Topley Pike (Derbys.), 31
Torbarrow Hill (Glos.), 48
Tower of London, 141–2
Treasure Guardians, 51, 70–1, 186
Tregeagle, 197
Treble, Mary, 130
Tree superstitions, 180–1
Tunstead Milton (Derbys.), 32–3
Turner, Anne, 67
Turpin, Dick, 59, 83–4, 96, 115

Uffington (Berks.), 117
Umbrella, superstition of the, 189–90
University College (London), 146
Uplyme (Devon), 186
Utkinton Hall (Cheshire), 18

Vaughan, Thomas, 57
Verney, Sir Edmund, 135
Viking ship, spectral, 104

Walberswick (Suffolk), 108
Walkern (Herts.), 133
Wallington Hall (Northumberland), 23
Walsh, John, 169–70
Waltham Abbey (Essex), 83
Walthamstow Museum, 147
Walton, Charles, 67
Walton-on-Thames (Surrey), 159
Wanstead (Essex), 147
Warboys (Hunts.), 97–8
Ware (Herts.), 128–9, 132
Warminster (Wilts.), 179

Warton (Lancs.), 15
Warwickshire cases, 66–72
Watton (Yorks.), 29
Waverley Abbey (Surrey), 158
Wayland Wood (Norfolk), 101
Weather lore, 125–6
Wellow (Somerset), 183
Wells, healing and holy, 12, 16, 31, 42, 125, 138, 160, 162, 169, 182
——, Cursing, 182
Wenham, Jane, 133
Weobley (Hereford), 57
Werewolf, 30
Wesley, Rev. John, 46, 194
West Aukland (Durham), 26
Westminster Abbey (London), 142–3
Westmorland cases, 10–12
Wayland the Smith, 116–17
West Wratting (Cambs.), 79
West Wycombe (Bucks.), 140
Whispering Knights, the, 123–5
Whitchurch (Salop), 38
White ladies, 23, 42, 62, 88, 100–1, 106, 115, 154, 183
Wicca, 20, 125, 134, 150–1, 161–2, 168
Wickham-Skeith (Suffolk), 109
Wilkinson, 'Iron-Mad', 41
Willingham (Cambs.), 79–80
Wilmington, Long Man of, 161–2
Wiltshire cases, 174–9
Winchcombe (Glos.), 52
Winchester (Hants.), 168
Windsor (Berks.), 118–20
'Winwick Pig', 15
Wistow (Leics.), 58
Witch balls, 155, 196
Witch bottles, 79, 160
Witchcraft, *see* individual entries
Witch posts, 27
Woburn Abbey (Beds.), 114
Woodcroft Castle (Northants.), 62–3
Woodford (Northants.), 64
Woodhouse Eaves (Leics.), 59
Woodstock (Oxon.), 127–8
Wookey Hole (Somerset), 184
Woolacombe (Devon), 189
Woolpit (Suffolk), 110
Worcestershire cases, 72–6
Worcester Cathedral, 72
Worms, *see* DRAGONS

Yorkshire cases, 26–30

Zennor (Cornwall), 194